Wellington at Bay

The Battle of Villamuriel, 25 October 1812

Garry David Wills

Helion & Company

Helion & Company Limited
Unit 8 Amherst Business Centre
Budbrooke Road
Warwick
CV34 5WE
England
Tel. 01926 499619
Email: info@helion.co.uk
Website: www.helion.co.uk
Twitter: @helionbooks
blog.helion.co.uk

Published by Helion & Company 2020
Designed and typeset by Mach 3 Solutions Ltd (www.mach3solutions.co.uk)
Cover designed by Paul Hewitt, Battlefield Design (www.battlefield-design.co.uk)

Cover: *Colonel* Jean-Pierre Béchaud, commander of the 66e Ligne, riding across Villamuriel to organise the response to the Allied counterattack. Original artwork by Christa Hook (www.christahook.co.uk) © Helion & Co. 2020

ISBN 978-1-913118-95-2

British Library Cataloguing-in-Publication Data.
A catalogue record for this book is available from the British Library.

For details of other military history titles published by Helion & Company Limited, contact the above address, or visit our website: http://www.helion.co.uk

We always welcome receiving book proposals from prospective authors.

To my wife Susan, who after 40 years is still patiently waiting for my all-consuming passion for the Napoleonic Wars to fade, and in memory of Drummer John Wills, 1st Battalion, 9th Regiment of Foot, a veteran of Villamuriel.

Contents

List of Maps

Foreword

On 18 June 1816 the second battalion of the 30th Foot, stationed at Limerick, celebrated the first anniversary of the Battle of Waterloo in fine style. Lieutenant Edward Neville Macready, an ensign at the time of the battle, described in his journal how the Assembly Rooms had been adapted for the occasion. He noted that:

> the grand dancing room was beautifully festooned with mingled flowers and laurels; beneath these were two transparencies at equal distance bearing the names Salamanca and Badajoz; Fuentes d'Onor and Villamuriel which occupied each side of the chamber; while its ends were ornamented with two particularly brilliant ones bearing the inscriptions of Quatre Bras and Waterloo.

When a General Service Medal was finally issued in 1848, however, the survivors of those who had served with the Fifth Division in Spain and Portugal received no clasp for Villamuriel. Furthermore, later accounts of that period of the Peninsular War, the autumn of 1812, have tended to gloss over the action at Villamuriel as a minor event during the allied retreat from Burgos. It might be argued that an action that involved only one division, with some Spanish support, was indeed too minor to deserve the award of a clasp. Yet clasps were awarded for Sahagun and Benevente, actions that involved far fewer combatants, and Benevente, like Villamuriel, happened during a retreat.

In this new work, Garry Wills has finally given the events of 25 October the attention they deserve. He has focused both on the action itself and on the troops who were involved. The reason the action took place is carefully contextualised in terms of the retreat which followed the failure to take Burgos. Thus, the significance of the Fifth Division holding and then destroying the bridge over the Carrion emerges clearly from the narrative. Furthermore, the narrative itself, supported by a wealth of contemporary material, clearly establishes the course of events and offers some solutions to the uncertainties that have hitherto remained unresolved. As someone who has written about one of the battalions in the division, as well as about the retreat itself, it is gratifying to discover the actual location of the all-important ford. Guesswork is no substitute for hard facts.

In addition to clarifying what actually happened and its significance to the progress of the retreat, Garry Wills also offers a detailed analysis of the Fifth Division and Maucune's French force, not merely statistical. This pleasing emphasis on the actual combatants, not always a feature of military history, ensures that the reader will never lose sight of the human element. As a result, we are able to evaluate the action from the French as well as the Allied perspective. We may well conclude, after reading this account, that dogged determination was the quality most on display.

As for why no clasp was awarded for Villamuriel after the division had held the position long enough for the rest of the allied army to affect its departure (even if eventually the French did indeed cross the river), there can only be supposition. Perhaps Wellington did not wish to be reminded of his worst scrape, as he himself entitled it. Yet, as Lieutenant Colonel William Gomm, on the divisional staff, wrote to his sister: 'We lost nearly 600 men, but did, I believe, all that was expected of us'. He was in a position to know and would certainly have approved of this work, which gives both sides the credit they deserve.

Carole Divall
September 2019

Preface

Several years ago, I was having coffee with Carole Divall and her husband John while demonstrating my wargame of the Battle of Boxtel 1794, the subject of my first book, *Wellington's First Battle*. As she was leaving Carole recommended that I look at the battle of Villamuriel. Given that the Peninsular War has been studied so minutely and for so long, I initially thought that it would make a nice magazine article. However, it soon became clear how little was readily available about this small but significant action and this rewarding project was born. The action at Villamuriel de Cerrato is of interest for several reasons including the involvement of the 5th Division of Wellington's army and Maucune's 5e Division of the Armée de Portugal, only three months after the former broke the latter at Salamanca. Béchaud's account of the 15e Ligne deployed entirely as skirmishers is often cited but without the context of the action itself, in which the British counterattack was delivered partly in column formation. The action at Villamuriel was also part of the controversy surrounding the publication of Napier's *History* in the 1830's.

This account attempts to pull together memoirs and documents from all sides, both published and archival sources, to give a balanced description of the combat that took place at Villamuriel on 25 October 1812 as Oswald's 5th Anglo-Portuguese Division, together with Liñan's 1ª Sección, 1ª Division, 6º Ejército (Galicia y Asturias), fought to repel Maucune's assault.

In March 1813, when describing the events at Villamuriel, the *Royal Military Chronicle* asked 'why do not such acts call forward an historian worthy to record them?' Such worthiness is the aspiration of this author.

Acknowledgement and Sources

While research and writing are solitary endeavours I have been greatly assisted by many people, some that I have never met. I would like to acknowledge and thank Carole Divall for the inspiration and providing some of her own research; Jorge Planas Campos for generously providing his own photographs of the *contrôles des officiers*, casualty information, his help in identifying Montbertrand and in translating Liñan's report; Jose Arcon and Ian Brooks who alerted me to Oman's mistake regarding the involvement of Losada's Division at Villamuriel; Professor Charles Esdaile for sharing his knowledge of the Spanish literature; Stephen Summerfield for his help with the Dickson Manuscripts and all things artillery; Tom Holmberg for providing John Kenneth Mackenzie's obituary; Tony Broughton for providing the relevant pages of the history of the 66e Ligne; Ron McGuigan for help with the quarterly pay-lists and James Ward's death; Steven Smith for providing histories of the French cavalry regiments and information regarding Camp d'Orique; Robert Burnham for Spry's after action report from Salamanca; Dominique Timmermans for providing a biography of Desfossés; Moises Gaudencio for biographical information regarding *Coronel* Tavares. Most of these contacts came via the extremely useful Napoleon Series Discussion Forum and I would also like to thank all the contributors who have added to my research. The Napoleon Series also hosts the invaluable Peninsula Roll Call by Challis. The staff of the National Archives, Kew, the York Minster Library, University of Manchester Library and the British Library, Ben Fellows of the National Army Museum and James Whittaker of the Staffordshire Regiment Museum have all been very helpful. The staff of the Hartley Library, University of Southampton, the *Archivo Histórico Militar*, Lisbon and the *Archivo Histórico Nacional de Madrid* have also helpfully fulfilled my requests from afar. Christophe Pénichon provided photographs of the *Situations*. I must also thank David Bruton who generously allowed me to study Sir John Oswald's correspondence in his family's archive.

Thanks are also due to Andrew Bamford for gently but effectively guiding me into and through the Helion publication process.

I would like to thank my wife Susan for proofreading the manuscript and my son George for his help with the translations, all remaining errors remain my responsibility. Finally, I would like to thank my son James for accompanying me when walking the battlefield in 2017.

Two sources are particularly worthy of comment:

The *Journal of Colonel Béchaud* was published in 1913 by Jean Colin in the *Revue des études napoléoniennes*. Béchaud wrote his account in January 1813, in response to the publication of Wellington's own dispatches regarding the campaign, when Béchaud was in Salamanca.[1] Written before Napoleon's final defeat, this account is thus particularly useful. It has often been referenced but has not been published in English, the excerpts here are placed in their full context.

Also used throughout this study is *The Journal of James Hale, Late Sergeant in the Ninth Regiment of Foot*, which was published in 1826. However, the 9th Foot's pay-list, records that Corporal James Hale of Cirencester, who wrote the journal, was absent sick in Salamanca in October, in Viseu in November, and in Lisbon in December (Hale was promoted to sergeant on 21 June 1813, the day of the battle of Vitoria). Hale did not record any of these incidents of sickness in his Journal.[2] His account of Villamuriel is at least as extensive and detailed as his account of Salamanca and is consistent with other accounts. It appears that James Hale of Cirencester was the victim of mistaken identity. Private James Hale of Shepton Mallett was also recorded as sick in Salamanca in October and in Viseu in November and December, thus the pay-list may have confused the two men. James Hale of Shepton Mallet enlisted in 1811 and is the man in the Military General Service Medal roll with clasps for Salamanca and San Sebastian.

The battlefield maps included with this volume are based on an interpretation of the available sources with the units portrayed on their footprints as if deployed in line. Skirmishers are shown in company sized units with their local reserves. The maps are scaled in paces with one pace equal to 28 inches.

1 Jean Colin, 'Journal du Colonel Béchaud de l'Armée de Portugal Octobre 1812', *Revue des études napoléoniennes* (1913) Vol.I, p.114.

2 The National Archives, Kew (TNA), WO12/2665.

1

The Retreat from Burgos

For Lieutenant General the Marquis of Wellington, 1812 was marked by one of his greatest victories, even perhaps his 'masterpiece', the Battle of Salamanca.[1] The defeat of *Maréchal* Marmont in July led to the liberation of Madrid and the French evacuation of Andalusia. With the French in some disarray, Wellington advanced to Burgos in northern Spain.

Here Wellington was joined by the 6° Ejército (Galicia y Asturias). Captain John Freemantle (Coldstream Guards), who later joined Wellington's staff as aide de camp on 31 October, recorded that 'General Castanos with 12,000 men joined us yesterday [12 September 1812]'.[2] At this time Castanos was *capitán general* commanding the 5°, 6° and 7° Ejércitos.[3] However, Wellington complained that the two armies had effectively marched past one another. *Mariscal de Campo* José María Santocildes y Llanos, commander of the 6° Ejército, had attempted to make the agreed rendezvous, at Valladolid, but was five or six days late, by which time Wellington had advanced to Palencia and Magaz. Consequently, the junction of the two armies occurred only on 16 September.[4]

By late October 1812 Wellington, with his Anglo-Portuguese army, comprising the 1st, 5th, 6th and 7th Divisions, Pack and Bradford's Independent Portuguese brigades, Anson's light cavalry brigade together with Bock and Ponsonby's dragoon brigades, was retreating from the failed siege that had cost him 2,000 men.[5] Wellington's Anglo-Portuguese

---

1 *Army List*, 1813, p.5; E. Longford, *Wellington: The Years of the Sword* (Frogmore: Panther, 1971), p.425; Wellington became a Duke on 3 May 1814.

2 G. Glover (ed.), *Wellington's Voice, The Candid Letters of Lieutenant Colonel John Freemantle, Coldstream Guards 1808–1837* (Barnsley: Frontline, 2006), p.124.

3 A.M.L. Martinez, *Diccionario Biografico del Generalato Español: Reinados de Carlos IV y Fernando VII (1788–1833)* (Villatuerta: Foro para el Estudio de la Historia Militar en España, 2012), p.196.

4 C. Oman, *History of the Peninsular War* (London: Greenhill, 1996), Vol.VI, p.16; J. Gurwood (ed.), *Dispatches of Field Marshal the Duke of Wellington* (London: John Murray, 1852), Vol. VI, pp.68, 70.

5 Oman, *History*, Vol.VI, pp.3, 5, 741; C.J. Esdaile and P. Freeman, *Burgos in the Peninsular War, 1808–1814; Occupation, Siege, Aftermath* (Basingstoke: Palgrave Macmillan, 2015), pp.84–125.

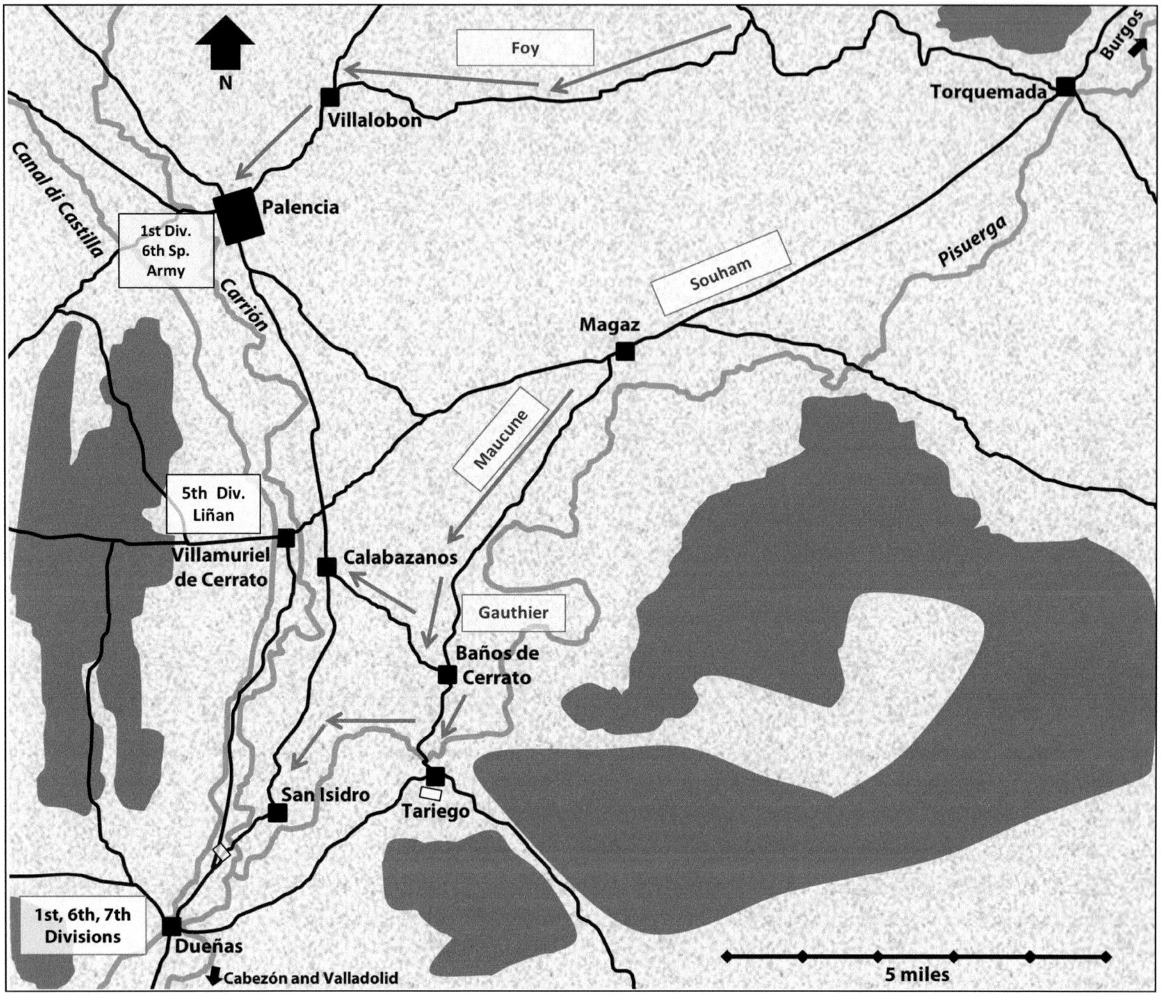

Map 1 Campaign Map – Morning.

army had 24,000 men 'present under arms', while the 6º Ejército was 12,500-strong.[6]

For the army, the retreat was 'the most dangerous and unpleasant operation we have had' and eventually ended back in Portugal, where the campaigns of 1812 had begun.[7] The retreat was marked by several small battles and skirmishes, of which the Battle of Villamuriel is just one, albeit the deadliest.[8]

Wellington was pursued by *Général de Division* Joseph Souham's Armée de Portugal, together with *Général de Brigade* Baron Pierre Gabriel d'Aussenac's brigade of seven infantry battalions (3,500 men strong), detached from the Réserve de Bayonne, and *Général de Division* Marie-François Auguste de

6 *Archivo Histórico Nacional de Madrid* [AHNM], *Diversos/Colecciones*/144/n32 (October monthly state).

7 G. Glover (ed.), *Eyewitness to the Peninsular War and the Battle of Waterloo, the Letters and Journals of Lt. Colonel the Honourable James Stanhope, 1803–1825* (Barnsley: Pen and Sword, 2010), p.103.

8 C. Divall, *Wellington's Worst Scrape: The Burgos Campaign 1812* (Barnsley: Pen and Sword, 2012), pp.3–5, 24, 79–80; Oman, *History*, Vol.VI, p.153.

Cafferelli du Falga's newly arrived field force of the Armée du Nord. Caffarelli's field force comprised parts of *Général de Division* Edmé-Martin Vandermaesen's 2e Division as well as *Général de Division* Baron Pierre Dumoustier with *Général de Brigade* Baron Régis Barthélemy Mouton-Duvernet's brigade of Jeune Garde and Garde Nationale de la Garde (together 9,500 of a total of 16,500 infantry in the Armée du Nord), together with *Général de Brigade* Louis-Marie Levesque de Laferrière's cavalry brigade of 11 squadrons. *Colonel* Antoine François Eugène Merlin's brigade of six squadrons from the Armée du Nord had also been with the Armée de Portugal since July. Souham thus deployed a combined force of 53,000 men, a total that excludes approximately 16,000 men on detachment and in hospital.[9] The men of the allied army were particularly concerned by the preponderance of cavalry that Souham was able to deploy, approximately 6,000 versus less than 3,000.

At this key moment, Lieutenant General Sir Edward Paget arrived and was appointed to command the 1st Division on 11 October 1812. Paget was senior to lieutenant generals Stapleton Cotton, Hill and Beresford by six months and was therefore effectively Wellington's second in command.[10]

The French offensive began on 18 October when Souham's advanced guard from Maucune's 5e Division surprised the outpost at the village of Santa Olalla. Although he had received orders to await the arrival of King Joseph with significant reinforcements before bringing on a general action, Souham pressed on. Writing at the beginning of October, he believed that his army was safer in attack than in defence; '... if lord Wellington is not in retirement, I will be forced to attack him. I see less risk to advance than to retire. In a moment where the morale of the soldier starts to improve any retirement produces the worst effect'.[11]

On 20 October, Souham sent Maucune's and Chauvel's divisions against Wellington's centre, the 7th Division, in front of the villages of Quintana Palla and Olmos to the north east of Burgos. As Maucune's leading division was remote from Souham's main force, Wellington directed Paget, to lead his own 1st Division and the 5th Division in an attack from the left wing on Maucune's flank. Despite being 'hotly engaged' to his front, Maucune managed, at the last minute, to scramble his division away without serious loss, just 80 men, while the British 7th Division lost 47 men. Martinien records that three officers of the 86e Ligne were wounded at this combat of Monasterio de Rodillo. A further officer, *Sous Lieutenant* J.L. Prat from the 86e Ligne was also wounded there, as was an officer from the 82e Ligne on 21 October.[12] At this time, Wellington received intelligence from Hill in Madrid

9 Oman, *History*, Vol.VI, pp.54–55, 743, 744.

10 2nd Duke of Wellington (ed.), *Supplementary Despatches, Correspondence and Memoranda of Field Marshal Arthur, Duke of Wellington, K. G.* (London: John Murray, 1872), Vol.XIV, p.126; *Army List,* 1813, p.7.

11 W.F.P. Napier, *History of the War in the Peninsula and in the South of France from the year 1807 to 1814* (London: Constable, 1993), Vol.V, p.602.

12 Oman, *History*, Vol.VI, pp.64–66; A. Martinien, *Tableaux, par corps et par batailles, des officiers tués et blessés pendant les guerres de l'Empire (1805–1815)* (Paris: Charles-Lavauzelle, 1899), pp.167, 271, 293, 299; *Service Historique de la Défense*, Paris, (SHD) 2Yb 411, *Contrôle des Officiers*, 86e Ligne, p.241.

that Soult had begun to advance on that city, and subsequently concluded that the safety of the army required him to lift the siege and retreat to the line of the river Duero. Wellington himself dates this intelligence to the morning of the 21st whereas Gordon puts it earlier on the night of the 19th. Wellington elsewhere refers to letters received from Hill dated both 17 and 19 October 1812, with the decision to retreat made on 21 October.[13]

The retreat from Burgos then began and on 21 October the 5th Division of Wellington's army received orders to retreat via Quintanadueñas and Villalón, both to the northwest of Burgos. Lieutenant Colonel William Maynard Gomm, Assistant Quartermaster General, was assigned to the 5th Division and in charge of the movement of the 5th Division and two Spanish Divisions from Burgos to Palencia and Villamuriel.[14] There followed the lively cavalry action at Venta del Pozo and the combat at Villodrigo on 23 October.[15]

Writing to his sister on 2 November 1812, Lieutenant Peter Le Mesurier (1/9th Foot, Barnes's Brigade, 5th Division) described the beginning of the retreat:

> Our time has been most disagreeably occupied lately. About the middle of last month, the French moved down to relieve Burgos.
>
> On the 21st ulto: [October] the siege was raised and we began our retreat the same night at dark, and marched till four o'clock next morning over ploughed fields, ditches etc, etc, the men to their knees in mud. After a few hours' rest we recommenced marching and halted about four in the afternoon.
>
> On the 23rd ulto: we marched from six in the morning till midnight to Cordovilla. [Cordovilla la Real, on the high road, 4 miles NE of Torquemada] We left an immense number of stragglers in the rear, having marched upwards of 8 leagues in bad roads.
>
> On the 24th ulto: we had a march of seven leagues (the road was strewed on both sides with men completely knocked up) and we arrived after dark at Villa Muriel, a village situated on the Carrion River between Duenas and Palencia. We were buoyed up with the hopes of a halt on the 25th.[16]

In Barnes's Brigade, Ensign George Young (2/38th Foot) gives us more details of the conditions of the march in a letter, written on 10 December to his brother from Lamego:

> We marched all night [of the 20th], all the next day, and till 5 o'clock of the morning following without a halt which tired us not a little. We were ordered to commence cooking, and indeed very little we had, however little as it was, we began, but

13 R. Muir (ed.), *At Wellington's Right Hand – The Letters of Lieutenant Colonel Alexander Gordon* (Stroud: Sutton, 2003), p.333; *The London Gazette*, 16,669, 17 November 1812, p.2319; Gurwood, *Dispatches*, Vol.VI, p.133.

14 F.C. Carr-Gomm (ed.), *The Earlier Letters and Journals of Sir William Maynard Gomm* (London: John Murray, 1881), p.288.

15 Oman, *History*, Vol.VI, pp.69–77.

16 A. Greenwood (ed.), *Through Spain with Wellington, the letters of Lieutenant Peter Le Mesurier of the fighting Ninth* (Stroud: Amberley, 2016), p.137; a league was approximately three miles, originally the distance walked in an hour.

> to our surprise in a little time after what should we see coming on like vultures but the enemy's cavalry. Well tired as we were, we could not help again pursuing our wearisome way, with hearts rather sad, as at that time the hungry worm bit pretty keenly. By this time the men began to fall off pretty quickly, and I assure you I have seen many a brave soldier through excess of fatigue fall down in the ranks and expire, with horses, mules, asses and bullock, all were indiscriminately strewed [sic] on the road, the beast had the same grave as the man.[17]

Widespread drunkenness occurred in both armies as they marched through Torquemada because of the readily available local wine.[18] Major Robert Lawson, who commanded the artillery attached to the 5th Division, wrote the following entry in his diary:

> 23rd. Moved to Torquemada where such a scene of drunkenness occurred as would have disgraced even a Billingsgate rabble. The wine vaults were broken open by the troops and hardly 500 men in all the troops consisting of my brigade, the 1st and 6th divisions, were effective. I had left the 5th division at Tardajos [6 miles WNW of Burgos], as it marched by the heights on our right and I moved into the plain.[19]

On 23 October the 1/9th Foot and the 2/38th Foot of the British 5th Division reported losing their 'sick cars' during the retreat.[20]

At Torquemada on 24 October, the Allied rearguard made a brief stand to defend the bridge. Maucune, leading the French advanced guard, brought forward 'a superior artillery' comprised his own artillery and those of one or more other divisions, and sent his skirmishers to the riverbank and the arches of the bridge, forcing the defenders to continue their retreat.[21]

The same day, Wellington occupied a position along the rivers Carrión and Pisuerga, from the city of Palencia on his left, to Dueñas on his right where the 1st and 6th Divisions were posted. The 1st Division had camped near Dueñas overnight and stayed there until after noon on the 25th when they moved up on the heights overlooking the Carrión towards Villamuriel. From this vantage point they watched the advance and massing of the French army.[22] The artillery of the 1st Division, however, had already, at least in part,

---

17 K.E. Younge, 'Some Peninsular Letters', *United Service Magazine (USM)*, Vol.LII (New Series), October 1915–March 1916, pp.511–512; see Appendix III for the identification of this officer.

18 Napier, *History*, Vol.V, pp.298–300.

19 J.H. Leslie, *The Dickson Manuscripts* (Cambridge: Ken Trotman, 1990), Vol.IV, p.712.

20 TNA, WO17/148 November monthly return 2/38th Foot; WO12/2665, pay-list 24 December 1812, 1/9th Foot.

21 Colin, 'Béchaud', p.405; Martinien, *Tableaux*, p.639; Jorge Planas Campos, personal communication citing SHD GR 2Yb 1000; SHD C8 468; *Lieutenant* Paul Davezac, 3e Régiment d'Artillerie à Pied, shot in the right foot, and *Capitaine* Flavien Graillat, 5e Régiment d'Artillerie à Cheval of Boyer's dragoon division, were both wounded at the bridge of Torquemada on the 24th (*Archives Nationale*, Paris, *Base de Données Léonore* (LEONORE), LH/1184/75). Companies of Davezac's regiment supported the 2e (15e Compagnie), 3e (9e) and 7e (10e) Divisions of the Armée de Portugal, although of these only the 15e and 10e Compagnies were with the army when Davezac was previously wounded on 3 May 1811.

22 G.F. Burroughs, *A narrative of the retreat of the British army from Burgos: in a series of letters: an introductory sketch of the campaign of 1812 and military character of the Duke of*

moved further south to Cabezón de Pisuerga.[23] Ross-Lewin describes his regiment of the 6th Division being posted overlooking the position at San Isidro and Dueñas, while others in the 6th Division were deployed across the Carrión in the convent of San Isidro until withdrawn on the approach of the French.[24] The 5th Division, then under the command of Major General William Pringle,[25] had marched to the heights above the village of Villamuriel de Cerrato, where there was a bridge across the river Carrión. This final stage of the march was not without its frustrations, as described by an officer of Pringle's Brigade of the 5th Division:

> On the 24th of October 1812, the army, under Lord Wellington, was retiring by the main road from Burgos to Valladolid. In the evening the 5th division was turned off to the right to occupy the village and bridge of Villa Muriel, on the right bank of the river Carrion; apparently, the officer whose duty it was to inform the general commanding the division of its position for the night of that day [presumably Gomm or his ADQMG Captain Nathaniel Gledstanes], had forgotten or neglected to do so, for the division had nearly reached the bridge of Devenas [Dueñas], when it had to march back about three or four miles before it reached its bivouac, and after crossing Villa Muriel bridge and taking up its ground, it was quite dark. There were no rations served out, and there was nothing either for officers or men to eat or drink; some marauders, broke into the wine vaults close to the village, which had the appearance of grave vaults.[26]

Corporal Hale of the 1/9th Foot (Barnes's Brigade) gives a similar account, but differs in that he implies that his battalion marched on a more northerly route through Palencia on its way to Villamuriel:

> [S]o we remained on our ground till about seven o'clock in the evening [22 October], when we began to retreat, and continued on till four o'clock the next morning, when we halted and lay down about two hours; but finding the enemy advancing very rapidly, we stood to our arms again, and continued retreating all day till it was nearly dark, then we formed our camp, and remained till about four o'clock in the morning: we then stood to our arms in the usual way, and continued our retreat till nearly sun-set in the evening, when we arrived on the other side of Palencia, towards Valladolid: there our division formed our camp

Wellington (Bristol: Joseph Routh, 1814), pp.20–24; George Frederick Burroughs served as surgeon to the 2/24th Foot, 1st Division (*Army List*, 1813, p.181).

23 G. Glover (ed.), *The Peninsular War and Waterloo Journals of Lieutenant William Ingilby, Royal Horse Artillery, 1810–15* (Godmanchester: Ken Trotman, 2014), p.56.

24 H.Ross-Lewin, *With the 32nd in the Peninsular and other Campaigns* (Dublin: Hodges, Figgis and Company, 1904), p.202; Glover (ed.), *Eyewitness*, pp.96–7; G. Glover (ed.), *Wellington's Lieutenant, Napoleon's Gaoler–The Peninsular War Letters and St. Helena Diaries of Sir George Ridout Bingham* (Barnsley: Pen and Sword, 2004), p.162. Bingham was lieutenant colonel in the 2/53rd Foot, and at this time commanded the 1st Brigade, 6th Division.

25 University of Manchester Library (UML), GB 133 Eng MSS 1273, item 24; Wellington to Pringle, as commander of the 5th Division, 19 October 1812.

26 McK, 'The Affair of Villa Muriel', *United Service Magazine* (1850), pt.1, p.542; 'McK' is Lieutenant (later Lieutenant Colonel) John Kenneth Mackenzie of the 1/4th Foot – see Appendix IV.

> very convenient to the river Pisuera [Carrión], at about four miles distance from Palencia, where was a bridge, near Villa Muriel.[27]

The pay-lists of the British battalions of the 5th Division show that they lost between one and nine percent of their men missing, and four men dead, during the three days of this retreat, with an average loss of four percent.[28] It is noteworthy that a comparison of the October monthly returns and the 21 October morning state, suggests this loss was only one percent.

By the evening of 24 October Souham had advanced to Magaz de Pisuerga.[29] The next morning, Foy, with his own 1er Division and the 7e Division together with a strong detachment of cavalry was sent by Souham from Torquemada via Villalobón to take the crossings of the Carrión at and around Palencia on his right.[30] Foy's cavalry comprised Laferrière's brigade (Armée du Nord, 11 squadrons; Lanciers de Berg, two; 1er Légion de Gendarmerie d'Espagne, six; 15e Chasseurs à Cheval, three) and *Colonel* Baron Redmond Shée's brigade (from Curto's light cavalry division; four squadrons of the 13e and three of the 14e Chasseurs à Cheval).[31] On his left, Souham sent Maucune, with his own 5e Division and Gauthier's 8e Division, to probe the line of the river Carrión from Villamuriel de Cerrato to the monastery at San Isidro near Dueñas and that of the Pisuerga at Tariego. While Gauthier led his division against the bridge at Tariego, supported by 'some squadrons' of Boyer's dragoon division,[32] Maucune himself led the 5e Division in a reconnaissance of the centre right of the river line at the village of Villamuriel de Cerrato, supported by Desfossés's light cavalry brigade, previously Curto's brigade. Meanwhile Souham followed the royal road towards Tariego with the rest of the army, a further five infantry divisions and three other brigades.[33]

---

27 J. Hale, *The Journal of James Hale, Late Sergeant in the Ninth Regiment of Foot* (Cirencester: Philip Watkins, 1826), p.93.

28 TNA, WO12/2012, 2206, 2265, 2665, 4646, 5184, 5245, 5716, battalion pay-lists; the dead men were Privates William Stubbins, John Townsend (2/30th), Sergeant Edward Bridgman (1/38th) and Private Joel Ball (2/38th).

29 Oman, *History*, Vol.VI, p.78.

30 Oman, *History*, Vol.VI, p.744; R. Burnham, *Charging against Wellington* (Barnsley: Frontline, 2011), p.76; Martinien, *Tableaux*, p.597; Wellington, *Supplementary Despatches*, Vol.XIV, pp.147, 149; H.Magon de la Giclais, *Historique du 15e Régiment de Chasseurs à Cheval* (Paris: Berger-Levrault, 1895), p.156; SHD C8 467/8; A.L. von Ardenne, *Bergische Lanziers, Westfälische Husaren nr.11* (Berlin: Mittler, 1877), pp.73–5; E. Martin, *La Gendarmerie Française en Espagne et en Portugal. (Campagnes de 1807 à 1814)* (Paris: Léautey, 1898), p.319; Cafferelli's dispatch to the Minister of War (30 October) places the Lanciers de Berg from Laferriére's brigade 'near Palencia', while the history of the 15e Chasseurs à Cheval states that this regiment spent 25 October 'capturing the crossings of the Carrión between Palencia and Villamuriel'. Martinien has *Lieutenant* Nicol, 13e Chasseurs à Cheval, 'as wounded 25 October 1812, near Palencia'.

31 Eugène Redmond Shée was his son, see page 2 of his son's record, LEONORE LH/2512/54. The father's record (LH/2512/55) contains little information.

32 Wellington, *Supplementary Despatches*, Vol.XIV, p.150; Souham's report, 1 November 1812; Burnham, *Charging*, p.76.

33 Oman, *History*, Vol.VI, pp.743–746; Clausel's 2e Division, Taupin's 3e, Sarrut's 4e, Pinoteau's 6e, 2e Demi-brigade Provisoire (en route to the Armée du Midi), Aussignac's brigade of the

The 1/1st Foot Guards joined the allied army at Dueñas, in the evening of 24 October,[34] as described by Lieutenant William Staveley (Royal Staff Corps) in a letter to his mother:

> When I wrote to you from Corunna I told you I was on my way back to Burgos with the Guards but on our arrival at Palencia we found the Army was retiring and we joined them at Duenas. I had just the pleasure of seeing the French in full pursuit and was immediately summoned to attend Lord Wellington who ordered me back again to Corunna to meet the 91st Regiment, which had landed and conduct them to the Army, directing their route according to the circumstances.[35]

The 7th Division started the 25th at or near Dueñas but in the morning was ordered south, de Bernewitz's Brigade to Venta de Trigueros and Halkett's Brigade to Cabezón. The October monthly return of the Chasseurs Brittaniques, of de Bernewitz's Brigade, reports the unit as being camped near Dueñas on the 25th. Green has the 68th Foot, also of de Bernewitz's Brigade arriving in Valladolid on the evening of the 24th, while Wheeler, of the 51st Foot of the same brigade, has his regiment pushed on by forced marches from Burgos to Valladolid. Likewise, Deputy Assistant Commissary General Daniel of the headquarters staff reported that he was sent on to Valladolid on the 24th.[36] On the other hand von Kortzfleisch has the move to Valladolid happening only after 26 October.[37]

However, this difficult retreat had not been without its distractions:

> On the day before this action, [the 24th] while the French were pressing the British hard with their cavalry, the printing press of the Spanish General Castanos stuck in passing a small stream, and the light companies on rear guard, were compelled to halt to rescue it. The Marquis of Wellington coming to see what was the matter, up jumped a hare, when a brace of greyhounds belonging to Lieutenant Robert Grier, of the 44th, happening to be at hand, started off, followed by his Lordship and an orderly. It was a pretty course and seen by all present. Wellington made the

---

Réserve de Bayonne and from the Armée du Nord, Vandermaesen's Division and Dumoustier's Jeune Garde brigade.

34 G. Glover (ed.), *With the 1st Foot Guards in the Peninsular and at Waterloo, The Letters of Lieutenant Colonel Henry Packe, 1806–16* (Godmanchester: Ken Trotman, 2016), p.53.

35 National Army Museum (NAM), Acc. No. 1999-06-149 item 8; letter, 14 December 1812; Burroughs, *Narrative*, p.22, Burroughs dates this to 25 October.

36 J.E. Daniel, *Journal of an Officer in the Commissariat Department of the Army...* (London: Author, 1820), p.174; *Army List*, 1813, pp.59–60 for rank.

37 G.von Kortzfleisch, *Geschichte des Herzoglich Braunschweigischen Infanterie-Regiments und seiner Stammtruppen 1809–1867* (Braunschweig: Limbach, 1896), Vol.I, pp.239, 241; A. Nicols, *Wellington's Mongrel Regiment* (Staplehurst: Spellmount, 2005), p.86; J. Green, *The vicissitudes of a soldier's life; or, A series of occurrences from 1806 to 1815* (Louth: Author, 1827), pp.121–2; B.H. Liddell Hart (ed.), *The Letters of Private Wheeler, 1808–1828* (Adlestrop: Windrush, 1993), p.99; Anon., 'Record of the Services of the 51st (Second West York) or King's Own Light Infantry Regiment', *USM* (1869), pt.1, Vol.CXIX, pp.370–371; Napier, *History*, 1993, Vol.V, p.303; A.F. Mockler-Ferryman, *The life of a regimental officer during the great war, 1793–1815 comp. from the correspondence of Colonel Samuel Rice, C.B., K.H. 51st Light Infantry, and from other sources* (Edinburgh: W. Blackwood and Sons, 1913), pp.214–219.

> orderly dismount and sent back the dead hare. The dogs were afterwards brought to England. Lieutenant Pearce had a Welsh Spaniel named Brush that would run up and down the whole division, frequently flushing game to the amusement of the men. Poor Brush died on service.[38]

Wellington's chief engineer, Fletcher, had been recovering from the wound received at Badajoz and repairing the fortifications there, consequently he did not re-join the army until 26 October. In his place was Brevet Lieutenant Colonel John Fox Burgoyne, who related in his journal how, on the 24th, he was:

> At 9pm sent for by Lord Wellington, and ordered to mine the bridges of Dueñas, Tariego, Villa Muriel, and Palencia. Sent officers off for the purpose. At Tariego, the cavalry officer at our outposts and a little in rear of the town, reported to Lieutenant Pitts [Lieutenant Thomas James Hiblethwaite Pitts, Royal Engineers] that the enemy was in possession of the bridge, and he retired without attempting anything in consequence. We have troops at Villa Muriel, and the Royals and two guns, in front of Palencia.[39]

However, as we shall see the Royals were not to arrive in Palencia until the morning of the 25th.

On 24 October, Colonel James Willoughby Gordon, Wellington's Quartermaster General, issued the following orders:

> Movements of the army on the 25th October 1812
> The army will halt tomorrow the 25th inst.
>
> The baggage with the exception of the officer's tents and canteens and the camp kettles and cattle for tomorrow must be sent behind Dueñas at 6 o'clock in the morning.
>
> The troops are to cook at day light and as it is probable that they may be wanted they must be kept in the lines, and sober if possible, throughout the day. Guards must be put over all the wine cellars in the neighbourhood of the camp.[40]

Wellington also ensured that the 5th Division had sufficient reserves of musket ammunition, with Lord Fitzroy Somerset, his military secretary, writing to Colonel Robe, Royal Artillery, 'Lord Wellington begs you will take care that the 5th division are provided with plenty of musquet ammunition besides the reserve they now have with them'.[41]

The scene was now set for the combat that took place at Villamuriel on 25 October as Oswald's 5th Anglo-Portuguese Division, together with Liñan's 1ª Sección, 1ª Division, 6º Ejército (Galicia y Asturias), fought to repel the assault of Maucune's 5e Division, Armée de Portugal.

---

38 T. Carter, *Historical Record Forty–Fourth or East Essex Regiment of Foot* (Chatham: Gale and Folden, 1887), p.68.

39 G. Wrottesley, *Life and Correspondence of Field Marshal Sir John Burgoyne, Bart* (London: Richard Bentley, 1873), Vol.I, pp.183, 240–2.

40 Leslie, *Dickson*, Vol.IV, p.778.

41 Leslie, *Dickson*, Vol.IV, p.777; letter from Villamuriel 25 October.

2

Orders of Battle

French

Infantry

The 5e Division, Armée de Portugal was commanded by *Général de Division* Antoine-Louis Popon Baron de Maucune.[1] His chief of staff was *Chef de Bataillon* Étienne-François Girard and his artillery commander was *Chef de Bataillon* Charles Blanzat of the 2e Régiment d'Artillerie à Cheval. Maucune's *aides de camp* were *Capitaine*s Pierre Lafont and Alexandre Lachapelle.

The division comprised two brigades each of two regiments. The first brigade was commanded by *Général de Brigade* Pierre-Louis d'Arnauld, whose seniority dated to 17 November 1808. He was supported by his *aides de camp Capitaine* Louis Antoine Marie Demailly, who had served in this role since July 1809, and *Lieutenant* Douence.[2] D'Arnauld's two regiments were the 15e Régiment d'Infanterie de Ligne (15e Ligne) and the 66e Ligne.

The 15e Ligne was commanded by *Major* Jacques-Louis Dornier and comprised the first and second battalions, the men of the third battalion having been used to reinforce the other two in August. Most of the men of the fourth battalion were used similarly in October with the cadre returning to France to recruit.[3] However, the grenadier and *voltigeur* companies of the fourth battalion feature separately in 15 October *situation*, as present with the regiment. The sources do not make it clear whether these men served during the battle as discrete companies of the fourth battalion or were distributed amongst the first and second battalions, although Béchaud's reference to 'eight companies' of *tirailleurs* suggests the latter. The 1/15e Ligne was commanded by *Capitaine* Jean Lafitte and the 2/15e Ligne by *Chef de Bataillon* Alexandre François Frémin.

The 66e Ligne was commanded by *Colonel* Jean Pierre Béchaud (*Baron de l'Empire*, 1809) and comprised the fourth battalion, commanded by *Chef de*

1 SHD C8 468; *Armées en Espagne …1er Janvier 1813*; contains the *Situation* of the *Armée de Portugal* for the 15 October 1812; Oman, *History*, Vol.V, p.602, Vol.VI, p.743.

2 LEONORE, LH/723/40, *Capitaine* Demailly, 36 years old, 47e Ligne.

3 Marie Louis Adrien De Tarragon, *Historique du 15e Régiment d'Infanterie* (Paris: Charles-Lavauzelle, 1895), pp.216, 221.

Bataillon Michel Izambard, and the sixth battalion, commanded by *Capitaine* Leopold Daniel Charlemont.

Maucune's second brigade was commanded by *Général de Brigade* Jacques Montfort, previously *colonel* of the 82e Ligne before his promotion on 6 August 1811. The brigade comprised the 82e Ligne and the 86e Ligne.[4] The 82e Ligne was commanded by *Colonel* Joseph Jacob van Geen and comprised the fourth battalion, commanded by *Chef de Bataillon* Michel Lefizelier, and the fifth battalion, commanded by *Chef de Bataillon* Jean Baptiste Dupré. The 86e Ligne was commanded by *Colonel* Claude Joseph Pélecier and comprised the first battalion, commanded by *Chef de Bataillon* Jean Luzinier, and the second battalion, commanded by *Chef de Bataillon* François Adam Eys.

Artillery

The artillery of the *5e Division* comprised only one company, the 11e compagnie, 8e Régiment d'Artillerie à Pied, which was commanded by *Capitaine* Joseph Marie Alexis Vincent Genta.[5] The company had five guns: two 8-pounder cannon, two 4-pounders, one 6-inch howitzer.

The division was also supported by men of the 2e compagnie, 2e (bis) Train Bataillon, commanded by *Lieutenant* Pierre Levaillant, and men of the 5e and 6e compagnies, 12e Train Bataillon, commanded by *Lieutenant* Jean Massot.[6]

However, this was not the only artillery available to Maucune on 25 October. Several British accounts, for example Oswald and MacKenzie, reported heavier and superior French artillery fire.[7] Other accounts are more quantitative: the obituary of Colonel Hamilton, 30th Foot, reported 'seventeen pieces of cannon', the history of the 30th Foot, reported eighteen guns reinforced by a further 10 'Young Guard' guns and Ensign George Young (2/38th Foot) writing in December 1812 describes a 'heavy cannonade' involving 'a large park of howitzers', and in a second letter written at the same time, he describes how at 10:00 a.m., 'the French brought down about forty pieces of cannon with a great number of howitzers'.[8]

Souham's entire army was accompanied by 59 guns from the Armée de Portugal and a maximum of 19 guns from the Armée du Nord, for a combined total of 78 guns and howitzers.[9] Thus, Ensign Young was suggesting that more than half of the French guns available were concentrated at Villamuriel, in

4 P. Desachy, *Les Cahiers du Colonel Girard, 1766–1846* (Paris: Plon, 1951), p.205, has Montfort leading the first brigade, however this is contradicted by the *situation*.

5 SHD C8 466; named in *situation* of 15 June 1812.

6 LEONORE LH/1623/78; Pierre Louis Adrien Stanilas Levaillant born 23 December 1782, Paris, volunteered *soldat* 1802; LH/1785/43, SHD 2Yb 1050 *CdO* train battalions; *Lieutenant* Jean François Alexandre Massot born 28 March 1770, joined as *lieutenant* December 1792.

7 J. Oswald, 'Affair at Villa Muriele', *United Service Journal* (1837), pt.1, pp.266–7; 'McK', 'The Affair of Villa Muriel', pp.542–544.

8 Anon., 'Obituary of Colonel Alexander Hamilton', *United Service Journal* (1838), pt.2, p.431; N. Bannatyne, *History of the Thirtieth Regiment now the First Battalion East Lancashire Regiment, 1689–1881* (Liverpool: Littlebury, 1923), p.28; Younge, 'Some Peninsular Letters', p.512.

9 SHD C8 468; G. Nafziger Orders of Battle available from The Ike Skelton Combined Arms Research Library, Digital Library (NAFZIGER), *North, 15 October 1812*.

support of only one of Souham's ten-and-a-half divisions, which would have constituted a massed battery on a scale seen only at the larger battles. Given that his pursuit of the allies was in three directions via Palencia, Tariego, and Villamuriel, it seems highly unlikely that Souham would have allocated more than one of his three reserve companies (two horse and one foot) to the attack on Villamuriel. Elsewhere in the same letters, written two months after the events described, Ensign Young inflated the size of the French Army, putting Souham's force at 100,000 infantry, 10,000 cavalry and 100 guns; approximately double the numbers of infantry and cavalry and 25 percent more artillery.

Regarding the involvement of the Jeune Garde, the order of battle for the Armée du Nord, shows that Dumoustier's Jeune Garde brigade was not supported by any artillery, their usual artillery support, the Canonniers Conscrits, having all been redeployed to Russia.[10]

Girard, Maucune's chief of staff, recorded that the French artillery comprised a '*batterie de dix canon*' while Béchaud described how the French artillery initially deployed 'at the gallop', which implies the presence of some horse artillery. Likewise, Burgoyne stated the French infantry were 'protected by a cannonade of ten guns from a hollow way near the village.'[11]

Taken together the evidence suggests that Souham allocated to Maucune one of his three available Batteries de Réserve, the 6/2e Artillerie à Cheval, the 7/3e Artillerie à Cheval or the 19/1er Artillerie à Pied. Similarly, on 23 October, Souham supported Maucune's advanced guard with both light cavalry and horse artillery.[12] Of the three companies, the 1er Batterie de Réserve is the most likely, since *Lieutenant* Robillard, 6/2e Artillerie à Cheval was wounded at Villodrigo with Maucune on 23 October, the sixth being the only company of the 2e Régiment present with the Armée de Portugal.[13]

This company was commanded by *Capitaine* Joseph Viard,[14] and was supported by detachments from the 3e Compagnie, 5e (bis) Train Bataillon and the 5e Compagnie, 12e Train Bataillon, commanded by *Sous Lieutenant* Barbier and *Lieutenant* Pierre Chéron respectively.[15]

The general artillery park of the Armée de Portugal comprised three 12-pounder cannon, twelve 8-pounders and seven 6-inch howitzers, consequently the long guns of Viard's Batterie de Rèserve, or of the alternative 2e Batterie de Rèserve, are likely to have been three or four 8-pounders, assuming the 12-pounders were with the 3e Batterie de Réserve. The balance of the five guns would have been 6-inch howitzers.[16]

10 NAFZIGER, *Grande Armée, 1 August 1812*.

11 Desachy, *Girard*, p.205; Colin, 'Béchaud', p.406; Wrottesley, *Burgoyne*, p.241.

12 Colin, 'Béchaud', p.401; '*artillerie légère*'.

13 A. Martinien, *Tableaux, par corps et par batailles, des officiers tués et blessés pendant les guerres de l'Empire (1805–1815): Supplément* (Paris: L.Fournier, 1909), p.103.

14 Martinien, *Tableaux*, p.107; SHD 2Yb 1015 *contrôle des officiers*; KIA at Dresden 26/08/1813, while serving in the Garde Impériale.

15 LEONORE LH/519/17; Pierre François Chéron, born 24/12/1769 in Villejust; enlisted 1792.

16 SHD C8 468.

Cavalry

Oman remarks that Maucune's divisions 'retained Curto's light horse', by which he meant the Armée de Portugal's light cavalry division. Similarly, on 13 October, Béchaud identifies the cavalry supporting Maucune's advanced guard of two infantry divisions as Curto's light cavalry division.[17] The light cavalry division comprised two brigades, *Colonel* Shée's brigade and Curto's own brigade (3e Hussards, 22e, 26e and 28e Chasseurs à Cheval, a total of 7 squadrons), then commanded by *Colonel* François Michel Desfossés of the 22e Chasseurs à Cheval.[18] Desfossés's father's surname was Michel but he preferred his mother's surname Desfossés and he was known by the form shown here.[19] Béchaud has Desfossés leading six squadrons at Monasterio on 13 October.[20] Although Mermet is said to have arrived to take command of the division from Curto on 8 September and the *situation* for 15 October shows him in command, a report written 4 November, by Souham's chief of staff, Baron de Lamartinière, is clear that Curto retained command of the Armée de Portugal's light cavalry division on 23 October.[21] Furthermore a note on the *situation* of the army for the 15 December 1812, reports that Mermet arrived from France only on the 4 December 1812.[22] Thus at Villamuriel, *Colonel* Desfossés is described by Béchaud as arriving with his brigade around 1:00 p.m.[23] The brigade comprised two squadrons each of the 3e Hussards, commanded by *Major* Amedée Marie Joseph Heina, Desfossés own 22e Chasseurs à Cheval, and the 26e Chasseurs à Cheval, commanded by *Capitaine* Jacques Felix Franquin Govon, and a small detachment of the 28e Chasseurs à Cheval, commanded by *Sous Lieutenant* Joseph Pinelli.

Summary

The strengths of the French forces involved at Villamuriel are summarised in the following table. The numbers represent those men present under arms as given in the *situation* of 15 October, reduced to reflect likely casualties from the period 15 October to 24 October, based on Martinien's list of officer casualties, using Oman's proportional technique.[24]

17 Colin, 'Béchaud', p.389.

18 Burnham, *Charging*, p.76.

19 Anon., *État des donataires totalement dépossédés: qui en droit á l'indemnité fixée par la loi proposée aux Chambres en 1821* (Paris: Imprimerie Royale, 1821), p.128; LEONORE LH/1869/22.

20 Colin, 'Béchaud', p.391.

21 Burnham, *Charging*, p.76; Gurwood (ed.), *Dispatches* (London: Parker, Furnivall and Parker, 1845), Vol.VI, p.774.

22 SHD C8 469 *Situation* Armée d'Espagne, 15 February 1813.

23 Colin, 'Béchaud', p.407.

24 Oman, *History*, Vol.V, p.605; Martinien, *Tableaux*, pp.293, 299, 606, 618, 808; Martinien, *Supplément*, p.103; R. Muir, *Salamanca 1812* (New Haven: Yale University, 2001), pp.253–6.

Formation	Unit	*Situation* 15 October Present under arms		Estimated losses 16–24 October		Estimated Strength 25 October 1812	
		Officers	Other ranks	Officers	Other ranks	Officers	Other ranks
1re Brigade, 5e Division D'Arnauld	1/15e Ligne	22	655			22	655
	2/15e Ligne	15	644			15	644
	4/15e Ligne	6	234			6	234
	4/66e Ligne	22	493			22	493
	6/66e Ligne	17	450			17	450
2e Brigade, 5e Division Montfort	4/82e Ligne	24	441	1	10	24	431
	5/82e Ligne	24	458		10	23	448
	1/86e Ligne	20	621	4	75	17	547
	2/86e Ligne	12	592		77	11	515
Artillery 5e Division	11/8e à Pied*	2	75			2	75
	Train	2	124			2	124
Totals						161	4,615
1re Brigade Cav. Légère Desfossés	3e Hussards	17	249	1	16	16	233
	22e Chasseurs	15	339	1	23	14	316
	26e Chasseurs	19	337			19	337
	28e Chasseurs	3	18			3	18
1re Batterie de Réserve	6/2e Art. à Cheval	4	85	1		3	85
	Train	2	137			2	137
*incl. 4 Ouvriers of the 4e Cie							
Totals						218	5,741
							5,959

Martinien includes lightly wounded individuals who may have returned to the ranks by 25 October, therefore these numbers may slightly understate the strengths for the units affected. However, there is no evidence that any of the wounded officers concerned served at Villamuriel. Furthermore, the infantry casualties for the period 16–24 October are likely to have been less concentrated in the 86e Ligne. The *registres matricules* record 56 casualties for the 86e Ligne during this period, but also record two for the 15e Ligne and nine for the 66e Ligne, suggesting that the strength of the 86e Ligne is underestimated by 25 men and vice versa.

Brief biographies of the regimental and battalion commanders are given in Appendix I.

Anglo-Portuguese

The 5th Division comprised two British brigades and the Portuguese Brigada N.3.[25] Major General John Oswald commanded the division in the absence of Lieutenant General James Leith who was recovering from the wound he received at Salamanca.

25 C. Oman, *Wellington's Army 1809–1814* (London: Edward Arnold, 1913), p.359.

The first brigade was commanded by Brigadier General Edward Barnes. He was appointed to the command of Hay's Brigade in General Orders only on 28 October 1812, but he served at Villamuriel, as confirmed by Wellington in his dispatch of 26 October.[26]

The brigade comprised the 3/1st (Royal Scots) Foot, 1/9th (East Norfolk) Foot, 1/38th (1st Staffordshire) Foot and the 2/38th Foot.

The light companies of these battalions were removed, in compliance with Wellington's General Orders,[27] to form a battalion, together with the 2nd Company, the Duke of Brunswick Oels Light Infantry.[28] According to his biography, the light battalion was commanded by Captain Thomas Willshire of the 38th Foot.[29] However it is worth noting that Hale was in the light company of the 9th Foot, which according to the pay-list and his discharge papers, was Captain Ferrars's company. Ferrars was more senior than Willshire by 25 days and would have been expected to command the light infantry battalion. This suggests that as the second most senior officer in the battalion, Ferrars was performing the role of a major in the 1/9th Foot. Similarly, in 1813 Hale has Lieutenant John Ogle commanding the light company, 1/9th Foot.[30]

The second brigade was commanded by Major General William Henry Pringle, who had commanded the division until Oswald arrived on 25 October. The brigade comprised the 1/4th (King's Own) Foot, 2/4th Foot, the 2/30th (Cambridgeshire) Foot, and the 2/44th (East Essex) Foot.

The light companies of these battalions were also used to form a battalion, together with the 10th Company, the Duke of Brunswick Oels Light Infantry. The light battalion was probably commanded by Major Alured Dodsworth Faunce of the 4th Foot, who had commanded it at Salamanca and is reported to have commanded it until the end of 1812.[31]

Brigada N.3 was commanded by *Brigadeiro* William Frederick Spry, a 42-year-old veteran of Seringapatam. The brigade comprised the Regimento de Infantaria N.3, 1º de Olivença, (RI N.3), commanded by *Coronel* João António Tavares, the Regimento de Infantaria N.15, 2º de Olivença, (RI N.15), commanded by *Coronel* Luís do Rêgo Barreto, and the Batalhão de Caçadores

26 Wellington (ed.), *Supplementary Despatches*, Vol.XIV, p.146.

27 J. Gurwood, *The General Orders of Field Marshal the Duke of Wellington* (London: W. Clowes, 1832), pp.187–8.

28 Kortzfleisch, *Geschichte*, Vol.I, pp.158, 239, 250; neither the 2nd or 10th companies were the sharpshooter company, which was numbered 3 and served with the 4th Division. This unit is known by several names; the *Army List* 1812 refers to them as the Duke of Brunswick Oels Corps including the Hussars, while in modern accounts they are widely referred to as Jagers. I have chosen the contemporary description of the Duke of Brunswick Oels Light Infantry as shown, for example, in Wellington (ed.), *Supplementary Despatches*, 1871, Vol.XIII, pp.472, 636.

29 C.R. Low, 'Memoir of General Sir Thomas Willshire', *United Service Magazine* (1879), pt.2, pp.69, 75.

30 Hale, *Journal*, p.39, 110; TNO, WO12/2665, WO97/306/79.

31 Anon.,'Fourth (or the Kings Own) Regiment of Foot', *United Service Magazine* (1830), pt.2, p.563; R. Cannon, *Historical Record of the Fourth Regiment of Foot* (London: William Clowes, 1839), p.106; UML, GB 133 Eng MSS 1273, item 16; Faunce is named as such in Pringle's correspondence regarding Salamanca. Faunce's full name from his will (TNA, PROB 11/2111/265).

de Trancoso N.8 (Caçadores N.8), commanded by the 25-year-old *Major* Dudley St. Leger Hill.[32] The two line regiments had two battalions in the field.

In June 1812 Le Mesurier wrote that the 5th Division had been reinforced by the 2/58th Foot and that the 2/4th, 1/9th and 2/58th Foot were then brigaded together. However, at Salamanca in July, the 2/58th Foot was with the 1st Division. On 20 October 1812, the 2/58th Foot was assigned to Brigadier General Denis Pack's command comprising his own Portuguese brigade and eight other battalions. Pack's command was designed to blockade the castle of Burgos and when the retreat was ordered the next day, the 2/58th Foot returned to the 1st Division.[33]

The 5th Division's artillery was provided by Major Robert Lawson's brigade of the Royal Artillery. Lawson's company was part of the 8th Battalion. The guns were five heavy 6-pounders and one iron 5½-inch or 24-pounder howitzer.[34]

The howitzer is described as a 5½-inch howitzer from the brigade's arrival at Oporto in August 1811 and as a 24-pounder howitzer from December 1811. Originally the brigade would have had a brass heavy 5½-inch howitzer, but in September 1811, Wellington ordered them to be replaced with iron howitzers in order that the heavy brass howitzers could be used to replace their light equivalents in the troops of the Royal Horse Artillery. On 26 September 1812, during the siege of Burgos, Lawson's diary records that his howitzer was sent to Captain Gardinier and does not explicitly record its return. However, Lawson implied its return before 3 October and certainly had a howitzer again in January 1813.[35]

Spanish

Oman stated that Losada's 3ª Division was present at Villamuriel, however *Brigadier* Don Pascual de Liñan's report of the action records that his sección (brigade), from Barcena's 1ª Division, 6º Ejército, was the one involved and specifically names the Regimiento de la Corona as present.[36] Sañudo names those regiments from Liñan's sección, which were present, as the Regimiento 1º Asturias and the 2º Voluntarios de la Corona.[37]

---

32 A. Halliday, *The present state of Portugal, and of the Portuguese Army* (Edinburgh: G.R.Clarke, 1812), p.160; Castro Alves, Pinto da Silva, Cordeiro Simões, *A História do Regimento de Infantaria N.º15*, p.65, available at <http://ri15.paraquedistas.com.pt/publicacoes/livro200anos/200anos.html>, accessed 4 February 2014.

33 Oman, *Army*, p.363; R. Muir, R. Burnham, H. Muir, R. McGuigan, *Inside Wellington's Peninsular Army, 1808–1814* (Barnsley: Pen and Sword, 2006), pp.192–3; Greenwood, *Le Mesurier*, pp.111–2; Gurwood (ed.), *Dispatches*, Vol.IX, pp.503–4; Anon.,'Notes on the History and Services of the Fifty-Eighth Regiment of Foot', *USM* (1878), Vol.CXLVII, pt.2, p.87.

34 Leslie, *Dickson*, Vol.IV, pp.696, 699; TNA, WO10/916, muster roll for October 1812; N. Lipscombe, *Wellington's Guns – The Untold Story of Wellington and his Artillery in the Peninsula and at Waterloo* (Oxford: Osprey, 2013), p.256.

35 Leslie, *Dickson*, Vol.III, pp.439–40, 448, 462–3, 468–9, 524, Vol.IV, pp.685–6, 699, 711, 715, 730.

36 AHNM, *Diversos/Colecciones*/101/n63 (Liñan's report); AHNM, *Diversos/Colecciones*/144/n32 (October monthly state); the Spanish renamed their brigades as *seccións* earlier in 1812.

37 J.J. Sañudo, *Base de datos sobre las unidades militares en la guerra de la independcia Española* (Madrid: Ministerio de Defensa, 2012).

1° Asturias

This is not the original line regiment named Asturias (Regimiento N. 22) which went with Romana to Denmark in 1807 and did not return.[38] While Nafziger has this regiment raised on 5 August 1812, Sañudo's database states that the regiment was raised by the French born, former *soldado distinguido, Coronel* Pedro Dejoui, between 5 March and 14 April 1811, based around the absorption of four older units, three of which he separately associates with the 2° rather than the 1° Asturias, but it was certainly in the order of battle at the end of 1811. Kortzfleisch gives the commander of the 1° Asturias at Villamuriel, as *Coronel* Miranda, but was presumably referring to Dejoui's subordinate, *Teniente Coronel* Don Manuel Miramón.[39]

2° Voluntarios de la Corona

The October monthly state identifies the regiment present in Barcena's 1ª Division as the similarly named Regimiento de la Corona. Modern lists of Spanish units include three similarly named units; two pre-war line regiments, the Regimiento de la Corona and the Voluntarios de la Corona, and a further unit also called the Voluntarios de la Corona. Clonard gives the name, Cazadores de la Corona, as the 1812 name for the pre-war Voluntarios de la Corona.[40] Of these the Regimiento de la Corona was part of the 3° Ejèrcito.[41] A unit named Voluntarios de la Corona features in an 1811 order of battle for the 6° Ejército,[42] and in the 1ª Division, 6° Ejército for April 1811, October 1811 and January 1812.[43] In 1811, this unit is not listed among the line regiments but as part of the 'additional' units, thus suggesting that this is not the line regiment raised in 1795. Sañudo's database first mentions the 2° Voluntarios de la Corona in June 1812, following the 'dispersal' of the original unit at the action of Pajares on 17 May 1812. Sanudo describes this regiment as light infantry but the evidence for this is unclear. In July 1812, the regiment was commanded by *Coronel* José Quiroga y Quindos. In December 1813, the '2° de la Corona' was reported in the 4ª Division, 4° Ejército.[44]

The third unit in Liñan's sección was the Cazadores del Rey, but this light infantry unit had been detached to Poza de la Sal, approximately 30 miles north east of Burgos.

---

38 G.Nafziger, *The Armies of Spain and Portugal 1808–1814* (West Chester: Author, 1993), p.59; R.Partridge, M.Oliver, *Napoleonic Army Handbook – British Army and her Allies* (London: Constable, 1999), pp.317, 347; Anon., *Estado militar de España* (Madrid: Imprenta Real,1812), p.72, (1815), p.54, (1816), p.73.

39 Kortzfleisch, *Geschichte*, Vol.I, p.240.

40 Partridge and Oliver, *Handbook*, p.368; Conde de Clonard, *História orgánica de las armas de infantería y caballería españolas desde la creación del Ejercito permanente hasta el día* (Madrid: Castilla, 1858), Vol.XII, pp.194, 216.

41 Anon., *Estado*, 1811, p.144.

42 Anon., *Estado*, 1811, p.154.

43 Anon., *Estados de la Organizacion y Fuerza de los Ejercitos Espanoles Beligerantes en la Peninsula, Durante la Guerra de Espana contra Bonaparte* (Barcelona: Viuda e hijos de Antonio Brusi, 1822), pp.103, 132, 140.

44 Anon., *Estados*, p.214.

Coronel Sañudo's database also suggests that other Spanish units were present at Villamuriel, namely the Milicia Provinciale de Monterrey (2ª Sección, Barcena's 1ª Division, 6º Ejército), the Regimiento 1º Toledo and the Milicia Provinciale de Oviedo (both from Cabrera's 2ª Division) and the Regimiento 2º Asturias (Losada's Division de Reserva). However, the other sources suggest that these units were present at and around Palencia, rather than Villamuriel itself, as part of the larger Combat on the Carrión.

Allied Unit Strengths

British Infantry

The October monthly returns for the British battalions are dated from the day of the action at Villamuriel, so we have an accurate picture of these battalions.[45] In the following table, the battalion strengths are given as the total fit and present at headquarters for all ranks, excluding staff officers, as reported in the monthly returns for each regiment reduced by a tenth to allow for the detachment of the light company.

Unit	Officers	Men	Total
Barnes's Brigade			
3/1st Foot	20	356	376
1/9th Foot	16	288	304
1/38th Foot	14	270	284
2/38th Foot	14	144	158
Light Battalion	7	118	125
2nd Coy. Brunswick Oels Light Infantry	2	45	47
Totals	73	1,221	1,294
Pringle's Brigade			
1/4th Foot	25	330	355
2/4th Foot	20	282	302
2/30th Foot	15	191	206
2/44th Foot	14	135	149
Light Battalion	8	104	112
10th Coy. Brunswick Oels Light Infantry	2	37	39
Totals	84	1,079	1,163

The historical record of the 9th Foot described the battalion as 'not numbering more than 300 men', but Le Mesurier wrote on 2 November 1812 that the 1/9th Foot had only 168 rank and file in the field on the 25th, a full 112 men fewer than the 280 fit for duty at headquarters as shown in the October monthly return (338 men of all ranks, excluding the assistant surgeon). Together with the officers, sergeants and drummers, Le Mesurier's total would suggest a total strength for the battalion of only 226 men of all ranks. At the same time Le Mesurier refers to two companies being detached from the battalion and it is not clear whether he is including these men in his

45 TNA, WO17/96 (1st Foot); WO17/110 (9th); WO17/148 (38th); WO17/101 (4th); WO17/138 (30th); WO17/156 (44th); WO12/11654 (Brunswick Light Infantry).

figure of 168 rank and file. Hale gives the battalion strength in excess of 200 men. In a later letter Le Mesurier stated that the 1/9th Foot had only lost one man to straggling in the retreat before Villamuriel, so it is unlikely that he was referring to some unrecorded straggling.[46]

The actual strength of the 2/30th Foot on this day is left uncertain by the arrival of a detachment of five officers (Captain Thomas G. Richardson (1st Battalion – first mentioned in the November muster roll), Lieutenant Theophilus O'Halloran, Ensigns Samuel R. Poyntz, George Madden and Francis Kelly) and 90 non-commissioned officers and men. The monthly return of 25 October clearly states that all these men were 'on the way to join now in Portugal'. However, Madden is listed as wounded at Villamuriel. Bannatyne has the detachment arriving after the battle, the exception being Madden who he gives as arriving separately.[47] It seems more likely that the whole detachment arrived at the close of the action and helped guard the bridge as witnessed by Lieutenant Elers Purnell Hopkins (1/4th Foot) with Madden wounded in the final skirmishing at the bridge.[48] Other candidates for Hopkins's detachment are the 3/1st (208 men), 1/4th (60 men) and the 2/44th (44 men) who each showed significant numbers of men joining, as recorded in their November monthly returns, but none of these detachments were recorded on 25 October as *en route* to their units. The strength for the battalion shown here is the strength at the beginning of the day as shown in the monthly return, before the addition of Richardson's detachment of 5 officers and 90 other ranks.

The adjutant's roll for the 2nd Company, the Duke of Brunswick Oels Light Infantry, gives the number of men present under arms on 24 October, at one captain (Georg David von Sternfeld), one lieutenant, five sergeants, three corporals, one drummer/fifer and 36 privates, although the muster is dated 8 November 1812.

The adjutant's roll of the 10th Company for 24 October, again dated 8 November 1812, gives the strength at one captain, five sergeants, four corporals, one drummer/fifer and 59 privates but, unlike that of the 2nd Company, does not specify the men who were absent due to sickness. However, the 1 November fortnightly state shows that the company had 34 men sick absent and three men sick present on this date. Based on the equivalent data for the 2nd Company, 32 of the men of the 10th Company are assumed sick on 25 October.

None of the officers recorded in the adjutant's roll were in fact with the company, Captain von Gillern (Ludwig von Nassau had taken his place) and Ensign Müller were in England, Lieutenant von Lisnewsky had been taken prisoner on 18 October at Santa Ollala and Lieutenant Sonntag, whereabouts unknown, possibly absent sick. Lieutenant Karl Hartwig is not mentioned in

46 TNA, WO12/2665; R. Cannon, *Historical Record of the Ninth or East Norfolk Regiment of Foot 1685–1847* (London: William Clowes, 1848), p.62; Greenwood, *Le Mesurier*, pp.139, 145–6; Hale, *Journal*, p.94.

47 Bannatyne, *Thirtieth*, pp.285–289.

48 Napier, *History* (London: Murray, 1840), Vol.VI, p.xviii; TNA, WO17/101, October monthly return, 1st battalion.

the adjutant's roll for the 2nd or 10th company but was present at Villamuriel, having transferred from the 7th Company. In total, for the 10th Company, the present under arms strength is estimated as 39.[49]

Portuguese

The overall strength of Brigada N.3 is taken from 23 October morning state, although the information for the 5th Division is dated 21 October. This shows that, on this date, the total men present, for Spry's Brigade, excluding staff, was 1882 men of all ranks. This strength has been reduced to 1,806 men based on the pay-list returns for the British battalions, which show a loss of approximately four percent during the retreat between 21 and 25 October, assuming the Portuguese battalions suffered in the same proportion.[50]

A regimental history of the RI N.15 regiment gives its total strength on 25 October 1812 at 741 men of all ranks.[51] In the following table, the battalion strengths are estimated based on Oman's order of battle for Salamanca, the regimental strength given for the RI N.15, together with Foster's battalion strength data after the battle of Salamanca.[52]

Brigada N.3	Officers	Men	Total
1/RI N.3	17	370	387
2/RI N.3	12	265	277
1/RI N.15	19	419	438
2/RI N.15	13	290	303
Caçadores N.8	18	384	402

Royal Artillery

The establishment of a Royal Artillery company at this time was five officers, 17 NCOs, three drummers and 120 gunners, a total of 145 men. The muster roll for 31 October 1812, records 117 men in the company of whom 48 were present, 11 guard, 12 duty, 24 on command or otherwise away, and 22 sick. Also present was Lieutenant James Sinclair, giving a total of 118 men. Of these perhaps 72 were available for duty at Villamuriel.[53] While Lawson's muster roll contains no information regarding the drivers, this information is detailed in his diary. Taking into account the various reinforcements and losses between 21 May 1812 and 25 October 1812, we can estimate that Lawson's company was supported at Villamuriel, by a detachment of the Corps of Royal Artillery Drivers, comprising one staff sergeant (Corbett, assuming he retained his rank following his court martial on 21 August), one sergeant (Rotherway), three corporals, 53 drivers, two trumpeters and nine artificers, a total of 69 men, together with 123 horses and 30 mules.

---

49 TNA, WO12/11654, WO1/256.

50 TNA, WO1/256, p.103, morning state 23 October 1812.

51 Alves, *História*, p.71.

52 Oman, *History*, Vol.V, p.598; R. Foster, 'Notes on the Portuguese Infantry of the Peninsular War 1807-1814: 3rd Regiment of Olivenza (Beira) and 15th Regiment of Olivenza (Beira), and 8th Caçadores' *Napoleon Series*, available at; <http://www.napoleon-series.org/military/organization/portugal/Infantry/Notes/c_NotesonPortugueseInfantry3.html>, accessed 15 January 2015.

53 Leslie, *Dickson*, Vol.IV, p.697; TNA, WO10/916, muster roll for October 1812.

This is consistent with Adye's statement that a heavy six pounder brigade required 53 drivers. Using a similar rate of sickness as the gunners, perhaps some 14 men were absent sick. This is consistent with the diary, where in the entry for 13–16 October, Lawson remarks that his fit drivers each had three horses rather than the usual two, implying that only around 40 drivers were effective. Subsequently on 11 March 1813, Lawson recorded in his diary that a total of 79 drivers and 165 animals were present at a review by Major General Andrew Hay.[54]

Royal Artillery	Officers	Men	Total
Lawson's Brigade			
Gunners	3	69	72
Drivers		55	55
Total	3	124	127

The staff and regimental officers of the 5th Division are detailed in Appendix II.

Spanish

The October monthly state of the 6º Ejército gives the strength of the 1ª Division as 4,804 men. The division comprised nine regiments, each of a single battalion of eight companies, with therefore an average battalion strength of 534 men.[55]

In summary, the strength of the allied Army by brigade was;

Unit	Officers	Men	Total
Staff	15		15
Barnes's Brigade	73	1,221	1,294
Pringle's Brigade	84	1,079	1,163
Spry's Brigada N.3	68	1,739	1,807
Lawson's Brigade, RA	3	124	127
5th Anglo-Portuguese Division	243	4,163	4,406
Liňan's Sección			1,068
Grand Total			5,474

Oman gives the division strength dated 23 October 1812, as 3,638 rank and file present under arms. The 25 October monthly returns demonstrate that the 23 October morning state only applies to the British and Portuguese foot regiments and excludes not only their officers, sergeants and drummers but also the Duke of Brunswick Oels Light Infantry and the artillery.[56]

54 Leslie, *Dickson*, Vol.IV, pp.696–727; C. Franklin, *British Napoleonic Field Artillery* (Staplehurst: Spellmount, 2007), p.140, citing Adye, 1813.

55 AHNM, *Diversos/Colecciones*/144/n32; Anon., *Estados*, pp.162–3; the latter gives an average battalion strength of approximately 800 men.

56 Oman, *History*, Vol.VI, p.746.

3

Commanders and Troop Quality

In this chapter, a brief overview is given of each commander's military experience leading up to, and in some cases beyond, Villamuriel, as background for an assessment of their ability.

Troop Quality

The quality of the troops making up the various units is a key determinant of the outcome of any battle. For the purposes of this discussion three categories based on training and experience have been chosen:

Inexperienced troops: with less than six months training and combat experience.

Experienced troops: with more than six months training and combat experience.

Veteran troops: with experience of two or more campaigns, or 24 months training and combat experience. Two campaigns was the minimum requirement for entry to the Garde du Directoire. In 1800, Napoleon increased it to three campaigns for the Garde Consulaire.[1]

British

Commanders

John Oswald was born in Dunnikier, Kirkcaldy, Fife on 2 October 1771. Six feet tall, popular, powerful and handsome, he attended the military school at

1 J. Lynn, *Bayonets of the Republic* (Urbana: University of Illinois, 1984), p.223; H. Lachouque, A.S.K. Brown, *The Anatomy of Glory* (London: Arms and Armour, 1978), pp.5, 7.

Brienne before joining the 23rd Royal Welch Fusiliers as second lieutenant.[2] His progress through the ranks was as follows:[3]

second lieutenant	23rd (Royal Welch) Fusiliers	February 1788
lieutenant	7th (Royal) Fusiliers	January 1789
captain	Independent Company	January 1791
captain	35th (Sussex) Foot	March 1791
major	35th (Sussex) Foot	September 1795
lieutenant colonel	1/35th (Sussex) Foot	March 1797

Oswald, commanding the grenadier company, 35th Foot, served in the West Indies on Martinique, St Lucia and Guadeloupe in 1794, as part of Grey's 2nd Grenadier Battalion.[4] In 1799, he was seriously wounded at Krabbendam during the Battle of Bergen and in 1800 he served on Minorca and took part in the capture of Malta, remaining there until 1805.[5] A brevet colonel in October 1805, he joined Sir James Craig's force on Sicily, commanding at Melazzo. In 1806 he served with Sir John Stuart, leading the first troops ashore in the Bay of St. Euphemia before commanding the 3rd Brigade, which formed the reserve, at Maida. Twenty days later he successfully took Scylla Castle.[6] In 1807 Oswald, at the head of his regiment, served with Major General Mackenzie Fraser in the unfortunate expedition to Alexandria and Rosetta in Egypt. Returning to Sicily, Oswald was appointed to the command in Augusta. In 1808 Oswald was promoted to the local rank of brigadier general and in 1809 led successful expeditions to the island of Procida (as part of Stuart's larger attack on the island of Ischia, near Naples), the Ionian Islands and, in 1810, to the island of Santa Maura.[7] In 1811 Oswald was appointed colonel of the Duke of York's Greek Light Infantry Regiment, a corps that he had organised locally. Leaving the Ionian Islands, he was promoted to major general in June 1811 and placed on the staff of the Western District.[8]

Following the Burgos campaign, Oswald commanded the 5th Division at Osma in June 1813 and during heavy fighting for the bridge at Gamarra Mayor during the Battle of Vitoria.[9] Also in 1813, he commanded the successful storming of San Bartolomé and the 'disaster' of the July assault during the First Siege of San Sebastian, receiving his share of the blame

2 Second lieutenant was used in the Army List for this regiment until 1796, when it changed to ensign.

3 *The Scots Magazine* (1791), Vol.LIII, p.41; *London Gazette*, 13,278, 1 February 1791, p.63; *Army List*, 1793, p.111.

4 S. Brown, *By Fire and Bayonet, Grey's West Indies Campaign of 1794* (Solihull: Helion and Company, 2018), pp.63, 87, 200, 216.

5 R. Trimen, *An Historical Memoir of the 35th (or Royal Sussex) Regiment of Foot* (Southampton: Southampton Times Newspaper, 1873), pp.74–82.

6 R. Hopton, *The Battle of Maida 1806: Fifteen Minutes of Glory* (Barnsley: Pen and Sword, 2002), pp.101–102; J.W. Fortescue, *A History of the British Army* (Uckfield: Naval & Military, 2004), Vol.V, p.339.

7 *London Gazette*, 16,321, p.1927, 16,294, p.1412.

8 G. Glover, *The Forgotten War against Napoleon, Conflict in the Mediterranean 1793–1815* (Barnsley: Pen and Sword, 2017), p.129–182, for Oswald's Mediterranean campaigns.

9 Oman, *History*, Vol.VI, pp.377, 424–426.

for 'losing his nerve' while directing the assault, while he, in turn, blamed the engineer and artillery staff.[10] However, when Leith resumed command of the 5th Division on 31 August 1813, Oswald volunteered to serve as an aide de camp in the successful assault of San Sebastian during which he was wounded in the face.[11] Knighted in 1815, Oswald received Army Gold Medals for Maida, Vitoria, and San Sebastian.

Fortescue in his account of Maida describes Oswald along with Cole, Kempt and Ross, as 'taken together a far abler lot of officers than were generally to be found in a British force. Any one of the four would have made a better commander than Stuart'.[12] A more contemporary assessment was provided by Lieutenant General Sir Thomas Graham in his dispatch following the successful siege of San Sebastian:

> Your Lordship will now permit me to call your attention to the conduct of that distinguished officer, Major General Oswald, who has had the temporary command of the fifth division in Lieutenant General Sir James Leith's absence, during the whole campaign, and who resigned the command of the division on Sir James Leith's arrival on the 30th ultimo. Having carried on with indefatigable attention all the laborious duties of the left attack, no person was more able to give Sir James Leith the best information and assistance. This Sir James Leith acknowledges he did with a liberality and zeal for the service in the highest degree praiseworthy, and he continued his valuable services to the last, by acting as a volunteer, and accompanying Lieutenant General Sir James Leith to the trenches on the occasion of the assault. I have infinite satisfaction in assuring your Lordship of my perfect approbation of Major General Oswald's conduct...[13]

A subordinate's perspective was provided by Lieutenant Le Mesurier (1/9th Foot) writing shortly after Villamuriel, 'we have a new Division Genl:[Oswald] and Brigade Genl:[Barnes] just come out from England and that annoy us greatly. They wish to parade us continually. We have not one single day we can call our own. Immediately after a march, instead of a rest we have a parade'.[14]

However, Wellington's General Orders include the following 'the Commander of the Forces particularly requests that no battalion in this army may at any time be dismissed from a parade without performing some one or other of the manoeuvres prescribed by His Majesty's Regulations'.[15]

Thus, although not a famous member of Wellington's Peninsular staff, John Oswald was an experienced and competent commander, a veteran of 15 years foreign service before Villamuriel, including four years as a general officer.

---

10 Oman, *History*, Vol.VI, pp.571, 574–585; Vol.VII, p.16; Lipscombe, *Guns*, p.309, citing Ross.

11 Oman, *History*, 1997, Vol.VII, p.25.

12 Fortescue, *History*, Vol.V, p.339.

13 J.A. Hall, *A History of the Peninsular War, Vol.VIII; the Biographical Dictionary of British Officers Killed and Wounded, 1808–1814* (London: Greenhill, 1998), pp.453–4.

14 Greenwood, *Le Mesurier*, p.142.

15 Gurwood, *General Orders*, p.94; dated 7 October 1811.

Edward Barnes was born in 1776, the son of John, formerly governor of Senegal, and Ann Barnes. He joined the army in 1792 and his progress through the ranks is summarised in the following table:[16]

ensign	47th (Lancashire) Foot	November 1792
lieutenant	Captain Colman's Independent Company of Foot	March 1793
lieutenant	86th Foot	October 1793
captain	99th Foot	February 1794
major	99th Foot	November 1794
brevet lieutenant colonel	half pay, late 99th Foot	January 1800
major	79th (Cameron Volunteers) Foot	February 1800
lieutenant colonel	46th (South Devonshire) Foot	April 1807
brevet colonel	46th (South Devonshire) Foot	May 1810

With the 99th Foot Barnes served on the Isle of Man in 1794. The regiment, in 1795, went to Saint Domingue (Haiti) in the West Indies and took part in the capture of the Dutch colony of Demerara in South America in 1796, although Barnes appears to have missed this expedition as his name is missing from the prize money list.[17] Barnes was placed on half pay when the regiment was disbanded in Demerara in 1797.[18]

In August 1800 the 79th Foot took part in Sir James Pulteney's abortive expedition to Ferrol and Vigo.[19] In 1801, Barnes served with the 79th Foot in the expedition to Egypt, which culminated in the Battle of Alexandria, and he was awarded a gold medal by Sultan Selim III. The regiment formed part of the garrison of Minorca until June 1802, when it returned home to Kirkcaldy, before moving to Ireland in February 1803 to perform garrison duties until November 1805 and then, in 1806, to England.[20]

In April 1807, the 46th Foot was serving on the island of Dominica in the West Indies.[21] Barnes commanded the brigade which took St. Pierre during the capture of Martinique in 1809.[22] He was thus on the island at the same

16 Philippart, *Royal Military Calendar* (London: Valpy, 1821), Vol.III, pp.227–8; 'Obituary', *The Gentleman's Magazine*, August 1838, p.214; *Army List*, 1793, p.123; *London Gazette*, 13,514, p.252; *Army List*, 1794, p.97; R. Cannon, *Historical Record of the Eighty-Sixth or the Royal County Down Regiment of Foot* (London: John W. Parker, 1842), p.10; *Army List*, 1795, p.204; TNA, WO17/221, monthly return August 1794; *Army List*, 1800, pp.31, 633; 1802, p.304, 1804, p.222, 1806, p.267, 1812, p.225, 1813, p.9.

17 TNA, WO164/108; the monthly returns for the regiment after August 1794 have not survived (see WO17/221); Fortescue, *History*, Vol.IV, Pt.1, p.468.

18 *Army List*, 1798, pp.32, 317; T.E.K.,'Sketch of the Formation and Services of the various regiments of the line raised and disbanded since the commencement of the Seven Years War', *USM* (1851), pt.1, p.558.

19 Fortescue, *History*, Vol.IV, Pt.2, p.789; TNA, WO17/200, monthly return August 1800; L. Maclean, *Indomitable Colonel* (London: Shepheard-Walwyn, 1986), pp.156–159.

20 T. Mackenzie, J. Ewart, C. Findlay, *Historical Records of the Seventy-Ninth Queens Own Cameron Highlanders* (London: Hamilton, Adams, 1887), pp.16–18, 20–6, 207.

21 *Army List*, 1808, p.202; R. Cannon, *Historical Record of the Forty Sixth or South Devonshire Regiment of Foot* (London: Parker, Furnivall and Parker, 1851), pp.44–45.

22 Cannon, *Forty-Sixth*, p.46; R. Burnham, R. McGuigan, *The British Army Against Napoleon: Facts, Lists and Trivia, 1805–1815* (Barnsley: Frontline, 2010), p.40.

time as his future opponent Montfort. Barnes served as Lieutenant Governor and Governor of Dominica, 1809–12, remaining in post until March 1812.[23]

Barnes joined the army in Spain and was appointed brigadier general on Wellington's staff on 7 October 1812.[24]

After Villamuriel, Barnes was promoted to major general in June 1813 having moved to command a brigade in the 7th Division, comprising the 1/6th Foot, the 3rd Provisional Battalion and the Duke of Brunswick Oels Light Infantry. At Echalar in August 1813, Barnes led his brigade with great distinction, despite being outnumbered four to one, as described by Wellington himself:

> Major General Barnes's brigade was formed for the attack, and advanced before the 4th and Light divisions could co-operate, with a regularity and gallantry which I have seldom seen equalled, and actually drove two divisions of the enemy from the formidable heights, notwithstanding the resistance opposed to them.
>
> It is impossible that I can extol too highly the conduct of Major General Barnes, and of these brave troops, which was the admiration of all who were witnesses of it.[25]

The French corps commander, *Lieutenant Général* Clausel, described his men, from the divisions of Conroux (4e) and Vandermaesen (5e), as demoralised.

Barnes was made Knight Commander of the Bath and awarded an Army Gold Cross with three clasps for his service at Martinique, Guadeloupe, Vitoria, Pyrenees, Nivelle, Nive and, Orthez.[26]

Overall Barnes developed a reputation as a very competent and aggressive brigade commander:

> 'The British soldiers, their natural fierceness stimulated by the remarkable personal daring of their general Barnes'.[27]
>
> 'Barnes set at the French as if every man had been a bulldog and himself the best bred of all' [A distinguished officer, referring to the assault at Echalar].[28]
>
> 'Our fire eating Adjutant General'.[29]
>
> 'A very thunderbolt of war'.[30]

Barnes ended his career as a lieutenant general, commander in chief in India. However, although Barnes had plenty of experience in the army by the time of Villamuriel, his combat experience was limited to three campaigns as a

23 Anon., P*arliamentary Papers, House of Commons, Finance accounts of Great Britain and Ireland, Session 8th November 1814 to 12th July 1815* (London: House of Commons, 1815), Vol.VIII, p.62.

24 Burnham, McGuigan, *British Army*, p.38; R. Burnham, R. McGuigan, *Wellington's Brigade Commanders: Peninsular and Waterloo* (Barnsley: Pen and Sword, 2017), p.35; Wellington (ed.), *Supplementary Despatches*, Vol.XIV, p.146.

25 Gurwood (ed.), *Dispatches*, Vol.X, pp.597–8.

26 Burnham, McGuigan, *British Army*, pp.244, 256, 263–4, 284, 289, 294, 298, 301.

27 Napier, *History*, 1993, Vol.VI, p.161.

28 C. Dalton, *The Waterloo Roll Call* (London: Eyre and Spottiswoode, 1904), p.29.

29 Dalton, *Waterloo*, p.29.

30 Oman, *History*, Vol.VI, p.637.

regimental officer followed by the Martinique campaign in command of a brigade.

William Henry Pringle's year of birth is unclear. Accounts give different dates between 1771 and 1773. Pringle's Parliamentary biography suggests 1771 while his burial record at All Souls, Kensal Green gives his age at death as 67 years and a birthday in 1773. His obituary gives his age at death as 68 giving a birthday in 1772. In 1771 his father's regiment was serving in Ireland but in 1772 and 1773, he was serving in Minorca. Given the sources, 1772 seems his most likely year of birth.[31] He was educated in Drogheda, Ireland, before joining the army as a cornet in the 16th Light Dragoons in July 1792.[32] His progress through the ranks is summarised in the following table:[33]

cornet	16th (Queen's) Light Dragoons	July 1792
lieutenant	16th (Queen's) Light Dragoons	February 1793
captain	Independent Company of Foot	October 1794
major	111th Foot	February 1795
major	reduced on full pay	February 1796
major	4th (King's Own) Foot	August 1799
brevet lieutenant colonel		1 January 1800
lieutenant colonel	4th (King's Own) Foot	18 January1800
captain and lieutenant colonel	2nd (Coldstream) Guards	September 1802

Pringle served with the 16th Light Dragoons in Flanders from April 1793 until September 1794. On 18 May 1794, during the Battle of Turcoing, when the Duke of York's column was overwhelmed by the French, Lieutenant Pringle and his detachment of the 16th Light Dragoons were credited with escorting the Duke to the safety of *Feldmarschalleutnant* Otto's column.[34]

The 111th Foot formed part of the garrison of Dublin when the Duke of York determined, in the summer of 1795, to reduce all regiments whose number was greater than 100. Pringle then served with the 4th Foot in the

31 Burial record available at <http://home.ancestry.co.uk/>, accessed 15 September 2014; E. Burke, *The Annual Register* (London: Rivington, 1842), Vol.LXXXIII, p.177; W. Wheater, *A Record of the Services of the Fifty-first (Second West York), the King's Own Light Infantry Regiment* (London: Longman, 1870), p.34.

32 J. D'Alton, *History of Drogheda with its Environs...* (Dublin: Author, 1844), Vol.I, p.xvi; *Army List*, 1792, p.50.

33 *Army List*, 1794, p.50, 1795, p.247, 1796, p.326, 1798, p.321, 1800, p.118, 1802, p.118; *London Gazette*, 13,714, p.1050, 13,753, p.169, 15,167, p.797, 15,218, p.2, 15,222, p.48; S. Reid, *British Redcoat (2) 1793–1815* (London: Osprey, 1997), pp.4–5; S. Brown, *Ephemeral Corps*; TNA, WO12/10053, muster rolls 110th–135th Foot 1794–5; *Army List 1796* dates his promotion to major to September 1794; *Army List*, 1801, 1802 and 1803 all date his promotion to lieutenant colonel in his regiment to 5 December 1799, but this is not supported by the *Gazette*.

34 R. Cannon, *Historical record of the Sixteenth, or Queen's Light Dragoons, Lancers; containing an account of their formation in 1759 and their subsequent services to 1841* (London: J.W. Parker, 1842), p.41; J. Grehan, M. Mace, *British Battles of the Napoleonic Wars, 1793–1806* (Barnsley: Pen and Sword, 2013), p.60, Duke of York's dispatch to Dundas, 19 May 1794.

Duke of York's expedition to North Holland but was taken prisoner by the French in the confused fighting around Castricum on 6 October 1799.[35]

In 1805, Pringle was with the 1/Coldstream Guards when they joined Lord Cathcart's diversionary expedition to Bremen in North Germany, returning in February 1806. He then took part in the expedition to Copenhagen in 1807. In December 1808 he exchanged out of the Coldstream Guards to the 1st Foot and was subsequently appointed Inspecting Field Officer of Militia in Canada. In 1809, Pringle was promoted to colonel in the army.[36]

Promoted to major general in January 1812, Pringle left Portsmouth in April for the Peninsula, arriving in Lisbon in May.[37] Pringle then led Walker's Brigade of the 5th Division at the Battle of Salamanca in July 1812. During Leith's successful assault on Maucune's division, Pringle's brigade was divided between the two lines, suffering approximately 17 percent of the division's casualties.[38] Following Leith's wounding, Pringle took command of 5th Division and had his horse killed beneath him.[39]

After the battle Pringle retained command of the division until 31 July when Major General Richard Hulse arrived to take command of Hay's Brigade and the division by seniority. However, within a month Hulse contracted typhus and died on 6 September. During August, Pringle thereby resumed command of the 5th Division until Oswald arrived.[40]

During the advance to Burgos, on 6 September during the crossing of the Duero near Valladolid, Pringle was blamed for the cancellation of an attack on the French, when Lawson's artillery was misdirected and delayed. Peter Le Mesurier (1/9th Foot) described these events:

> Owing to some negligence of the staff of our division [again presumably Gomm or Gledstanes], our artillery was delayed some hours, the necessary orders not having been given, which were to follow the 6th Division over a ford where carriages might pass, whereas at the place where we crossed, horses could with difficulty pass, on account of the steepness of the banks on both sides. It was reported that the Marquis [Wellington] gave these gents a severe lecture for their negligence, as we were to have attacked immediately after crossing with another division [the 6th], and when the artillery came up it was too late in the evening…[41]

Lawson also described these events in his diary for 6 September:

> Marched and crossed [the Cega by] the bridge of Conquistilla in the rear of the 6th division and also passed the Douro at the ford of Herrera. Some very

---

35 Cannon, *Fourth*, 1839, p.78; Fortescue, *History*, Vol.IV, pt.2, p.697.

36 D. MacKinnon, *Origins and Services of the Coldstream Guards* (London: Richard Bentley, 1883), Vol.II, pp.90–92, 96, 506–7; *Army List* 1803, p.98, 1809, p.18, 1810, p.16, 1811, p.62.

37 *Army List*, 1812, p.14; UML, GB 133 Eng MSS 1273, items 2 (letter, Portsmouth 8 April) and 3 (letter, Lisbon 20 May).

38 Oman, *History*, Vol.V, pp.446–451.

39 UML, GB 133 Eng MSS 1273, item 5; letter to his wife Harriet.

40 Oman, *History*, Vol.VI, p.52; Oman, *Army*, p.363; Burnham, McGuigan, *Commanders*, p.145; Glover (ed.), *Bingham*, p.145.

41 Greenwood, *Le Mesurier*, p.129.

> unpleasant occurrence owing to the non-receipt of orders, for after the brigade passed the bridge of Conquistilla, not receiving any further directions it followed the division to a ford on the Douro, impassable for carriages. The consequence was a detention of 2 hours beyond its time.[42]

Further, on the 11th: 'Moved to Duenas. Had a very unpleasant message from Lieut. Colonel Gomm relative to the brigade, which obliged me to go to General Pringle….'[43] Interestingly, in his own letters Gomm makes no mention of this incident, despite his own role as Assistant Quartermaster General for the Division. Furthermore, in his own dispatch to Earl Bathurst on 7 September, Wellington merely glossed over the incident.[44]

For his service in the Peninsula, Pringle received an Army Gold Cross for Salamanca, the Pyrenees, Nivelle and Nive and was made Knight Commander of the Bath in 1815.[45] Pringle was among those who received the thanks of Parliament, in February 1813, for Salamanca[46] and again in June 1814 for the Pyrenees, Nivelle and Orthez,[47] although he in fact missed Orthez while recovering from a wound.

The opinion of Pringle's performance amongst his contemporaries is somewhat mixed:

> 'I fear we shall not see him [General Leith] with the army for some time. I regret it exceedingly, for I value his single presence at 10,000 men in any field. In the meantime, we are commanded by a man [Pringle] who is liked by all the world in private life, and respected by no one in public.' [Gomm, September 1812].[48]
>
> 'The coolness displayed by General Pringle, who commanded at the hard-fought action at Maya, with two British brigades against two French divisions, was admirable… Our brigade suffered a severe loss in its gallant leader, General Pringle, who was shot through the body…' [Lieutenant Colonel Charles Cadell, 28th Foot, who served with Pringle in 1813 and 1814].[49]
>
> '…appears a very dull man, and never has been in any situation which enabled him to exhibit the sort of ability which is required'. [Charles Williams-Wynn, President of the Board of Control responsible for overseeing the East India Company, when discussing Pringle's suitability to command in India in 1825].[50]

42 Leslie, *Dickson*, Vol.IV, pp.709.

43 Leslie, *Dickson*, Vol.IV, pp.709–10.

44 Burnham, McGuigan, *Commanders*, p.243; Thompson, *Ensign*, p.197; Glover (ed.), *Bingham*, p.148; Carr-Gomm, *Gomm*, p.286, Gurwood (ed.), *Dispatches*, Vol.VI, pp.57–8.

45 Burnham, McGuigan, *British Army*, pp.244, 279, 289, 294, 298.

46 Anon., *Journals of the House of Commons* (London: House of Commons, 1813), Vol.LXVIII, p.17.

47 Anon., *Journals of the House of Commons*, 1814, Vol.LXIX, pp.380–1.

48 Carr-Gomm, *Gomm*, p.287.

49 C. Cadell, *Narrative of the Campaigns of the 28th Regiment… from 1802 to 1832* (London: Whittaker, 1835), p.165; see also p.210 regarding Garris.

50 Parliamentary biography available at <http://www.historyofparliamentonline.org/volum/1820-1832/member/pringle-sir-william-1771-1840>, accessed 14 September 2014.

Thus, in summary, Pringle had plenty of experience in the army by the time of Villamuriel, but his combat experience was limited to three campaigns as a regimental officer followed by the Salamanca campaign as a general officer.

Troop Quality

The British troops included men of long experience, for example Lawson's company of the Royal Artillery included Gunner Thomas Rollands, who became distinguished as the member of the Royal Artillery with the most clasps, thirteen, on his Military General Service Medal, 1793–1814.[51]

The monthly returns of the British infantry battalions provide a useful starting point for the evaluation of the experience of the units during the two years leading up to Villamuriel.

Monthly Return Data for the British 5th Division Battalions, November 1810 to October 1812[52]

Unit	Dates arrived in the Peninsula	Effectives Nov.1810	Sick Nov.1810	Effectives June 1812	Sick June 1812	Replacements	Total Losses	Sick Oct.1812	Effectives Oct.1812
3/1st Foot	1808 and 1810	602	293	711	349	509 (35%)	448 (31%)	574	360
1/9th Foot	1808 and 1810	571	236	600	320	380 (31%)	361 (30%)	544	280
1/38th Foot	1808 and 1812	–	–	723	45	0	118 (15%)	344	274
2/38th Foot	1810	353	152	252	120	55 (9%)	223 (38%)	193	130
1/4th Foot	1808 and 1810	707	99	368	298	236 (23%)	381 (36%)	322	313
2/4th Foot	1812	–	–	671	165	15 (2%)	72 (8%)	279	481
2/30th Foot	1809	528	84	301	229	201 (22%)	321 (35%)	310	176
2/44th Foot	1810	319	181	217	172	137 (21%)	276 (42%)	243	126
Brunswick Oels Light Infantry	1810	353	152	692	297	815 (60%)	458 (34%)	248	641

Notes:

1. All data refers to rank and file excluding officers, staff, sergeants and drummers.
2. The replacements are estimated using the monthly fluctuation of the total strength of the battalion allowing for total losses. The percentage refers to the proportion of the sum of the initial total strength (i.e. effectives, those on command and those sick) plus the replacements.
3. Total Losses includes dead, deserters and men sent home, plus prisoners of war and other missing men. The percentage is the proportion of the total of the initial strength (both effectives and sick) plus the total replacements. For example during this period, the 2/30th Foot had four main drafts of reinforcements, late September 1811– 5 officers, 2 sergeants, 1 drummer and 45 rank and file, including 38 new recruits; February 1812– 2 sergeants and 33 rank and file; July

51 Lipscombe, *Guns*, pp.413–414; M.G.S. Medal Roll: his clasps were for Roleia, Vimeiro, Talavera, Busaco, Fuentes de Oñoro, Ciudad Rodrigo, Badajoz, Salamanca, Vitoria, Pyrenees, San Sebastian, Nivelle, Nive. However, the October muster, dated 31 October 1812, reports him as sick.

52 A. Bamford, 'British Army Unit Strengths: 1808–1815, The Peninsular War', *Napoleon Series*, at <http://www.napoleon-series.org/military/organization/Britain/Strength/Bamford/c_BritishArmyStrengthStudyPeninsular.html> accessed on 7 July 2015.

1812– 1 officer and 26 rank and file, including 15 new recruits and 7 volunteers from the militia; October 1812– 90 NCOs and rank and file.[53]
4. The data for the Duke of Brunswick Oels Light Infantry is for the entire regiment and not just the two companies at Villamuriel.
5. Another change during this period was the number of men absent 'on command'; 3/1st Foot– 51 increasing to 74; 1/9th– 32 to 44; 1/38th– 0 to 32; 2/38th– 28 to 45; 1/4th– 2 to 27; 2/4th– 4 to 23; 2/30th– 8 to 112; 2/44th– 26 to 20; Brunswick Oels Light Infantry– 28 to 4.

The battle experience of the battalions before October 1812 is summarised in the following table:[54]

	Representative Battle Experience; 1807 to October 1812	Dates arrived in the Peninsula
3/1st Foot	Corunna, Walcheren, Buçaco, Fuentes de Oñoro and Salamanca	1808 and 1810
1/9th Foot	Roliça, Vimeiro, Corunna, Walcheren, Fuentes de Oñoro, Ciudad Rodrigo, Badajoz and Salamanca	1808 and 1811
1/38th Foot	Montevideo, Roliça, Vimeiro, Corunna, Walcheren and Salamanca	1808 and 1812
2/38th Foot	Buçaco, Fuentes de Oñoro, Ciudad Rodrigo, Badajoz and Salamanca	1810
1/4th Foot	Corunna, Walcheren, Fuentes de Oñoro, Badajoz and Salamanca	1808 and 1810
2/4th Foot	Salamanca	1812
2/30th Foot	Torres Vedras, Fuentes de Oñoro, Badajoz and Salamanca	1809
2/44th Foot	Torres Vedras, Fuentes de Oñoro, Ciudad Rodrigo, Badajoz and Salamanca	1810

Note:

The 5th Division was covering Fuerte de la Concepción during the battle of Fuentes de Oñoro and this action is often excluded from lists of their battle honours. However, members of the 5th Division were awarded a total of 177 Military General Service Medal clasps for this action (c.f. 829 for Salamanca). The light companies of the division were directly engaged, and we might expect that the MGSM clasps were exclusively awarded to men of the light companies. However, for example, those men of both the 2/30th and 2/44th Foot who held the Fuentes de Oñoro clasp, were from seven different companies, in each battalion, in the pay-lists of 1812.

These data suggest that the majority of the men of six of the eight British battalions at Villamuriel were veterans of the previous two years of campaigning in the Peninsula. Of the other two battalions, the 1/38th Foot would still include men with experience from their previous service in the Peninsula and on the ill-fated Walcheren expedition. The 2/4th Foot, however, had more limited experience having spent the period 1810 to 1812 in garrison in Gibraltar and then Ceuta in North Africa.

Including both the 21 regimental staff and the five officers of the 2/30th Foot, who arrived at the end of the action, the experience of the 213 officers present at Villamuriel on 25 October 1812, can be summarised using Challis's Peninsula Roll Call:

53 C. Divall, *Redcoats Against Napoleon* (Barnsley: Pen and Sword, 2009), pp.67, 105, 118; Bannatyne, *Thirtieth*, pp.262, 281, 289.

54 Oman, *History*, 1996, Vol.IV, p.339; I. Fletcher, *Wellington's Regiments–The Men and Their Battles from Roliça to Waterloo, 1808–1815* (Staplehurst: Spellmount, 1994), pp.138, 140, 143, 151, 155, 159.

Unit	No. of officers at Villamuriel	Years since first foreign service (mean)	Mean service in the Peninsula (months)	No. of officers with 6 months or less service in the Peninsula	No. of officers with 7 to 23 months service in the Peninsula	No. of officers with 24 or more months service in the Peninsula
5th Division Staff	15	10	24	4 (27%)	2 (13%)	9 (60%)
3/1st Foot	23	2	20	5 (22%)	7 (30%)	11 (48%)
1/9th Foot	19	3	30	1 (5%)	5 (25%)	13 (70%)
1/38th Foot	21	4	7	11 (52%)	10 (48%)	0
2/38th Foot	17	3	25	1 (6%)	5 (29%)	11 (65%)
Totals – Barnes				18 (23%)	27 (34%)	35 (44%)
1/4th Foot	32	3	16	9 (28%)	10 (31%)	13 (41%)
2/4th Foot	24	2	10	12 (50%)	8 (33%)	4 (17%)
2/30th Foot	25	2	20	6 (24%)	6 (24%)	13 (52%)
2/44th Foot	18	2	21	1 (6%)	9 (50%)	8 (44%)
Totals – Pringle				28 (28%)	33 (33%)	38 (38%)
Brunswick Oels Light Infantry	4	3	25	0	0	4 (100%)
Royal Artillery	3	7	39	0	0	3 (100%)
Brigada N.3	12	4	27	0	4 (31%)	8 (62%)
Totals	213			50 (23%)	66 (31%)	97 (46%)

Notes:

1. The data is for all officers who were present with the regiments as recorded in the October 1812 monthly returns however, Challis's Peninsula Roll Call does not always agree with this approach. The following officers are not given the Villamuriel battle honour by Challis: 3/1st Foot; Ensign Joseph Jefferies (Challis has him leaving the Peninsula in November 1812), Captain Lawrence Aguimbeau.1/9th Foot; Lieutenant Thomas Shepherd (Challis has him in the Peninsula until November 1813). 1/38th Foot; Ensign Edward Byam (Challis has him in the Peninsula until April 1814). 2/30th Foot; Lieutenant James Eager (Challis has him in the Peninsula until February 1813), Lieutenant Theophilus O'Halloran, Ensigns Samuel Poyntz, George Madden and Francis Kelly (Challis has them arriving in November 1812). 2/44th Foot; Surgeon Henry Job (Challis has him with the 5th Dragoon Guards from 5 November 1812).
   Conversely Adjutant John Garland of the 2/30th has been included based on Challis and his own obituary, although the monthly return has him as 'sick absent'.
2. Amongst the staff, both Oswald and Barnes arrived in the Peninsula only after Salamanca. *Capitão* Capèto's service data is excluded from the 'Years since first foreign service' and 'Mean service in the Peninsula' metrics.
3. For the 1/9th Foot, these data exclude Lieutenant Robert William Dallas, whom both Challis and the monthly returns suggest was present. Le Mesurier however records that he was left behind with the sick on 21 October and missed Villamuriel. For completeness, Dallas arrived in the Peninsula in 1810.
4. Ensign James Smith arrived with the 2/44th Foot in 1810. Challis records only his one-month service as an officer.[55]
5. For the Brunswick infantry the data excludes any service in Germany from 1805 to 1809.
6. The data for Brigada N.3 is based only on the British officers.

Again, these data highlight the relative lack of experience of the 1/38th Foot and the 2/4th Foot with approximately half of their officers having only a

55 TNA, WO12/5715, pay-lists for 2/44th Foot, sergeant.

few months experience in the Peninsula, three times the average of the other units.

Michael Glover's analysis suggests that, based on averages for the army as a whole, the 213 British officers who fought at the Battle of Villamuriel would include 12 officers who had been promoted from the ranks, a very different picture from the French army.[56]

Challis identifies two of these officers as Ensign James Smith (2/44th Foot) and *Alferes* William Hill (RI N.3):

> Ensign Smith was a whip maker in St. Clement Danes, London when he joined the 44th Foot on 12 May 1802. He was then more than 18 years old.[57] He became a sergeant on 11 August 1802. At the beginning of 1805 Smith was serving in Andrew Johnston's company of the 2/44th Foot before moving to that of Robert Blakeney in May 1805. He was present with the battalion until June 1810 when he was promoted to sergeant major and then until his promotion to ensign on 20 August 1812. From 1805 to 1810 he would therefore have served in the Channel Islands before joining Wellington's army in the Lines of Torres Vedras via Cadiz. He would have fought in all the battalion's actions, including Ciudad Rodrigo, Badajoz and Salamanca. He died on 30 October 1812 of wounds received at Villamuriel.
>
> William Hill was Quartermaster Sergeant in the 88th Foot (Connaught Rangers) when he was commissioned into the RI N.3 on 20 June 1810. Hill was then appointed adjutant on 23 March 1813. He served with this regiment at Buçaco, Fuentes de Oñoro, Badajoz, Salamanca and Vitoria before being wounded in the first assault on San Sebastian and then killed in action during the second assault.[58]

Other British officers promoted from the ranks and present at Villamuriel include:

> Lieutenant and Adjutant James Cluffe, 3/1st Foot, promoted to ensign from sergeant major on 29 January 1805 and then to lieutenant and adjutant on 5 July 1806. He served in the Walcheren expedition and nine Peninsular actions before he was killed in action at San Sebastian, 25 July 1813.[59]
>
> Quartermaster Thomas Southall, 1/38th Foot, promoted from sergeant major on 24 April 1806. He arrived in the Peninsula in April 1812.[60]

56 M. Glover (ed.), *A Gentleman Volunteer, The Letters of George Hennell from the Peninsular War 1812–1813* (London: Heinemann, 1979), p.1–2.

57 TNA, WO25/982, 1806 statement of service; WO12/5713–6, pay-lists.

58 R. Cannon, *Historical Record of the Eighty-eighth Regiment of Foot, or Connaught Rangers* (London: William Clowes, 1838), p.17; Halliday, *Portugal*, p.224; the historical record describes William Hill as being promoted from the rank of Quartermaster Sergeant but does not specify the Portuguese regiment concerned. Halliday describes him as a British subject rather than a British officer.

59 *London Gazette*, 15,775, p.126, 15,933, p.829; Hall, *History*, p.125.

60 *London Gazette*, 15,972, p.511; listed as Southwell.

> Adjutant and Lieutenant Thomas Barker, 1/4th Foot, promoted from sergeant major to adjutant and ensign on 8 June 1805. He was later killed in action at Vitoria in 1813.[61]
>
> Quartermaster John Jenkins, 1/4th Foot, promoted from quartermaster sergeant on 20 August 1811. He arrived in the Peninsula in September 1811.[62]
>
> Adjutant and Ensign William Richardson, 2/4th Foot, also promoted on 20 August 1811 from sergeant major. He arrived in the Peninsula in July 1812.[63]

A further man, Ensign Joseph Pickering, 2/4th Foot, was promoted from sergeant major in the first battalion on 8 October 1812. Although he was recorded as being with the second battalion in the December monthly return of the first battalion, Pickering does not feature in the monthly returns of either battalion for 25 October 1812. Pickering enlisted on 19 July 1799 and was a sergeant in 1806, during his service he was wounded at Alkmaar (1799), Corunna (1809) and Badajoz (1812). The latter wound was severe, and he therefore missed both Salamanca and Villamuriel. Pickering's MGSM had clasps for Corunna, Fuentes de Oñoro and Badajoz.[64]

This list excludes those men such as Ensign Francis Tincombe, 2/30th Foot, who had been gentlemen volunteers, serving in the ranks. Tincombe filled a vacancy to become an ensign in June 1812.[65] Other ex-gentlemen volunteers present at Villamuriel include Henry Andrews and Denis McCrohan (2/4th Foot), Samuel Poyntz (2/30th Foot) and John O'Reilly (2/44th Foot). Glover's analysis suggests that 10 of the British officers at Villamuriel could have been, at one time, gentleman volunteers.

Finally, an analysis of the medal roll of the Military General Service Medal, 1793-1814, gives us a window on the experience of the British infantry battalions at Villamuriel on an individual soldier basis.

The MGS Medal Roll is not always accurate, containing errors of both commission and omission. For example, in their study of the 95th Foot, Caldwell and Cooper demonstrate the following using the regimental pay-lists.[66]

Clasp	Clasps actually awarded	Errors of omission	Errors of commission
Talavera	11	1	8
Buçaco	163	47	21
Barossa	110	15	6
Fuentes de Oñoro	154	59	13

In summary, the authors record a total of 437 clasps officially awarded, whereas the actual entitlement was 513.

61 *London Gazette*, 15,813, p.746.

62 *London Gazette*, 16,514, p.1618.

63 *London Gazette*, 16,514, p.1618.

64 TNA, WO25/915 and WO25/771; statements of service 1806 and 1828; WO17/101 monthly returns September to December 1812, 4th Foot.

65 Divall, *Redcoats*, p.105; *Army List*, 1813, p.196.

66 G. Caldwell, R. Cooper, *Rifle Green in the Peninsula* (Leicester: Bugle Horn, 2006), Vol.II, pp.42–3, 212–234, 260.

Ten of the infantry officers who served at Villamuriel received Army Gold Medals for actions in the Peninsular War, but only four also received the MGSM; Faunce, Miles, Wilson and Hill. The six officers excluded from the following analysis are Lieutenant Colonel Colin Campbell (3/1st Foot; gold medals for Salamanca and Vitoria), Lieutenant Colonels Brooke and Piper (1/4th Foot, both for Salamanca), Lieutenant Colonel Williamson (2/4th Foot, Salamanca), Lieutenant Colonel Nugent (2/38th Foot, Buçaco and Badajoz) and Major Harding (2/44th Foot, Salamanca).[67]

In this context, a comparison of the medal roll with the pay-list data for each regiment suggests the following, for the men present at Villamuriel.

Unit	Men present who received the Badajoz, Fuentes de Oñoro, Salamanca and/or Vitoria clasps	Veterans at Villamuriel (One or more clasps before Ciudad Rodrigo)	Experienced men at Villamuriel (One or two clasps before Salamanca)	Less Experienced men at Villamuriel (No clasps before Salamanca)
Barnes:				
3/1st Foot	87	49%	10%	40%
1/9th Foot	91	70%	0%	30%
1/38th Foot	52	75%	0%	25%
2/38th Foot	29	66%	24%	10%
Pringle:				
1/4th Foot	77	53%	30%	17%
2/4th Foot	111	9%	9%	82%
2/30th Foot	55	40%	58%	2%
2/44th Foot	82	35%	62%	2%
Brunswick Oels Light Infantry	3	66%	33%	0%

This analysis is based on an interrogation of the medal roll,[68] the proportion represented by the sample varies significantly between units, in the range between 16 and 50 percent. The analysis also cannot include the experience of those men who died either in battle or of sickness during the war, perhaps 10 to 16 percent of the total numbers involved.[69] The experience of these men, at any one time, may have been less than that of the MGSM recipients, since the less experienced men are perhaps more likely to die of disease than the veterans, but the effect on the overall numbers is likely to be small. This analysis, by definition, also excludes those veterans who survived until 1847, but for whatever reason, chose not to apply for this medal; consequently, it rests on an assumption that these men had similar military experience to those that did apply.

The central assumption underpinning this analysis is that this subset of the veterans, who survived until 1847 to be awarded the medal, are a representative sample, with respect to military experience, of the men who served at Villamuriel. Despite the time gap, the sample is significant

67 Burnham, McGuigan, *British Army*, pp.255–282.

68 Available on the Dix Noonan Webb (MGSMR) website at <http://www.dnw.co.uk/resources/medal-rolls/medal-roll.php?medalroll_id=1>, accessed 9 January 2015.

69 Burnham, McGuigan, *British Army*, p.213.

comprising more than 20 percent of those involved. The data is specific to those men shown to be present with the regiments at the October muster of the relevant pay-list. However, the pay-list of the 2/44th Foot does not distinguish those men who were present from those who were absent sick or in the general hospital, who are therefore necessarily included in the sample, hence the larger proportion of men found.

Veterans: The Peninsula clasps before Ciudad Rodrigo (January 1812), in chronological order, are Albuhera and Fuentes de Oñoro, therefore men holding these clasps fulfil the two campaigns criterion. The percentage expressed is the ratio of those veterans with one or more clasps before Ciudad Rodrigo to the total number of MGSM holders identified in the pay-list.

Trained: These men will have served at Ciudad Rodrigo and/or Badajoz, as well as Salamanca, and will have at least 6 months training and experience.

Less experienced: These men will have fought no more than one campaign, i.e. Salamanca, having missed Badajoz in April 1812. Men who joined the army from August to mid-October 1812 are also included in this group. However, the muster rolls show that the numbers joining the regiments of the division between 25 August and the 24 October were either none or in single figures, with the exception of the 2/30th Foot, which had 90 rank and file joining on 25 October.[70] The October monthly returns also show that the battalion strengths were all between 10 and 50 percent lower than immediately after the Battle of Salamanca. Although '1,400 reinforcements reached the army between Salamanca and 24 October',[71] of these the 1/1st Foot Guards comprised 1,270 other ranks and 40 officers and the 2/30th Foot comprised another 90 other ranks and five officers (a total of 1,405 men).[72] The 3/1st Foot had 24 men who were present at Villamuriel (28 percent of their total recipients) whose first clasp was for Vitoria. The monthly return data shows that the 3/1st Foot received approximately 310 men as reinforcements, split into two groups in January and April 1812. However, over the period from December 1811 to July 1812, the number of men sick went up by more than 360.[73] Taken together the data suggests that the 3/1st Foot was still assimilating their new men in the third quarter of 1812. Overall, the men from all battalions, with perhaps the exception of the 2/4th Foot, in this category could not be considered 'inexperienced'.

Only one man from either the 2/30th Foot or the 2/44th Foot was awarded the Vitoria clasp, since these battalions were sent home to recruit in May 1813, having formed the 4th Provisional Battalion following Villamuriel.[74]

70 TNA, monthly returns; 3/1st Foot, 4; 1/9th, 2; 38th, 0; 4th, 5; 2/30th, 90; 2/44th, 7.

71 Wellington (ed.), *Supplementary Despatches*, Vol.VII, pp.507–8.

72 F.W. Hamilton, *The Origin and History of the First or Grenadier Guards* (London: John Murray, 1874), Vol.II, p.436.

73 Bamford, 'Unit Strengths'; January– 140 and April– 170.

74 Muir, *Peninsular Army*, p.218.

Although the numbers of the Duke of Brunswick Oels Light Infantry are small, the proportions approximately match those of all 26 men from the regiment who held the Salamanca and Vitoria clasps, of whom 73 percent would qualify as veteran, eight percent experienced and 19 percent inexperienced, at the time of Villamuriel.

The extra experience in Barnes's Brigade is emphasised by the fact that, based on those men present at Villamuriel, as represented by the pay-lists, 13 individuals in the sample from his regiments would receive four clasps for actions before Salamanca and six more individuals (all from the 1/9th Foot) would receive five such clasps. If the sample is representative, as many as five percent of Barnes's Brigade could have had this level of experience. The highest number of equivalent clasps in Pringle's Brigade is three, received by only five individuals.

Thus, the British infantry battalions at Villamuriel contained large numbers of very experienced soldiers who had taken part in several successful actions against the French.

Taking all this data together, the experience of the British infantry can be summarised as follows, determined by the experience of the majority of the unit:

	Unit rating
Barnes's Brigade	
3/1st Foot	Veteran
1/9th Foot	Veteran
1/38th Foot	Veteran
2/38th Foot	Veteran
Pringle's Brigade	
1/4th Foot	Veteran
2/4th Foot	Inexperienced
2/30th Foot	Veteran
2/44th Foot	Veteran
Brunswick Oels Light Infantry	Veteran

Although the 2/4th Foot was sent to Gibraltar in 1810, from March 1810 until May 1812 it was serving in garrison at Ceuta, North Africa. On the way to Gibraltar a transport was blown ashore by a gale and the battalion lost 300 men, who were made prisoners of war by the French. Until January 1811, the 2/4th Foot was commanded by Lieutenant Colonel Charles Bevan, whose correspondence suggests that this was depressing and unhappy posting for the battalion.[75]

Both battalions of the 4th Foot fought at Salamanca and therefore describing the second battalion as inexperienced may seem harsh as it had had plenty of time to perfect its training, but Wellington, even after Salamanca, in August, included the men of the 2/4th Foot amongst those he

75 A. Hunter, *Wellington's Scapegoat, the tragedy of Lieutenant Colonel Charles Bevan* (Barnsley: Pen and Sword, 2003), pp.85-104; L.I. Cowper, *The King's Own the Story of a Royal* Regiment (Oxford: University Press, 1939), Vol.I 1680 to 1814, pp.368–9; Bevan committed suicide, while commanding the first battalion, following the escape of the Almeida garrison in 1811.

described as 'very irregular'. Furthermore, the battalion was largely kept in reserve and out of the front line at Villamuriel, and despite this managed to lose seven percent of its men 'missing'. The cadre of 2/4th Foot was sent home at Christmas 1812, with the fit men transferring to the first battalion.

The 2/30th Foot and 2/44th Foot have fewer veterans than expected given their service. This is an artefact of the separate status of Fuentes de Oñoro for the 5th Division and because of their previous campaign history, the men of the 2/30th Foot and 2/44th Foot must have the Fuentes de Oñoro clasp to qualify in this analysis as veteran. The total number of Fuentes de Oñoro clasps is 40 for the 2/44th Foot and 41 for the 2/30th Foot (i.e. approximately 50 percent of those MGSM recipients present at Villamuriel), since none of the 2/30th Foot and only two men of the 2/44th Foot held the Egypt clasp. Conversely the 2/30th Foot and 2/44th Foot both have more Fuentes de Oñoro clasps than the other regiments.[76]

The low numbers of men present under arms in the monthly returns reveals another significant aspect, as Corporal John Douglas (3/1st Foot) recalled during the siege of Burgos:

> The number of killed and wounded at Salamanca, with sickness, had so thinned our ranks that out of 6 sergeants and as many corporals, there was not one present with the company but myself. Often at daylight, at which time the liquor was served out, I have drawn the company's allowance in two mess-tins, so that it may easily be conjectured we were not very strong; not more than 25 fit for duty in a company that, if all were present, numbered 100.[77]

The monthly returns of the 5th Division show that together the British battalions reported more than 2,900 men of all ranks as sick, which is more than half of the strength of the British brigades at the beginning of the retreat from Burgos. Hale attributed the high sickness rate to a lack of tents.[78]

In the autumn of 1812, the battalions of the 5th Division feature highly in the ranking of the units with the highest proportion of men absent sick. In September, October, and November, six or seven of the division's eight battalions feature in the top 10 units with the highest proportion of men sick. Their sickness ratio of approximately 60 percent was almost double the average for the army (32–35 percent). Five of the eight battalions were part of the Walcheren expedition in 1809 (i.e. 3/1st, 1/4th, 2/4th, 1/9th and 1/38th Foot) and therefore experienced the sickness issues associated with that expedition. However, this was not a clear determinant of the rankings as the three non-Walcheren units (i.e. the 2/30th, 2/38th and 2/44th Foot) also feature in the top 10 in October. In that month the eight British battalions

---

76 Fuentes de Oñoro clasps held by veterans of Villamuriel; 3/1st Foot–15, 1/9th Foot–14, 1/38th Foot–0, 2/38th Foot –3, 1/4th Foot –9, 2/4th Foot –2, 2/30th Foot –19 and 2/44th Foot –29.

77 S. Monick (ed.), *Douglas's Tale of the Peninsular War and Waterloo, 1808–1815* (London: Leo Cooper, 1997), p.53. The pay-list for the regiment spells his name 'Douglass' (TNA, WO12/2012 – 24 December 1812).

78 Hale, *Journal*, p.93.

ranged in sickness from 47 to 62 percent with an average of 58 percent.[79] In particular, as early as 4 August, the recently arrived 2/4th Foot and 1/38th Foot had come to Wellington's attention:

> I am sorry to say that the British troops are by no means healthy, notwithstanding the pains which have been taken to make moderate marches with them, and to encamp them in healthy situations, and that they have never failed to receive their regular food.
>
> The 5th and 38th regiments, and the troops recently arrived from England, are excessively unhealthy; and those arrived from the Mediterranean, viz., the 2nd batt. 4th regiment, from Ceuta, and the 82nd regiment, from Gibraltar, are not much better, although the latter have not yet joined the army, and are not on the returns.
>
> The truth is, that neither officers nor soldiers are accustomed to march. The soldiers are very irregular; and, owing to their irregularities, are not able to bear the labor of marching in the heat of the sun; and then the commanding officers of each of the 2nd batt. 4th, the 1st batt. 5th, 38th, and 82nd regiments, as well as the commanding officer of the 1st batt. 42nd regiment, have disobeyed the orders which were given to them, to have their men supplied with blankets before they marched from Lisbon, and they are consequently very inadequately protected, in comparison with the other soldiers, from the sun in the daytime, and from the dews at night.[80]

Returning to the artillery, Lawson's Brigade arrived in Portugal in 1808. Lawson arrived after Roliça and Vimeiro but was ultimately awarded an Army Gold Cross with a clasp for Talavera, Buçaco, Fuentes de Oñoro, Salamanca and Vitoria.[81] Lawson died before the Military General Service Medal, 1793-1814, was awarded but of his officers Lieutenant James Sinclair received clasps for Corunna, Badajoz, and Salamanca for actions before Villamuriel.[82] Lawson's other officer present, Lieutenant James Johnston, arrived in the Peninsula in 1808, serving at Roliça, Vimeiro and nine further actions, including Salamanca before Villamuriel, but like Lawson died before the MGSM was awarded.[83]

The analysis of the MGSM roll is less straightforward when applied to Lawson's company of 8/Royal Artillery, not least because four separate

---

79 R. Burnham, 'The British Expeditionary Force to Walcheren: 1809', *Napoleon Series*, at <http://www.napoleon-series.org/military/battles/c_walcheren.html>, accessed 7 July 2015; Bamford, 'Unit Strengths'.

80 Gurwood (ed.), *Dispatches*, Vol.IX, p.335; in August 1812, Bamford, 'Unit Strengths', shows that the 1/38th were ranked 3rd most sickly unit with 65 percent men sick and the 2/4th were 12th with 59 percent sick, compared to an army average of 36 percent.

81 J.H. Leslie, *The Services of the Royal Regiment of Artillery in the Peninsular War, 1808–1814* (London: H. Rees, 1908), Pt.1, p.5; Lipscombe, *Guns*, p.37; Burnham, McGuigan, *British Army*, pp.267–287.

82 MGSMR; he also received clasps for Vitoria, Pyrenees, Nivelle and Nive, seven in all.

83 W.H. Askwith, J. Kane, *List of Officers of the Royal Regiment of Artillery from the Year 1716 to the Year 1899* (London and Beccles: William Clowes, 1900), p.26.

companies from this battalion served in the Peninsular War.[84] A comparison of the October muster roll with the Military General Service Medal roll and cross-checking for potential duplicate names using the Royal Hospital Chelsea Soldier Service Records database,[85] and finally excluding those men holding the Orthez and Toulouse clasps, at which Lawson's company was not present, identified 37 potential candidates in the medal roll, of these men, 13 can be tied more directly to Lawson's company. Twelve of these men have from six to 13 clasps, with an average of eight clasps each; all of these men satisfy the veteran criterion.[86] The thirteenth man had five clasps, the first being Badajoz.

The drivers with the brigade are likely to have been significantly less experienced than the gunners themselves. Lawson's diary includes the surnames of some 60 drivers, of whom 19 have names that match the medal roll. Eliminating most of those men with duplicates on the medal roll and those holding the Orthez and Toulouse clasps, reduces the list of potential drivers at Villamuriel to seven men of whom one would be classed a veteran (Driver Thomas Clarke), one experienced (Driver James Scott) and five inexperienced (Drivers Robert Lord, James Pounder, Elias Cuthbert, Thomas Benforth and Robert Derbyshire).

The numbers of individual gunners and drivers identified are too small to make definite conclusions based on the MGS Medal roll alone. However, taking all the evidence together, Lawson's brigade should be considered a veteran unit at Villamuriel.

The 1/9th Foot: 'the light infantry manoeuvres for which we are getting famous'

The 1/9th Foot are not numbered amongst the specialist light infantry of the British army of the Napoleonic Wars, i.e. the regiments of the Light Division and their less-famous brethren, the 51st, 60th, 68th, 71st, 85th, and 90th. However, the letters and journals of two officers suggest that the 1/9th Foot at least aspired to light infantry status.[87] Le Mesurier, writing in a letter home in May 1813, described the regiment being inspected by two generals who reviewed and praised 'the light infantry manoeuvres for which we are getting famous.' In an earlier letter Le Mesurier also described the 1/9th Foot as being 'extended… in light infantry order' at the bridge of Villamuriel.[88] Lieutenant Colonel John Cameron described in his journal how, during the Battle of the Nive, on 11 December 1813, he deployed all of the companies of the 1/9th Foot to skirmish with the French near the village of Anglet, leaving

84 R. McGuigan, 'British Regiments in the Peninsular War 1808–1814', at <http://www.napoleon-series.org/military/organization/Britain/Strength/c_RegimentsinPeninsula.html>, accessed 6 November 2015.

85 TNA, WO97 series, which includes the names of 6,773 Royal Artillery men aged between 17 and 57 in 1812.

86 The first clasp of each of these men was Roliça, Corunna, Talavera, Buçaco or Fuentes de Oñoro.

87 Hale, *Journal*, pp.94, 125; although less explicit Hale confirms the accounts of these officers.

88 Greenwood, *Le Mesurier*, pp.138, 164.

only a small reserve. The 1/9th Foot was heavily engaged and Lieutenant Le Mesurier was amongst those killed in this action.[89]

This enthusiasm for 'light infantry manoeuvres' in the 1/9th Foot probably dates to 1806, when Lieutenant Colonel John Stuart took command of the battalion in Shorncliffe on his promotion from major in the 52nd Foot, whose conversion to light infantry he had been part of.[90] When Stuart was killed in action at Roliça in 1808 while leading the battalion to the attack, he was replaced by Lieutenant Colonel John Cameron, who had until 1807 served in the 43rd Foot, another of the light infantry converts.[91] As a young officer in 1794 Cameron had also served in the West Indies under Sir Charles Grey, a light infantry 'champion'.[92]

This use of men from the centre companies of the line battalions in light infantry roles is not unique, for example Private John Morris Jones of the 39th Foot recorded how, at the Battle of St. Pierre on 13 December 1813:

> The enemy's tirailleurs… were met by our rifles and light infantry companies, assisted by detachments of active good shots from the battalion companies… We threw out strong parties of skirmishers, which were frequently called in and relieved by others, so that most of us had a chance of a slap at the foe; but the main body, of our regiment at least, piled arms and lay down under the cover of the wall, until their turn came to relieve the skirmishers.[93]

Portuguese

Commander

William Frederick Spry was born in 1770, son of a Royal Engineer, Lieutenant General William Spry, and nephew of Lieutenant General Horatio Spry.[94] William Frederick's first commission was at the age of twelve as an ensign in the 70th Foot in 1782. He then features in the 1785 and 1786 Army Lists as a lieutenant on half pay, having been a member of the 2/73rd Foot, which was disbanded on 3 October 1783 following its service in the successful defence of Gibraltar in 1780–3.[95] This regiment was renumbered as the 71st Foot

89 G. Glover (ed.), *The Letters of Lt. Colonel Sir John Cameron, 1st Battalion, 9th Regiment of Foot, 1808–14* (Godmanchester: Ken Trotman, 2013), p.99.

90 Carter, *Historical Record*, p.43.

91 R.G.A. Levinge, *Historical records of the Forty Third Monmouthshire Light Infantry* (London: W. Clowes, 1868), p.301.

92 D.Gates, *The British Light Infantry Arm* (London: Batsford, 1987), pp.53, 63–4; J.F.C.Fuller, *Sir John Moore's System of Training* (London: Hutchinson, 1924), p.44; Fortescue, *History*, Vol.IV, pt.1, p.352; Brown, *Grey*, pp.165, 202; Grey's role as a trainer of light infantry as described by Fortescue and Fuller, but is challenged by Gates. Brown emphasises the shock role often given to Grey's converged light battalions, which were used interchangeably with the grenadier battalions.

93 E.O'Keefe, 'The Old Halberdier: From the Pyrenees to Plattsburgh with a Welshman of the 39th', *Journal of the Society for Army Historical Research* (2017), Vol.XCV, no.381, p.18, no.382, pp.142–3.

94 J.T.Centeno, *O Exército Aliado Anglo-Portuguès* (Parede: Tribuna da Historia, 2011), p.294.

95 *Army List*, 1783, p.29; 1785, p.340, 1786, p.328; R. Cannon, *Historical Record of the Seventy First Regiment, the Highland Light Infantry* (London: Parker, Furnivall and Parker, 1852),

in 1786. His next appointment was as lieutenant in the 64th Foot in 1786, before joining the 77th (East Middlesex) Foot in 1787 as a captain lieutenant and captain, serving in India from 1787 to 1807. While in India, Spry progressed through the ranks in both the regiment and the army; captain in 1789, brevet major in 1795, major also in 1795 and brevet lieutenant colonel in 1800.[96] Spry served at the Siege of Seringapatam in 1799 and during this campaign he had command of the regiment. Spry went on to lead the flank companies of the 75th and 77th Foot in the successful assault of the fort at Mangalore. In 1801 Lieutenant Colonel Spry led a column comprising the 77th Foot and the 6th Madras Native Infantry which surprised and captured the fortress of Caliarcoil. The 77th Foot subsequently joined the future Duke of Wellington's expedition to capture the city of Arrakaira in January 1802 but missed the Maharatta campaign and Assaye. The regiment returned to Chatham barracks in September 1807. The 77th Foot then formed part of the ill-fated Walcheren expedition in 1809, where half of the officers were struck down by fever and four died.[97]

Promoted to brevet colonel in July 1810, Spry went to the Peninsula, where he joined the Portuguese service commanding Brigada N.3 with the rank of *brigadeiro* from 16 August 1810. From October 1810, Spry's Brigade was attached to Leith's 5th Division.[98] In April 1812, Spry was present at the siege of Badajoz. At Salamanca, Spry's Brigade formed part of Leith's reserve line in the successful assault on Maucune's division and then was separately directed by Marshal Beresford to make the flank attack which halted Clausel's counterattack, for which he received the thanks of Parliament.[99] Following Villamuriel, Spry was promoted to major general in the general brevet of 4 June 1813, and to *mariscal de campo* in the Portuguese service on 10 July 1813.

In October 1813 Spry handed over command of his brigade to *Coronel* Luis do Rego Barreto of the RI N.15. Spry received Army Gold Medals for Salamanca, Vitoria and San Sebastián, but died on 16 January 1814 in the Peninsula as a result of illness and fatigue.[100]

In summary, Spry was a very experienced soldier who at the time of Villamuriel was in his 27th year of foreign service and third year as a general officer.

---

pp.6–33; R. Cannon, *Historical Record of the Seventy Third Regiment* (London: Parker, Furnivall and Parker, 1851), p.3; Spry is not in *Army List*, 1784, p.299.

96 *Army List*, 1787, p.127; the dates of the various commissions given are those found in the relevant army lists, which in some cases are different to Centeno's dates.

97 H.H.Woollright, *Records of the Seventy-seventh (East Middlesex): The Duke of Cambridge's Own Regiment of Foot* (London: Gale and Polden, 1907), pp.2–28.

98 Centeno, *Exército*, p.112. From this point onwards he often signed his name as Sprye (Ron McGuigan, Napoleon Series Discussion Forum, 2 November 2018).

99 Oman, *History*, Vol.V, pp.446–451, 459; Anon., *Journals of the House of Commons*, 1813, Vol. LXVIII, p.116.

100 Burnham, McGuigan, *British Army*, pp.232, 279, 284, 292; Divall, *Redcoats*, p.83; Anon., *Parliamentary Papers 1780–1849*, *Estimates of Army Services for the year 1816* (London: House of Commons, 1816), Vol.XII, p.48. While present at Badajoz in 1812, only Hill of the Caçadores N.8 from his brigade was awarded an Army Gold Medal for leading his battalion in the feint assault on the Pardeleras fort.

Troop Quality

Spry's Brigade had served together under this commander since March 1811 when the Caçadores N.8 had replaced the Caçadores N.6. Even before then they had served together at Buçaco, in 1810, when the Caçadores N.8 were in their previous incarnation as the 2/Leal Legião Lusitana.[101] At about this time, Gomm (1/9th Foot) wrote 'the 3rd and 15th battalions of the line have arrived from Coimbra… they are all young, full of spirit, and with enough discipline, even now, to promise everything that ought to be expected of them'.[102]

The brigade was present at Fuentes de Oñoro, Badajoz, Salamanca and the siege of Burgos, during this time the strength of the brigade declined from approximately 2,600 men down to approximately 1,900 men at Villamuriel. Throughout the period between May 1811 and July 1812, the battalions had received relatively small numbers of new recruits of perhaps 450 men (19 percent).[103]

This experience is also reflected in the records of the British officers present with the brigade at Villamuriel.

From RI N.3, three officers, *Major* Edward Ovens, *Capitão* Thomas Smith[104] and *Alferes* William Hill, all fought at Buçaco, Fuentes de Oñoro, Badajoz and Salamanca, with the first two men also present at Roliça and Vimeiro. A further officer, *Tenente* Alexander Campbell, was present at Badajoz and Salamanca.

Another officer who may have been present with RI N.3, but was not recorded as such by Challis, was *Major* Charles Stuart Campbell who served at Corunna with the 26th Foot. In June 1812, Campbell was appointed *major aggregado* (supernumerary major) in RI N.3. Challis does not specifically record Alexander Campbell's presence at Villamuriel; instead he is one of three British officers with Brigada N.3, described by Challis as being present at Burgos or the retreat therefrom, but not at Villamuriel. Thus, he may have been absent sick, as he does not feature amongst the casualty lists for Burgos. He commanded the regiment at Vitoria but missed Salamanca.

A final officer to be considered is *Major* Cassius Matthew Clanchy (Clenchy in the 1812 Army List). Clanchy is another of the three British officers with Brigada N.3, whom Challis described as being present at Burgos or the retreat therefrom, but not at Villamuriel. However, Clanchy was promoted in July 1811 to *major* at the general depot for recruits at Mafra. Consequently, he missed Salamanca and is unlikely to have been on the retreat from Burgos or at Villamuriel.[105]

101 Centeno, *Exército*, pp.112–3.

102 Carr-Gomm, *Gomm*, p.154; letter written on 8 July 1810.

103 R.Foster, 'Notes on the Portuguese Infantry of the Peninsular War 1807-1814: 3rd Regiment of Olivenza (Beira) and 15th Regiment of Olivenza (Beira), and 8th Caçadores', at <http://www.napoleon-series.org/military/organization/portugal/Infantry/Notes/c_NotesonPortugueseInfantry3.html>.

104 Hall, *History*, p.523.

105 A.N. Dos Santos, *Collecçao das Ordens do Dia do… Guilherme Carr Beresford…, Anno 1811* (Lisbon: Quartel General, 1811), p.142; Halliday, *Portugal*, p.217.

From RI N.15, *Major* Michael Murphy fought at Buçaco, Badajoz and Salamanca. *Major* Archibald Campbell had served on Dominica in 1805 with the 46th Foot and at Salamanca with RI N.15. Archibald Campbell is another of the three British officers with Brigada N.3, whom Challis described as being present at Burgos or the retreat therefrom, but not at Villamuriel. Thus, he may have been absent sick, as he does not feature amongst the casualty lists for Burgos.

Also from RI N.15, *Capitãos* Thomas O'Neale, Charles Fitzgerald,[106] and Edward Brackenbury[107] all fought at Buçaco, Fuentes de Oñoro, Badajoz and Salamanca. *Capitão* Charles Heatley fought at Corunna, Fuentes de Oñoro, Badajoz and Salamanca.

From Caçadores N.8, *Major* Dudley St. Leger Hill, formerly (until August 1810) of the 95th Rifles and who had served with them at Montevideo and Buenos Aires, fought at Roliça, Vimeiro, Buçaco, Fuentes de Oñoro, Ciudad Rodrigo, Badajoz and Salamanca. *Capitão* Charles Western had served at Buçaco, Fuentes de Oñoro, Badajoz and Salamanca. *Alferes* James Leech was present at Badajoz and Salamanca. *Capitão* Donald Macdonald was appointed *capitão* of the second company on 31 May 1812 and fought at Salamanca.[108] Challis has Macdonald present at Villamuriel, but Hill, in his report to Pringle, omits him from those British officers present with the Caçadores N.8 during the action; 'I however should be wanting in justice to the two British officers of the Battn (Captain Western and Adjt Leche) if I did not particularly mention them to you and who are both wounded'. This perhaps suggests that Macdonald was either present but not wounded, was absent sick, or was detached with Spry.[109] In 1814, Macdonald returned to the 21st Foot and was killed in action at New Orleans in January 1815.[110]

Coronel João Antonio Tavares of RI N.3 was born in Angola and he joined the army on 24 January 1780, as a *cadete* in the Regimento de Infantaria do Reino de Angola. He was subsequently promoted to *tenente* (9 January 1783), *capitão* (18 December 1788) and brevet *major* (10 October 1796) in the same regiment. In November 1807 Tavares was in Portugal as a *major* in RI N.4. When Junot disbanded the Portuguese army, Tavares became *tenente coronel* of the RI N.2 Legião Portuguesa. Choosing not to serve Napoleon, Tavares became a *tenente coronel* in RI N.4 (13 December 1808), in Hamilton's Portuguese Division. RI N.4 fought at Buçaco and Albuera. Tavares joined RI N.3 on his promotion to *coronel* in February 1811 and served with them at Badajoz and Salamanca. He was awarded the *Medalha de Distinção de Comando* (the Commander's Medal) with one 'olive leaf' for Salamanca. Tavares died at the headquarters of RI N.3, in Lamego on 23

106 *Army List*, 1813, p.317; *Army List*, 1822, p.651, captain on the half-pay list; CHALLIS.

107 Soldiers of Gloucester Museum, Accn No. GLRRM 04785.5, photocopy of an account of Sir Edward Brackenbury's career with the 61st Foot, in his own handwriting; *Hart's New Army List* (London: John Murray, 1845), pp.64, 87 note 127.

108 CHALLIS; Santos, *Ordens*, 1812, p.91.

109 Hartley Library, University of Southampton, MS 61 Wellington Papers WP1/353 (Wellington Papers); Hill to Pringle, 27 October 1812.

110 R. Cannon, *Historical Record of the Twenty First Regiment or Royal North British Fusiliers* (London: Parker, Furnivall and Parker, 1849), p.43.

April 1813. *Coronel* Tavares thus served for 33 years including the Angola campaigns, the *Campanhas do Certão*.[111]

Coronel Luís do Rego Barreto of RI N.15 was present at Buçaco, Fuentes de Oñoro, Ciudad Rodrigo, and had served with distinction at Badajoz and Salamanca as well as several smaller actions, Santo António de Cântaro, Mortágua, Pombal, Redinha, and Foz do Arouce, when commander of the Caçadores N.4. Barreto was promoted to *coronel* of RI N.15 in February 1812 and ultimately received the *Medalha de Distinção de Comando* with seven 'olive leaves', for Buçaco, Badajoz, Salamanca, Vitoria, San Sebastian, the Nivelle and the Nive.[112]

The experience of the other Portuguese officers is more difficult to trace but the following information regarding the seven officers of Caçadores N.8 who were casualties at Villamuriel gives us a small sample of the 90 officers in the brigade, as recorded in the 23 October 1812 morning state:[113]

Capitão Manoel Caetano Ferraz	Promoted to *capitão* 16 May 1810
Tenante Antonio Carlos Pereira de Macedo	Promoted to *capitão* 8 February 1813
Tenante João Baptista Ferreira	Promoted to *tenante* 15 July 1811
Tenante Domingos de Sá Pereira Farinha	Promoted to *tenante* 7 December 1811
Alferes José Fernandes dos Santos	Promoted to *alferes* 19 May 1812
Alferes João Salustiano da Costa e Sá	Promoted to *tenante* 8 February 1813
Alferes Rodrigo Navarro de Andrade	Promoted to *alferes* 8 January 1812

In his dispatch regarding the capture of Badajoz in April 1812, Wellington, as well as praising the 1/4th, 2/30th and 2/44th Foot, was fulsome in his praise of the men of Spry's Brigade; 'In the 5th division I must mention Major Hill of the 8th Caçadores, who directed the false attack upon the fort Pardaleras. It was impossible for any men to behave better than these did… the 15th Portuguese regiment under Colonel Luiz de Rego, likewise performed their part in a very exemplary manner'.[114]

Writing in November 1812, Sir Andrew Halliday, a physician who served as Assistant Inspector of Hospitals on the staff of the Portuguese Army from 1809, described the regiments of Spry's Brigade as follows:

> The Third Regiment… though in good order, is not so complete as many of the other corps of the army. It has always been a sickly corps, but nevertheless has always kept the field, and distinguished itself on various occasions during the last three years.

111 Santos, *Ordens*, 1812, p.67; Moises Gaudencio, Napoleon Series, 20 April 2017 citing the *Gazeta de Lisboa*, 83, 8 April 1820; Simão José da Luz Soriano, *Historia da guerra civil e do estabelecimento do governo parlamentar em Portugal, comprehendendo a historia diplomatica, militar e politica d'este reino desde 1777 até 1834, Guerra da Peninsula* (Lisbon: Imprensa Nacional, 1876), Vol.IV, pt.1, p.56; J. and D. Bromley, *Wellington's Men Remembered* (Barnsley: Pen and Sword, 2015), Vol.II, p.559.

112 Centeno, *Exército*, pp.230–1; Moises Gaudencio, Napoleon Series, 20 April 2017 citing the *Gazeta de Lisboa*, 83, 8 April 1820.

113 Santos, *Ordens*, 1810, p.105; 1811, pp.134, 223; 1812, pp.42, 84; 1813, p.26.

114 Gurwood (ed.), *Dispatches*, Vol.IX, p.45.

> I believe this regiment [the 15th] has suffered more from sickness than almost any other corps. It was so much reduced in June 1811 that Marshal Beresford was obliged to raise a second battalion at Oporto.
>
> The Eighth battalion [of Caçadores] was... formed from the Lusitanian Legion but was by no means as respectable a corps, in the first instance, as the last mentioned. [i.e. the Seventh Caçadores] It was commanded, on its first formation, by the late Major Offley... who was indefatigable in his exertions to bring it to perfection and left it as fine a battalion as any in the service. At present it is commanded by Major Hill under whom it behaved in a most gallant manner at the Battle of Salamanca.[115]

Douglas (3/1st Foot) was able to observe the Caçadores N.8 at first hand and endorsed Halliday's assessment as follows:

> Yet these new raised [Portuguese] regiments proved in a short time what discipline is able to accomplish with proper officers. I recollect one regiment, which belonged to our Division; commanded by Major Hill. This was the 84 [sic] Cassadores [sic] or light infantry. They were formed in Thomar late in 1810 and of all the collections that I have ever witnessed to make soldiers of they exceeded. That regiment at Salamanca behaved equal to the bravest of the British and every other regiment. But be it remembered, they were officered by the British.[116]

In his account of Salamanca, First Lieutenant Thomas Henry Browne (23rd Foot), serving as Deputy Assistant Adjutant General in the 4th Division from April 1812,[117] provides the following account of Spry's Brigade in action that day:

> The Portuguese of the 5th Division from being on the left took these battalions of the enemy completely in flank; but there was so much hallooing that instead of charging they began firing which was as dangerous to the British as to the French. Marshal Beresford and his staff put a stop to this firing, and he was making a disposition to charge the enemy in flank, which these regiments, the 3rd and 15th Portuguese were not willing to try – a few companies made a shabby charge which these French troops would scarcely have regarded but that the 4th Division again attacked and the 5th Division took them in rear. They then moved off and the greater part were killed or taken prisoner.[118]

Browne, who elsewhere is complimentary about the performance of the Portuguese troops,[119] is somewhat at odds with the account of Captain Edward Brackenbury, RI N.15:

115 Halliday, *Portugal*, 1812, front plate, pp.vii–x, 180, 190, 201; *Army List*, 1812, p.497.

116 Monick (ed.), *Douglas*, p.19.

117 *Army List*, 1813, p.177, R.N. Buckley (ed.), *The Napoleonic War Journal of Captain Thomas Henry Browne 1807–1816* (London: Bodley Head, 1987), p.321 note 79; Challis dates this to January 1813.

118 Buckley, *Browne*, pp.170–1.

119 Buckley, *Browne*, pp.144, 218.

> I fought with my Portuguese Regt. who behaved well and bayonetted a column of French, you will scarcely believe how I could have escaped when I assure you that I was cutting away with my common regulation sword but providence protected me as it did at Badajos.[120]

Another witness, Lieutenant Peter Le Mesurier (1/9th Foot) wrote the following about Spry's Brigade at Salamanca: '… the Portugeese [sic] of our division behaved uncommonly well when the cannon shots were thinning their ranks; not a man stirred. Their Coll: shewed them a fine example'.[121] In his after-action report Spry acknowledged that some confusion had occurred amongst RI N.15, which he attributed to the newer recruits, and that RI N.3, while remaining ordered, was reluctant to advance. However, he complimented the Caçadores N.8 on their excellent service throughout the day.[122]

Beresford chose to mention three officers from Spry's Brigade amongst the 15 officers mentioned and five others promoted, in his order of the day for 25 August 1812 celebrating Salamanca; *Capitão* Thomé de Avelar da Silva Capèto (aide de camp to Spry), *Capitão* Charles John Fitzgerald (brigade major to Spry) and *Capitão* Edward Brackenbury (RI N.15).[123]

On 5 October 1812, Wellington wrote to Beresford:

> Something or other has made a terrible alteration in the troops for the worse. They have lately, in several instances, behaved very ill; and whether it be owing to the nature of the service, or their want of pay I cannot tell; but they are not at all in the style they were. I am rather inclined to attribute their misbehaviour to the misery and consequent indifference of both officers and soldiers, on account of their want of pay.[124]

Friedrich Lindau (Lieutenant, 1st Light Battalion, King's German Legion) reported symptoms of this problem, which he observed while retreating during the night of 23/24 October:

> On this road we found many groups of Portuguese, five to ten men closely pressed together, wrapped up in their blankets, lying on the road. They could not or would not go further, as much as we urged them to and even used force, since the Portuguese are by nature a lazy and feeble people not in a condition to tolerate

120 Muir, *Salamanca*, p.157.

121 Greenwood, *Le Mesurier*, p.121, letter 3 August 1812; Spry was then still a brevet colonel in the British service. See also Lieutenant Colonel Henry Hollis Bradford's account, which emphasises the importance and superiority of the British officers (R.Muir, J.Reiter, 'A New Letter on the Battle of Salamanca 22 July 1812', *Journal of the Society for Army Historical Research* (2018), Vol. XCVI, no.385, p.24).

122 R.Burnham, personal communication.

123 Santos, *Ordens*, 1812, p.147.

124 Gurwood (ed.), *Dispatches*, Vol.IX, p.466.

> exertions as we are; they like best to lie on their backs and let the sun shine on their bodies.[125]

However, in his later summary of the Burgos campaign, written to Cooke, Wellington appears to rate the Portuguese regiments ahead of the German units in his army.

In July 1813, Wellington described the Portuguese troops generally in glowing terms as part of a letter to Earl Bathurst regarding the quality of the Spanish armies; '… the Portuguese are now the fighting cocks of the army, I believe we owe their merits more to the care we have taken of their pockets and bellies than to the instruction we have given them'.[126]

This high opinion of the Portuguese infantry dates to Buçaco in 1810, when Commissary August Schaumann described the performance of the Portuguese infantry, including specifically RI N.3: 'the Portuguese fought with conspicuous courage, and did great credit to Marshal Beresford who had trained them.' Specifically regarding the Caçadores: 'In this [skirmishing] the Portuguese displayed extraordinary bravery and skill…' Schaumann specifically mentions RI N.3, although Oman is clear that this regiment, while present, was never under fire and suffered no casualties.[127]

In summary, Spry's Brigade at Villamuriel predominantly comprised the surviving veterans, perhaps some 80 percent of the total, of the previous 2 to 3 years of campaigning, well-rated by their British allies although perhaps somewhat discouraged by the recent turn of events in the campaign. However, the remainder were likely to have been still learning their trade in October 1812.[128]

Spanish

Commander

Don Pascual Sebastián de Liñan was born in Teruel, a town in Aragon 188 miles east of Madrid, on 19 July 1775.[129] He was born into a

125 F. Lindau, *A Waterloo Hero – The reminiscences of Friedrich Lindau* (Havertown: Frontline Books, 2009), p.93.

126 Gurwood (ed.), *Dispatches*, Vol.X, p.569.

127 A.L.F. Schaumann, *On the Road with Wellington, the diary of a war commissary* (London: Greenhill, 1999), p.249; Oman, *History*, Vol.III, pp.378–9; I. Fletcher (ed.), *The Peninsular War–Aspects of the Struggle for the Iberian Peninsula* (Staplehurst: Spellmount, 1998), pp.178, 181–2.

128 R. Foster, 'Notes on the Portuguese Infantry of the Peninsular War 1807-1814…', at <http://www.napoleon-series.org/military/organization/portugal/Infantry/Notes/c_NotesonPortugueseInfantry3.html>; the men who had served throughout the 1811 and the 1812 campaigns comprised 82 percent of the 1/RI N.3, 73 percent of the 2/RI N.3, 69 percent of the 1/RI N.15, 95 percent of the 2/RI N.15 and 85 percent of the Caçadores N.8. These numbers must be treated with caution as they ignore the variations in the level of sickness in the regiments and the transfer of men between battalions of the same regiment. Halliday's comment regarding the raising of 'a second battalion' of the RI N.15 in June 1811 does not tally with either these numbers nor Beresford's *Ordens de Dio*.

129 Bernardo Blanco Pérez, *Pascual Sebastian de Liñan* (Madrid: Lit. de J. Donon, 1856), pp.21–24; Martinez, *Diccionario*, pp.495–6.

noble family, the son of Don Gonzalo Sebastián de Liñan, a knight or *caballero mesnadero.* In 1777, while still an infant, Liñan was enlisted in the venerable Order of the Knights of St. John on Malta as a Knight of Justice. In 1783, he was enlisted as a *cadete de menor* in the Real Guardias Españolas, with seniority from 1791. Liñan attended the Madrid academy for the cadets of the Real Guardias Españolas. In 1792 Liñan received permission to serve on the island of Malta in the galley fleet of the Knights of St. John. On the outbreak of war with France in 1793, Liñan returned to Spain and served with his regiment during the Roussillon War, as part of the Ejército de Cataluña in the Eastern Pyrenees, under *Capitán General* Antonio Ricardos. Liñan fought at the Battle of Mas Deu, in May 1793, which forced the French back to the fortifications at Perpignan, and in the unsuccessful assault on these fortifications in July 1793. In August Liñan took part in the crossing of the river Tet and the successful assault on the French camp at Corneilla de la Rivière. Then in September Liñan took part in the capture of Vernet close to Perpignan itself.[130] Later that month, Liñan fought with distinction at the Battle of Trouillas, which halted a French counterattack.[131]

In the first three weeks of October, Liñan, now in command of a company, was involved in the confused and disorderly fighting around the Camp of Boulou as Eustache Charles d'Aoust lead a further French counterattack.[132] In April 1794, Liñan was involved in fighting around Boulou once again, and in particular at Banyuls les Aspres, Tresserres and San Juan. During these combats he was wounded when a musket ball grazed his ankle.[133] At the end of May 1794, Liñan was captured by the French at the end of the siege of the coastal fortress of Collioure. He was, however, immediately released on parole until exchanged, which the Spanish commander-in-chief refused to honour.[134] Liñan was promoted to *alférez* in July 1794.

In July 1798 Liñan was promoted to *2° teniente*. From September until October 1800 he was stationed at San Roque near Gibraltar.[135] In mid-1801, during the War of the Oranges with Portugal, Liñan spent 40 days as part of the garrison of the Portuguese town of Arronches.

In June 1808, Liñan was promoted to *1° teniente*. On 21 June, during *Maréchal* Moncey's invasion of the Kingdom of Valencia, Liñan covered the Pajazo bridge over the River Cabriel near Contreras, as second in command of a detachment of 150 men. However, *Mariscal de Campo* Don Pedro Adorno's small garrison of 1,500 men, including local militia levies, was quickly forced back by superior French numbers. Subsequently Liñan joined *Mariscal de Campo* Pedro González Llamas's pursuit of the French

130 Chuquet, *Dugommier* (Paris: A. Fontemoing,1904), pp.132–134.

131 R.W. Phipps, *The Armies of the First French Republic and the Rise of the Marshals of Napoleon 1* (London: Oxford University, 1931), pp.152, 158–9.

132 Chuquet, *Dugommier*, p.137.

133 Chuquet, *Dugommier*, pp.246–66; D. Smith, *The Greenhill Napoleonic Wars Data Book* (London: Greenhill, 1998), p.77.

134 Smith, *Data Book*, p.81.

135 Martinez, *Diccionario*, p.495.

after Moncey's unsuccessful assault on Valencia on 28 June 1808.[136] Later that year on 23 November, Liñan was present at the battle of Tudela, and in the subsequent withdrawal of the army to Cuenca, from there to Valdepeñas and then to the Despeñaperros gorge with the División de Reserva, commanded by *Capitán General* Don Manuel de la Peña y Ruiz del Sotillo. During this time, Liñan distinguished himself by checking the advance of the French for two days with a detachment of 150 men of his own regiment plus one-and-a-half squadrons of cavalry.[137] In 1809 Liñan joined the light infantry of the second battalion of his regiment and was promoted to *capitán* in July.[138] In August he was appointed second-in-command of the column of light infantry of the fourth division in the Ejército de La Mancha. Liñan fought in the advanced guard of the army during the four days leading up to the Battle of Almonacid de Toledo on 11 August 1809.[139] Initially Liñan commanded the light infantry column, a squadron of the Regimiento de Caballería Santiago, and a 4-pounder cannon to contain the French skirmishers, while covering part of the poorly chosen main position. When the action became general, Liñan retired to the flank of the division, which was on the right centre of the Spanish line. Here he found the 5º Voluntarios de Sevilla infantry regiment surrounded by superior forces and close to surrender due to a lack of ammunition. Directed by *Brigadier* Castrejon and in the presence of the Conde de Castroterreno, Liñan led his troops in a bayonet charge on the French. Although facing 'five times his own numbers', Liñan put them to flight, thereby saving the 5º Voluntarios de Sevilla. Given that initially the French attempted only to 'contain' the Spanish centre and right flank, this incident presumably happened as the division was retiring to Venegas's second position on the Cerro de Castillo during which Oman describes the troops as being 'much disordered'. For this action Liñan received thanks for his bravery and boldness from both the Conde de Castroterreno and Don Manuel Maria de Medina Verdés y Cabañas, *Coronel*, 5º Voluntarios de Sevilla. Despite the heroics of Liñan and many others, the Spanish army was defeated and withdrew to the Despeñaperros gorge. When, in January 1810, King Joseph Bonaparte launched his invasion of Andalusia through the passes of the Sierra Morena and Despeñaperros, Liñan was involved with a

136 Oman, *History*, Vol.I, pp.134–138; Smith, *Data Book*, p.259; AHN, *Junta Central Suprema Gubernativa del Reino, Estado; 81. J. Control de Juntas territoriale, Requena*, < http://cronicas-historicas-de-requena.webnode.es/news/documento-historico-el-memorial-de-la-junta-de-requena-/> accessed 6 October 2014; J.G. de Arteche y Moro, *Guerra de la independencia, historia militar de España de 1808 á 1814* (Madrid: Credito de Comercial, 1875), Vol.II, pp.136–141; NAFZIGER, *Distribution of Spanish Forces, Zaragoza, Valencia and Murcia, June 1808*.

137 Oman, *History*, Vol.I, pp.437–449, 634; Oman describes La Peña's division as the 4th Division, Army of the Centre but does not include the Real Guardias Españolas; Arteche y Moro, *Guerra*, Vol.III, p.479, includes an order of battle that indicates that Liñan's battalion was the 3/Real Guardias Españolas.

138 This attribution to the 2/Real Guardias Españolas is based on the orders of battle available for Almonacid. The confusion that Partridge and Oliver (*Handbook*, p.313) point to over the fate of even the Spanish guards battalions may mean that Liñan's presence indicates that the battalion present was the third, although Sañudo's database states that in 1810 the Real Guardias Españolas had only two battalions.

139 Oman, *History*, Vol.II, pp.613–15, 655–6.

detachment of the 3/Real Guardias Españolas and the Milicia Provinciale de Plasencia, of Vigodet's 2ª Division, in defending the defiles of Despeñaperros, and then formed part of the rearguard covering the withdrawal of the Ejército del Centro.[140]

In August 1810, as *capitán* of the light infantry, Liñan joined General Lacy's feeble raid on Moguer.[141] For the rest of the year Liñan remained with the Ejército del Centro, under the command of *Capitán General* La Peña, as part of *Mariscal de Campo* Principe de Auglona's 2ª Division, including probably Blake's disaster at Baza in November.[142] On 5 March 1811 Liñan 'greatly distinguished himself' in the action amongst the pine groves of Chiclana and Barossa. He was wounded in the leg by a musket ball, when Auglona's division assaulted Villatte's division on the ridge of Torre Bermeja.[143]

In May 1811 Liñan was rewarded with promotion to *brigadier* and, in September, he was assigned to the 6º Ejército under the command of *Mariscal de Campo* Don Francisco Javier de Abadía.[144] This promotion from *capitán* to *brigadier* reflects the additional army rank that the guards officers held, thus the Pérez biography describes his promotion as being from *coronel capitán.* At the end of March 1812, Liñan was appointed second in command of the División de Reserva and general officer commandng the town of Vigo and its environs and then shortly after in the province of Tuy. At the end of May 1812, Liñan was sent on a tour of inspection of the irregular and guerrilla forces in part of Castile and the sixth military district with a view to reporting their state of discipline and training. When the French were forced to evacuate the Kingdom of Leon in June 1812, Liñan was appointed general officer commanding with responsibility for the demolition of the fortifications that had been built, for restoring legitimate government, and for bringing order and discipline to the guerrilla bands, which he accomplished with noted success despite the many difficulties associated with such a role.[145]

Given command of the 1ª Sección, 1ª División, 6º Ejército, Liñan took part in the successful siege of Astorga, which surrendered to the Spanish on 29 August 1812, he then joined the movement of part of the army to Burgos in support of Wellington's siege, reaching there on 16 September. During the siege, Liñan took part in the unsuccessful final assault of the castle with the 1º Asturias, supporting the attempt of the Caçadores N.9 to take the Church of San Roman.[146]

140 Oman, *History*, Vol.III, p.130; NAFZIGER, *Spanish Army of the Centre, December 1809*, shows the two battalions of the Real Guardias Españolas were the first and third, both in Giron's 3ª División (*Estado*, 1811, p.147, shows three battalions).

141 Oman, *History*, Vol.III, pp.329–330.

142 NAFZIGER, *Spanish Army of the Centre, September 1810*; Smith, *Data Book*, p.348; Oman, *History*, Vol.III, pp.337–8.

143 Oman, *History*, Vol.IV, pp.107, 614.

144 *Estados*, 1822, p.134; *Estado*, 1812, p.12; *Capitán General* Don Francisco Xavier Castaños, commander of the 5º Ejército, also had command of the 6º Ejército.

145 Oman, *History*, Vol.V, p.338; J.M. Maldonado, *Historia política y militar de la guerra de la independencia de España contra Napoleon Bonaparte desde 1808 á 1814* (Madrid: José Palacios, 1833), Vol.III, p.266.

146 Oman, *History*, Vol.VI, pp.16, 43, 47; Esdaile, Freeman, *Burgos*, pp.120, 198 note 124.

Following Villamuriel, Liñan's career continued and he rose to become *teniente general* and governor of Mexico City and then Ciudad Rodrigo and finally governor general of Madrid.[147]

Thus, prior to Villamuriel, Liñan had plenty of battlefield experience stretching back to 1793, had shown evidence of physical courage, and been twice wounded, but this experience was predominantly as a company officer and to a lesser extent a field officer. Indeed, it seems that Villamuriel was his first experience of taking a brigade into action in the open field.

Troop Quality

Understandably, given the invasion of their country, by the end of 1812 the armies of Spain had been through a cycle of occasional victories and many defeats, resulting in the repeated dispersion of the forces, which had then to be reassembled and recruited up to strength, before receiving the training necessary to build combat effectiveness. However, the Spanish armies had shown that, when the conditions and preparation was adequate, they could perform well including at Albuera and Sagunto in 1811, and later at Vitoria and San Marcial in 1813. In the 1812 campaign, *Major* José Miranda and the Milicia Provinciale de Monterey were praised for holding the castle at Alba de Tormes in November for 'many days' before escaping in a successful sally.[148]

In August 1812, Wellington wrote to the Earl Bathurst regarding his expectations of the Spanish in general:

> I do not expect much from the exertions of the Spaniards, notwithstanding all that we have done for them. They cry '*viva*', and are very fond of us, and hate the French; but they are, in general, the most incapable of useful exertion of all the nations that I have known; the most vain, and at the same time the most ignorant, particularly of military affairs, and above all of military affairs in their own country.[149]

This opinion had no doubt been coloured by the lack of strategic support that the 6º Ejército had been able to offer him throughout the campaign of 1812 to date.

In early to mid-1812, the 6º Ejército received significant supplies of clothing and arms from the United Kingdom as it rebuilt, a process that was significantly hampered by the Cortes in Cadiz requisitioning troops for service in the Americas. Nevertheless, its commander Santocildes advanced with part of his army to besiege Astorga from June until the end of August, albeit without adequate artillery.[150]

---

147 Martinez, *Diccionario*, pp.495–6; *Estado*, 1833, pp.14, 17.

148 C.J. Esdaile, *The Spanish Army in the Peninsular War* (Nottingham: Partizan Press, 2012), Reprise – the Army and the Liberals (unpaginated chapter); Oman, *History*, Vol.VI, p.125.

149 Gurwood (ed.), *Dispatches*, 1838, Vol.IX, p.366.

150 C.J. Esdaile, *The Peninsular War* (London: Allen Lane Penguin, 2002), pp.392–393, 410; R. Chartrand, B. Younghusband, *The Spanish Army of the Napoleonic Wars (3) 1812–15* (Oxford: Osprey Military, 1999), pp.12–13; Oman, *History*, Vol.V, p.337.

In August 1812, Sydenham described the troops that arrived to support Wellington's attack on Burgos, in a letter to Sir Henry Wellesley, British Ambassador to Spain:

> Astorga is not yet taken. Santocildes has left one division of his army to watch the place, and has moved on with the remainder. [The Marquis of] Anjenja speaks in high terms of the Spanish troops. Don Julian is no longer a leader of guerrillas, but his party has been brigaded with the other Spaniards. Such part of the army of Galicia as have joined Lord Wellington are described to be well clothed and in excellent order, particularly the cavalry. The cavalry of the different *partidos* are well mounted: they skirmish admirably, and they are very useful in the duties of the outposts.[151]

A month later, following a long discussion with Wellington, Sydenham was writing in somewhat different terms to the same correspondent:

> Lord Wellington declares that he has not yet met with any Spanish officer who can be made to comprehend the nature of a military operation. If the Spanish officers had knowledge and vanity like the French, or ignorance without vanity as our allies in India, something might be done with them. But they unite the grossest ignorance with the most insolent and intractable vanity. They can therefore be neither instructed, nor persuaded, nor forced to attend to their duty...
>
> The Galician army is a nominal one of nearly 30,000 men. At least nearly that number are supposed to be mustered, paid, and fed. But by Santocildes's return, which was only received this morning, it appears that he has with him but 11,000 infantry and 350 horse; and if Sir H. Douglas's report can be depended upon, this small number is ill-disciplined and miserably equipped.[152]

Lieutenant Colonel Sir Howard Douglas was a Commissioner in Galicia amongst whose duties was the supervision of the distribution of British military supplies to the 6° Ejército.

Finally, Captain the Honourable James Stanhope (1st Foot Guards, Assistant Quartermaster General, 1st Division), in writing to his friend Richard Heber in December 1812, presumably had Villamuriel in mind when he wrote, 'we have also seen that regular Spanish soldiers who for more than two years have been organising in the Galicias cannot stand against French conscripts who had been 20 days from Bayonne though they have British soldiers by their side as an example'.[153]

If, however, we focus on the two Spanish regiments that fought at Villamuriel, Stanhope's comments seem an overstatement of the case, since neither regiment had been together for more than two years.

The 1° Asturias was raised in March and April 1811. The regiment was involved in the manoeuvring around Astorga, in July and August 1811,

151 Wellington (ed.), *Supplementary Despatches*, Vol.VII, p.371.

152 Wellington (ed.), *Supplementary Despatches*, Vol.VII, pp.420–422; Esdaile, *Spanish Army*, p.118; Gurwood (ed.), *Dispatches*, Vol.IX, p.116.

153 Glover (ed.), *Eyewitness*, pp.90, 102.

including the actions at the passes of Manzanal (second battalion) and Foncebadon (first and second battalions).[154] In May 1812, they were present at the actions of Pajares and Puente de los Fierros, and in June, at the actions of Vega del Rey and Urbies before joining the siege of Astorga in July and August.[155] This may suggest that this regiment was an experienced unit. However, Wellington's observation that Liñan's brigade could 'neither advance nor retreat in order', with all their movements made '*à la débandade*' and Gordon's 'flock of sheep' characterisation, suggests that they still lacked the training and discipline of an experienced unit.[156]

The 2º Voluntarios de la Corona was raised only four months before Villamuriel, in June 1812, following the 'dispersal' of the original unit at the action of Pajares on 17 May 1812. Although the regiment was involved in the siege of Astorga in August, by the time of Villamuriel in October it remained an inexperienced and untrained unit.[157]

In summary the Spanish regiments at Villamuriel were both inexperienced units, in need of more training and improved discipline.[158] However, the willingness and desire of these units to engage with French was remarked on by all observers including Wellington, Stanhope and Liñan himself.

French

Commanders

Antoine Louis Popon Baron de Maucune was born in Brive on 21 February 1772. Maucune joined the Corps des Pionniers in 1786 as a *sous lieutenant* and was promoted *lieutenant* in 1787. At the outbreak of the revolution, he enlisted as a *grenadier* in the 1er Volontaires de Paris in July 1791. In May 1792 Maucune was wounded in the left chest at the taking of Menin, then in June became a *lieutenant* in the 23e Régiment d'Infanterie.[159] He received a bayonet wound in the right arm at Bardonèche in August 1793 with the Armée des Alpes. Promoted to *capitaine* in 1794, after the two amalgamations he was in the 39e Ligne with the Armée d'Italie in which he served until 1801. On 6 November 1796, during the Arcola campaign, as part of Vaubois's division, Maucune distinguished himself while leading the second company of grenadiers, at the head of the column during the retreat from Trento. Despite being on foot, armed only with his sabre, he fought, dismounted and defeated an enemy *uhlan* who had charged him.[160] Subsequently he was

154 Sañudo, *Base*; Oman, *History*, Vol.IV, p.470.

155 Sañudo, *Base*.

156 J.M. Queypo de Llano Ruiz de Saravia, Conde de Toreno, *Historia del Levantamiento, Guerra y Revolucion de Espana* (Paris: Europea de Baudry, 1838), Vol.III, pp.155–6.

157 Sañudo, *Base*.

158 Arsenio García Fuertes, *Nos Sin Nosotros: La aportación militar española a la victoria aliada en las campañas de 1811 y 1812 de la guerra peninsular* (Astorga: CSED Historia, 2018), Vol.I, p.596.

159 LEONORE LH2199/91.

160 G. Fabry, *Rapports historiques des régiments de l'armée d'Italie pendant la campagne de 1796–1797* (Paris: R. Chapelot, 1905), p.167.

promoted to *chef de bataillon* by Napoleon in December 1796. Maucune was wounded both in the right chest and the left shoulder at the first combat of Tauffers in March 1799 and he was promoted to *chef de brigade* on the battlefield, confirmed in 1800.[161] He was then wounded in the right foot, at Novi in August 1799. During the campaigns of the Grande Armée from 1805 to 1807 he served in the VI Corps under Ney, fighting at Elchingen, Jena and Eylau. Maucune was promoted to *général de brigade* in March 1807 and fought at Friedland. Napoleon then made him a *Grand Officier* of the *Legion d'Honneur* and Baron. He then moved with the VI Corps to Spain in 1808. In May 1809, Maucune was defeated and wounded when he tried to defend Santiago by advancing against superior numbers of Spanish regulars and partisans under *Brigadier* Don Martin de la Carrera.[162] However in November 1809, at the Battle of Alba de Tormes, he particularly distinguished himself in the pursuit of the fugitives and the capture of the defended bridge over the Tormes. Maucune was subsequently wounded again at Buçaco in 1810, while leading one of the brigades of Marchand's division against Pack's Portuguese brigade and twice more at Fuentes de Oñoro.[163]

Promoted to *Général de Division*, Maucune became the commander of the 5e Division, Armée de Portugal in May 1811. At Salamanca in July 1812, Maucune's division, particularly d'Arnauld's brigade, was broken by Leith's 5th Division and Le Marchant's heavy cavalry, during the collapse of the French left. Oman's, Fortescue's and other accounts assume that as each French division was beaten by the British it dissolved never to be rallied that day. However, there is evidence that Maucune managed to rally at least part of his division and participate in the rearguard action. Unlike the divisions around him Maucune's command escaped with its divisional artillery and all four of its regimental eagles. Furthermore, there was enough time to rally his division on the Monte de Azan, as suggested by Belmas, between his defeat 'in 40 minutes' at 05:00 p.m. and the final rearguard action, which took place between sunset (8:37 p.m.) and full dark at (11:00 p.m.). Girard's somewhat self-serving account has been discarded by some, but it is consistent with other sources regarding this phase of the battle.[164]

161 Smith, *Data Book*, p.148; C. Mullié, *Biographie des célébrités militaires des armées de terre et de mer…* (Paris: Poignavant, 1851), Vol.II, pp.278–280.

162 Muir, *Salamanca*, p.35; *The Scots Magazine* (1809), Vol.LXXI, p.553; Oman, *History*, 1995, Vol.II, p.385.

163 Oman, *History*, Vol.III, pp.382–383.

164 Fortescue, *History*, Vol.VIII, pp.486, 494; Napier, *History*, Vol.V, p.178; Oman, *History*, Vol.V, pp.435–7, 448–50, 463, 602, 604; Muir, *Salamanca*, p. 211; C-T. Beauvais, *Victoires, conquêtes, désastres, revers et guerres civiles des …* (Paris: C.L.F. Panckoucke, 1820), Vol. XXI, pp.78–9; Desachy, *Girard*, pp.201-2; Dumay, *Historique du 66e régiment d'infanterie, 1672–1900* (Tours: E. Arnault, 1900), p.59; P. Arvers, C. Brecht, *Historique du 82e Régiment d'Infanterie* (Paris: Lahure, 1876), p.127; Ross-Lewin, *With the 32nd*, p.184; W. Grattan, *Adventures with the Connaught Rangers, 1809–14* (London: Edward Arnold, 1902), pp.252–3; Hale, *Journal*, p.87; J-B. Lemonnier-Delafosse, *Campagnes de 1810, 11, 12, 13, 14 1815 en Portugal, Espagne, France, Belgique ou Souvenirs Militaires* (Havre: Lemale, 1850), p.163; P. Castel, *Relation de la bataille et retraite des Arapiles…* (Toulouse: Caseaux, 1854), p.20; J-V. Belmas, *Journaux des sièges faits ou soutenus par les Français dans la Péninsule* (Paris: Firmin Didot, 1836), Vol.I, pp.233–4; de Tarragon, *Historique*, p.219; Dumay, *Historique*,

Following the Burgos campaign, in June 1813, Maucune's troops were surprised by the Light Division at San Millán de la Cogolla, but, although he lost his baggage, he managed to extract his infantry through his 'presence of mind'.[165] Maucune's division missed the Battle of Vitoria but helped delay the Allied pursuit at Tolosa.[166] Following Soult's reorganisation Maucune's command became the 7e Division, but this division was scattered at 2nd Sorauren in late July 1813. At Echalar in August 1813, Maucune's now 'most dilapidated' division, the right flank guard of Soult's army, was brushed aside by the Light Division.[167] Maucune's division was scattered again at the Bidassoa in October and after these defeats, Marshal Soult replaced him with Jean François Leval.[168]

Maucune was wounded nine times in his 25-year career, with five years as a general officer before Villamuriel. Oman described him as 'a gallant but very rash leader' and 'a good fighter but habitually rash and careless'. Thus, Oman suggests that Maucune was 'careless' at San Millan and that Villamuriel was an example of his 'hazardous attacks'. However, he also stated that 'no discredit' could be attributed to the general for San Millan.[169] Girard describes him as having a reputation for being 'unbearable' to his subordinates and the views of Maucune's contemporaries are indeed somewhat mixed;

> 'General Maucune was a man of outstanding bravery' [Girard].[170]
>
> '[T]his general said that he prefers to observe the movements of the enemy closely with his own eyes, rather than from a distance, which increases and multiplies the objects; he still places himself between the line of skirmishers and the heads of his columns' [Béchaud].[171]
>
> 'We must greatly praise General Maucune for his activity and his value on the battlefield; his deployments were always those of an experienced general officer' [Lamartinière, referring to Maucune's performance on 23 October 1812 at Villodrigo].[172]
>
> '[S]o that General Maucune, notwithstanding the brilliant success which he had obtained was forced by superior numbers to retire' [Marmont, 25 July 1812].[173]
>
> 'Accordingly, I gave orders to the 5e Division to take a position on the extreme right of this plateau, the fire of which was perfectly connected with that of

---

p.59; Monick (ed.), *Douglas*, p.47; R. Cannon, *Historical Record of the Eleventh or North Devon Regiment of Foot* (London: Parker, Furnivall and Parker, 1845), pp.65, 68.

165 Oman, *History*, Vol.VI, pp.375–6; Smith, *Data Book*, p.426.

166 Smith, *Data Book*, p.432.

167 Oman, *History*, Vol.VI, pp.731–5.

168 Oman, *History*, Vol.VII, pp.124, 134–5.

169 Oman, *History*, Vol.VI, pp.66, 376; Vol.VII, pp.124, 134–5.

170 Desachy, *Girard*, p.215; Girard served as chief of staff to Maucune throughout 1812 and 1813, until after Vitoria.

171 Colin, 'Béchaud', p.403.

172 Gurwood (ed.), *Dispatches*, Vol.VI, p.773.

173 Anon., *The confidential correspondence of Napoleon Bonaparte with his brother Joseph...* (New York: Appleton, 1856), Vol.II, pp.232–3.

Arapiles… The 5e Division, after taking the indicated post, extended to the left without any motive nor reason' [Marmont, 31 July 1812].[174]

'[A] man of little ability, albeit a very brave soldier… it was in his character to get carried away in the moment when he marched on the enemy' [Marmont, 1857].[175]

'[A man] of distinguished talents, able to second, and able to succeed him [Souham] in command' [Napier].[176]

Finally, Souham wrote the following endorsement of Maucune following Villamuriel:

> General Maucune in all actions in which he takes part, manages to inspire the troops that he commands with the enthusiasm and dedication of which he has already given so much evidence.[177]

Maucune is one of the names inscribed under the *Arc de Triomphe*.

In summary, Maucune had a very mixed combat record; his early successes as a regimental commander were offset by several defeats as a brigade and division commander, albeit with the weaker French army of 1812–14, which led to his dismissal by *Maréchal* Soult.[178]

In contrast to his comments immediately after Salamanca, Marmont's later comment in his memoirs conforms to the headstrong, foolhardy and reckless characteristics often associated with Oman's 'rash' descriptor. However, Maucune's defeat at Salamanca, at least in part, resulted from forming his infantry in square formation, while Leith's infantry attacked. As to him extending too far to the left, Leith passed the Arapiles village to attack Maucune on the heights beyond, in the position he had been ordered to occupy. Oman's other label of 'careless' is probably a better fit with Maucune's record of being surprised on more than one occasion, including, as we shall see, by Wellington's counterattack at Villamuriel.

Pierre Louis Baron d'Arnauld was born on 13 May 1771 in Saint-Pierre on the island of Martinique.[179] In January 1788, he entered the army as a *cadet volontaire* in the chasseur company of the Bataillon de milice du Mouillage. He then became *sous lieutenant* in the Garde Nationale de Saint-Pierre in March 1790, *lieutenant* in the third battalion in February 1793, and *capitaine* of grenadiers in the same battalion in the following November. D'Arnauld was also appointed *aide de camp* to General Rochambeau in December

174 A. Du Casse, *Memoirs and political and military correspondence of King Joseph* (Paris: Perrotin, 1854), Vol.VIII, p.204.

175 A.F.L.V. de Marmont, *Memoires du Maréchal Marmont, Duc De Ragusa* (Paris: Perrotin, 1857), Vol.IV, pp.228–229, 238–9.

176 Napier, *History*, Vol.V, p.288.

177 Wellington (ed.), *Supplementary Despatches*, Vol.XIV, p.151.

178 Oman, *History*, Vol.VII, p.134.

179 J. Courcelles, *Dictionnaire historique et biographique des generaux Français: depuis le onzième siecle jusqu'en 1820* (Paris: Author, Arthus Bertrand and Treuttel and Wurtz, 1822), Vol.V, p.145; LEONORE LH/54/19, pp.2–3.

1793. Rochambeau then nominated d'Arnauld to be a *capitaine* in the 32e Régiment d'Infanterie in March 1794. D'Arnauld served at the siege of Fort Bourbon during the British invasion and conquest of Martinique in 1794. He next served in Victor Hugues's successful expedition to retake Guadeloupe from the British, between May and October 1794. In March 1795, d'Arnauld was appointed *aide de camp* to *Lieutenant Colonel* Cottin, commander of the expedition against St Lucia, and took part in the recapture and subsequent defence of this island, being wounded in the left leg by a shell fragment. In November 1795, d'Arnauld was appointed temporary governor of the city of Castries on St Lucia and provisionally promoted to *chef de bataillon* in May 1796. However, by the end of that month, he had been taken prisoner of war when Abercromby retook the island. D'Arnauld was taken to Barbados but managed to escape and landed in France in June 1797. Confirmed in his rank of *chef de bataillon* in June 1798, he was posted to the 81e Demi-brigade. D'Arnauld then joined *Général de Division* Desfourneaux's expedition to Guadeloupe, arriving in November 1798. He was commander of the garrison of French *Saint-Martin* in October 1799 but, despite an attestation of 'good conduct and distinguished zeal', was dismissed in March 1800, due to a misunderstanding with the commander of Dutch Sint Maarten.[180] In August 1801, d'Arnauld was recalled to the Armée de Guadeloupe and was appointed assistant chief of staff in February, and then chief of staff of the 1er Division, in May 1802. During the same month he distinguished himself, in the taking of a piece of artillery from the insurgents at Camp du Gray on Basse Terre, Guadeloupe, aided only by an engineer officer and two grenadiers.[181] In August, d'Arnauld was charged with the administration and the discipline of two battalions of the 66e Demi-brigade. In October he was made second in command of the second battalion of this demi-brigade and commander of the district of Grande-Terre (Guadeloupe). In May 1803, *Capitaine-Général* Ernouf gave d'Arnauld command of the island of Saint-Martin, but in June, having not been included in the new organization of the Armée de Guadeloupe, he went to France.[182] During the voyage, in July, d'Arnauld was taken prisoner of war by the British, however he eventually arrived at Morlaix in November 1803. From May 1804, d'Arnauld was employed as a senior staff officer in the camp of Montreuil, as part of the Armée d'Angleterre. In June, he received the *Legion d'Honneur*. D'Arnauld was then employed in the 1805 campaigns of the Grande Armée, on the staff of Ney's VI Corps. In October, he had a horse killed under him at Elchingen and was present at the capture of Ulm. After a spell at army general headquarters, in May 1806 d'Arnauld went back to the headquarters of VI Corps and fought at Jena before being given command of the combined grenadier and *voltigeur* companies, which formed the advanced guard of the corps. In November, he was given command of the 1er Bataillon, 3e Régiment Grenadiers et

180 The partition dates to 1648, however from 1795–1801 the French administered both parts of the island.

181 Fortescue, *History*, Vol.V, p.179.

182 A. Lacour, *Histoire de la Guadeloupe*, Vol.III *1798 à 1803* (Basse Terre: Gouvernement, 1858), p.412.

Voltigeurs Réunis and sent to Berlin and then to the siege of Danzig.[183] In June 1807, d'Arnauld fought at the head of his battalion, now the 5e Bataillon, 3e Régiment de Grenadiers, in Conroux's 2e Brigade of Oudinot's grenadier division, at the Battle of Friedland, where he was wounded twice and where his distinguished service, firmness and courage earned him the staff rank of *adjudant-commandant*.

In October 1807, he served on the staff of the 1er Corps d'Observation de la Gironde, which became the Armée de Portugal, VIII Corps of the Armée d'Espagne, and finally part of the II Corps, Armée de Portugal. In August 1808, d'Arnauld fought at Roliça, greatly distinguishing himself in multiple charges. He was wounded again but this did not prevent him from fighting until the end of the action with the utmost bravery.

Following Vimeiro, *Général de Division* Delaborde recommended d'Arnauld for promotion to *général de brigade*, which was confirmed in November 1808. In January 1809, d'Arnauld fought at the Battle of Corunna, leading the 2e Brigade, 3e Division, II Corps, Armée d'Espagne.[184] In the same month he was appointed *Officier* of the *Legion d'Honneur*. During the second invasion of Portugal, d'Arnauld fought at the capture of Oporto in March 1809, and then with distinction at the combat for the bridge at Amarante in April.[185] However in May, he was also present when Wellington retook Oporto and during the subsequent retirement to Galicia. In 1810, d'Arnauld spent time in Toledo to recover his health; he was also created a baron. In July 1812, he fought at the Battle of Salamanca commanding his brigade in Maucune's 5e Division. In the attack by Leith's 5th Division and Le Marchant's cavalry he had a horse killed under him and was taken prisoner. However, overnight, he managed to escape and re-join the army. After Villamuriel, in January 1813 he was appointed *Commandant* of the *Legion d'Honneur* and in August 1813 he was assigned to the Corps d'Observation d'Italie. There, after several successes against the Austrians, at the request of the viceroy, d'Arnauld was appointed *Chevalier* of the *Ordre de la Couronne-de-Fer*.[186]

D'Arnauld's career before Villamuriel comprised more than 20 years of service with four as a general officer. He fought with distinction on several occasions, was wounded four times and taken prisoner three times.

Jacques Montfort was born on 22 July 1770 at Sallanches, then part of the kingdom of Sardinia.[187] At the beginning of the revolution he enlisted as a *soldat* in the 4e Volontaires du Bas Rhin in 1792. He served with this unit in the Armée du Rhin and the Armée du Nord until 1801. Montfort

---

183 Napoleon Series at <http://www.napoleon-series.org/military/organization/c_oudinotgren.html>; accessed 27 August 2014, see 10 January and 1 June 1807 Orders of Battle (cites G. Nafziger, *Royal, Republican, Imperial, a History of the French Army from 1792–1815*, Vol.I).

184 NAFZIGER, *French II Corps, 15 January 1809*.

185 Oman, *History*, Vol.II, pp.267–271.

186 G. Nafziger and M. Gioannini, *The Defense of the Napoleonic Kingdom of Northern Italy, 1813–14* (Westport: Praeger, 2002), pp.197, 199.

187 Anon., *Revue Savoisienne: Journal publié par l'Association Florimontane d'Annecy: histoire, sciences, arts, industrie, littérature* (Annecy: Perrissin, 1876), p.13; Pigeard, *Étoiles*, p.493.

was appointed *capitaine* in June 1793, commanding the battalion's artillery company. Captured near Rheinzabern (20 August 1793) he managed to escape to Lauterbourg, bringing, with the aid of some gunners, two artillery pieces, which had been left on the battlefield. Montfort, then *capitaine* in the 44e Demi-brigade, became an *aide de camp* to *Général de Division* Claude Lecourbe, who commanded the 3e Division in Massena's Armée du Danube in 1799.[188] Montfort distinguished himself during the combat at Amsteg (14–16 August 1799) and it is reported that after the 2nd Battle of Zurich in September 1799, Massena promoted him on the battlefield to *chef de bataillon*.[189] However, the archives of the *Legion d'Honneur* date this promotion to 1802 with the 84e Demi-brigade. In September 1802, Noguès has Montfort in command of a battalion of the 46e Demi-brigade, stationed in Dunkirk.[190]

After the Peace of Amiens, Montfort was sent to Martinique and was appointed *colonel* of the 82e Ligne on 24 May 1805. In this capacity, he served in the defence of Fort Desaix, but was wounded and taken prisoner in February 1809.[191] However due to his injuries, Montfort was sent back to France on parole, arriving in Quiberon Bay on 1 March 1809.[192] Exchanged on 16 October 1810, he then served in Spain until 1813. He was promoted to *général de brigade* in the Armée de Portugal in August 1811. At Salamanca, while part of Maucune's disaster, his brigade escaped the worst effects of Le Marchant's cavalry charge.[193] Montfort was created baron in December 1812 and was thereafter styled de Montfort.[194] After Villamuriel and Vitoria, Montfort served in Soult's reorganised army, including the rout on the Bidassoa and the combat of Barrouillet during the Battle of the Nive, in defence of Bayonne, where he again fought the British 5th Division under Hay.[195] Montfort was then transferred to the VII Corps, with the Grande Armée in Champagne in 1814. Here he served with distinction, being wounded at Bar-sur-Aube and Arcis-sur-Aube, and was also present at Troyes.[196] Montfort, originally decorated in 1806, became a *Commandant* of the *Legion d'Honneur* in April 1814. During the Waterloo Campaign, Montfort became chief of staff to Lecourbe in the Armée du Jura and, in July 1815, took part in the combat of Offemont and the defence of Belfort.[197]

---

188 R. Günther, *Der Feldzug der Division Lecourbe im Schweizerischen Hochgebirge 1799* (Frauenfeld: J. Huber, 1896), p.27; C.Jones, *The Longman Companion to the French Revolution* (Harlow: Addison Wesley Longman, 1988), pp.147–9.

189 Smith, *Data Book*, p.164; A. Folliet, *Révolution française: les volontaires de la Savoie, 1792–1799* (Paris: L. Baudoin, 1887), p.351.

190 André, Baron de Mericourt, *Mémoires du Général Noguès, 1777–1853: sur les guerres de l'empire* (Paris: Lemerre, 1922), p.148; LEONORE LH/646/36, p.10.

191 S. Daney de Marcillac, *Histoire de la Martinique: depuis la colonisation jusqu'en 1815* (Fort Royal: E. Ruelle, 1846), Vol.VI, pp.319, 335.

192 Arvers, Brecht, *Historique*, p.95.

193 Oman, *History*, Vol.V, pp.450–1, 602, 604.

194 *Revue Savoisienne*, p.13.

195 Oman, *History*, Vol.VII, pp.122–127, 247–8; J. Vidal de la Blache, *L'évacuation de l'Espagne et l'invasion dans le Midi, juin 1813–avril 1814* (Paris: Berger-Levrault, 1914), Vol.II, p.169.

196 F.-G. Hourtoulle, *1814, The Campaign for France* (Paris: Histoire et Collections, 2005), pp.72, 132.

197 H. Bardy, *La dernière campagne du général Lecourbe: Belfort en 1815* (Saint-Dié: Humbert, 1889), pp.42, 46; F.F.G.de Vaudoncourt, *Histoire des campagnes de 1814 et 1815, en France*

> 'Former *aide de camp* of Lecourbe, Savoyard by birth, good officer but miserably ambitious' [*Général de Brigade* Antoine Noguès].[198]

In summary, Montfort had served with distinction for twenty years before Villamuriel, but with only one year as a general officer. Jacques de Montfort is another of the names inscribed on the *Arc de Triomphe*.

François Michel Desfossés was born on 29 January 1773 in Saint-Révérien, in the Niévre department of central France.[199] He was the son of Révérien Michel, a Tax Attorney, and Louise Desfossés, whose surname he later preferred to use. In March 1789 he volunteered into the Chasseurs de Bretagne, which became the 10e Chasseurs à Cheval in 1791.

Desfossés was steadily promoted during the revolutionary wars; *brigadier* in June 1794, *maréchal des logis* in January 1796 and *maréchal des logis-chef* in January 1797. With his regiment he served in the Armée du Centre in 1792, the Armée du Rhin and the Armée de la Moselle from 1792 until 1794, and in the Armée d'Italie from 1795 until 1797. On the first day of the Battle of Arcola, 15 November 1796, Desfossés distinguished himself in the affair of Saint-Michel before Verona. When leading a detachment of the regiment on reconnaissance; he found and charged the third battalion of the Hungarian Infanterie Regiment Alvinczy Nr.19, having his horse killed beneath him.[200] On 22 March 1797, during the Battle of Tarvis, he was made a prisoner of war, when attacked by superior numbers.[201] In 1799 Desfossés served in the Armée du Danube and the Armée d'Helvétie and he was promoted to *sous lieutenant*, still in the 10e Chasseurs à Cheval, in July 1799. Serving with the Armée du Rhin from 1800 to 1801, Desfossés fought at the Battle of Engen, 3 May 1800, where he charged the enemy twice and took 90 prisoners including two officers. He was further promoted to *lieutenant* in August 1802 and appointed *adjutant major* in June 1804 in the same regiment. A *legionnaire* of the *Legion d'Honneur* in November 1804, Desfossés served with the Grande Armée in the 1805 campaign and was promoted to *capitaine* in December 1805. Appointed *aide de camp* to *Général de Brigade* Auguste Colbert-Chabanais in January 1806, Desfossés was wounded in the thigh by grapeshot at the Battle of Jena, 14 October 1806. Promoted to *chef d'escadron* in the same regiment in November 1806, Desfossés returned to active service in December 1806 and took part in the Polish campaign of 1807. In February 1808 he was appointed an *Officier* of the *Legion d'Honneur*. In August 1808 after 19 years of service, Desfossés

---

(Paris: De Gastel, 1826), Vol.IV, p.294.

198 Mericourt, *Noguès*, p.148.

199 D. and B. Quintin, *Dictionnaire des Colonels de Napoléon* (Paris: S.P.M., 2013), p.614; LEONORE LH/1869–1822; SHD 2YB928; *22e Chasseurs à Cheval; Registre des Services des Officiers, 4e vol. an XII–1814*.

200 A.H. Jomini, *Critique et Militaire des Guerres de la Revolution* (Brussels: Petit, 1840), Vol. III, pp.53–57; Fabry, *Rapports*, p.543; A.F. von Wrede, *Geschichte der K. und K. Wehrmacht* (Vienna: Seidel 1898), Vol.I, p.252.

201 Fabry, *Rapports*, p.549; NAFZIGER, *French Army of Italy, 21st March 1797*; in Rampon's brigade, Massena's division.

was promoted to *colonel* in the 22e Chasseurs à Cheval at the age of 35. With this regiment, he served in Spain, Portugal and with the Armée des Pyrénées from 1808 until 1814, during which time he was wounded at the Battle of Salamanca on 22 July 1812. The 1812 campaign also offered his first experience in command of a brigade.

Troop Quality

In the third quarter of 1812, the Armée de Portugal was in the process of recovering from its major defeat at Salamanca. *Général de Division* Bertrand Clausel was in command, following the wounding of *Maréchal* Marmont, and to him fell the task of reorganisation. On 6 August 1812, he wrote to Clarke, the Minister of War in Paris, describing the challenge he faced:

> I have gathered most of the army between Torquemada and Palencia, while a division escorted our wounded and baggage to Burgos, and *Général* Foy, with his division, observed Aranda [de Duero, on the road from Madrid to Burgos]. I have had to find a position in which I could support the army, restore its morale, give it a few days off, form a new reserve supply of food, punishing some of the soldiers who were engaged in the most frightful disorders, scare others by examples of severity, and especially to overcome the desire, too often expressed, to cross the Ebro and to approach the borders of France. It is common to see, after a failure, an army discouraged; it is difficult to see one in which there is greater discouragement, and I cannot, and must not be silent to Your Excellency, regarding the bad spirit that is and has been in it for quite some time; disorder and the most outrageous excesses have marked every step of our retirement.[202]

Clausel was obviously the right man for this job, as six weeks later, Joseph's aide de camp, *Colonel* François-Alexandre Desprez wrote to the King from Paris; 'the Armée de Portugal has rallied; its losses are much lower than previously thought'.[203] Furthermore, Souham himself commended Clausel's work in his report of 1 November to the Minister of War.[204]

To understand the nature of the French troops at Villamuriel it is important to look at their service record under the First Empire. By the time of the battle of Fuentes de Oñoro in May 1811, each of the infantry regiments at Villamuriel had had four of their *bataillons de guerre* in the Peninsula. For the 15e and 86e Ligne, the first, second, third and fourth battalions all served in the Peninsula.[205] For the 66e Ligne, the third, fourth, fifth and sixth battalions of the re-formed regiment served there, the original regiment having been lost on Guadeloupe in 1810.[206] Similarly the fourth, fifth, sixth

---

202 Du Casse, *Joseph*, Vol.IX, pp.63–64.

203 Du Casse, *Joseph*, Vol.IX, p.91.

204 Wellington (ed.), *Supplementary Despatches*, Vol.XIV, p.151.

205 De Tarragon, *Historique*, pp.189–196; Anon., *Historique du 86e régiment d'infanterie* (Paris: Charles-Lavauzelle, 1886), p.26.

206 Oman, *History*, Vol.I, p.612; H. de Poyen-Bellisle, *Les Guerres des Antilles, 1793–1815* (Paris: Berger-Levrault, 1896), pp.276, 298, 391, 398; there were two third battalions at different times, one on Guadeloupe and the old depot battalion that went to Portugal.

and seventh battalions of the 82e Ligne served in the Peninsula, the first, second and third having been lost on Martinique in 1809.[207]

The following table shows the battles and engagements which comprise the experience of the infantry battalions at Villamuriel, drawn largely from Martinien's officer casualty data.[208]

Battles of the Regiments of the 5e Division, Armée de Portugal, 1805-1812				
	1 and 2/15e Ligne	4 and 6/66e Ligne	4 and 5/82e Ligne	1 and 2/86e Ligne
1807	Friedland			
1808	Medina del Rio Seco Gamonal			Evora Vimeiro
1809	Corunna 1st and 2nd Oporto	1st Oporto (4/66e Ligne)	1st Oporto (5/82e Ligne)	Corunna 1st and 2nd Oporto
1810	Astorga Buçaco Sobral	Astorga Ciudad Rodrigo Almeida/Coa Buçaco	Almeida/Coa Buçaco	Astorga Buçaco Casal Novo
1811	Fuentes de Oñoro	Fuentes de Oñoro	Fuentes de Oñoro (4 and 6/82e Ligne) Almeida (5/82e Ligne)	Fuentes de Oñoro
1812	Salamanca	Salamanca (4/66e Ligne)	Salamanca	Salamanca

Notes

1. During 1805–6, the 15e Ligne was based in Brest. Martinien shows casualties from the naval battle of Santo Domingo, but these were from the third battalion.[209] At Medina del Rio Seco, the 15e Ligne was in Reynaud's brigade of Mouton's division.[210] The fourth battalion served at Zaragoza.[211]
   At the 1st Battle of Oporto, 29 March 1809 against the Portuguese, the 15e Ligne was in Merle's Division, the 66e Ligne and 82e Ligne in Heudelet's Division, in reserve, and the 86e Ligne in Delaborde's Division.[212] The 15e Ligne was also present for Wellington's capture of Oporto on 12 May 1809.[213] Although Smith does not show the 15e Ligne at Buçaco, they were in Gratian's brigade with the 86e Ligne, in Solignac's division of Junot's corps.[214]
2. The 4/66e Ligne, 5/66e Ligne and the 5/82e Ligne served in the Corunna campaign in Heudelet's division but did not fight at the Battle of Corunna itself.[215]
3. At Vimeiro the 3/82e Ligne was also present but was subsequently sent to the West Indies, while the 3/66e Ligne and 4/66e Ligne were at Cascais, near Lisbon, and the 3/15e Ligne served at Saccavem and Lisbon, at this time. In August 1812, the 3/15e Ligne was dissolved into the first and second battalions.[216]
4. Although Martinien records that the 66e Ligne had an officer wounded in the final assault on Astorga, 21 April 1810, Oman does not mention the presence of the 66e Ligne. However, Loisin's

207 Arvers, Brecht, *Historique*, pp.95, 103, 110, 122.
208 D. Smith, *Napoleon's Regiments* (London: Greenhill, 2000), pp.65, 124, 136, 141.
209 Martinien, *Tableaux*, p.151; de Tarragon, *Historique*, 1895, pp.167, 175, 179.
210 NAFZIGER, *Medina del Rio Seco, 14 July 1808.*
211 De Tarragon, *Historique*, pp.193–5.
212 Oman, *History*, Vol.II, p.243–5, 625; Ch. Talandier, *Mémoires relatifs aux opérations du deuxième corps d'armée en Espagne et en Portugal, sous les ordres du Maréchal Soult dans les années 1808, 1809, 1810, et 1811* (Verdun: Lippmann, 1835), pp.91, 107–120.
213 De Tarragon, *Historique*, p.205; Oman, *History*, Vol.III, pp.441, 542 (Sobral 13 October 1810).
214 Oman, *History*, Vol.III, p.542.
215 Oman, *History*, Vol.I, p.585; NAFZIGER, *French II Corps, 15 January 1809.*
216 Oman, *History*, Vol.I, pp.243, 602; de Tarragon, *Historique*, p.219.

division of VI Corps, of which the 66e Ligne were part, was the initial force which attempted to take the city in February.[217]
5. Following the battle of Salamanca, the 4/66e Ligne and 5/66e Ligne were re-formed into one battalion, the 4/66e Ligne.[218]
6. Men of the 6/82e Ligne were absorbed into the fourth and fifth battalions in February 1812.[219]
7. At Fuentes de Oñoro the 15e Ligne and 86e Ligne were in Solignac's division, while the 66e Ligne and 82e Ligne were in Ferey's division and involved in the attacks on the village itself.[220]
8. The 86e Ligne were in Delaborde's division at Second Oporto but were detached at Baltar, halfway between Oporto and Amarante.[221] Martinien records a *Lieutenant* Delplatz (86e Ligne) as killed at the siege of Ciudad Rodrigo on 19 January 1812, but the regiment was not part of the garrison so the unfortunate lieutenant must have been present amongst the sick or for some other reason.[222]

Thus, of the regiments present at Villamuriel, only the 15e Ligne had been involved in the victories of Napoleon's Grande Armée. Furthermore, each of the regiments had been directly involved in the defeats, both tactical and strategic, suffered at the hands of the Anglo-Portuguese army. Thus, Muir's comments regarding the psychological inferiority, despite their veteran status, of these French battalions are likely to have been even more relevant in the aftermath of Salamanca, although such inferiority is clearly not reflected in the bravado intrinsic to the accounts of Béchaud or Girard.[223]

Throughout 1812, by reducing the number of battalions to the two that were present at Villamuriel, the regiments managed to maintain a high level of experienced men in the remaining battalions, despite arduous campaigning and the defeat at Salamanca.[224] The cadres of the other battalions were sent back to France, subsequently returning with men, who were then used to bring the two battalions with the field army up to strength. For example, the cadre of the 6/82e Ligne (20 officers and 96 men) departed from the environs of Valladolid on 8 February 1812 to return to France.[225] The rebuilt battalion then left Bayonne on 8 September 1812 to re-join the 5e Division, where its men were used to reinforce the fourth and fifth battalions. An inspection of the returns and regimental histories for these regiments throughout 1812, suggests that the regiments had approximately 30 percent recently arrived men. The new men comprised:

15e Ligne: troops which arrived with the 4e Bataillon, approximately 32 percent of the men present with the regiment. The return for 15 September shows that the battalion left Bayonne on 26 September 1812 with 754 officers and men, although 300 of these men were sick in hospital by 15 October.

217 Oman, *History*, Vol.III, p.225; Martinien, *Tableaux*, p.270.
218 Dumay, *Historique*, p.59; SHD C8 467.
219 Arvers, Brecht, *Historique*, p.123.
220 Oman, *History*, Vol.IV, p.626; J.H. Gill, 'Fuentes de Oñoro 1811: The French Order of Battle', pp.6–7, <http://www.sammustafa.com/honour/wp-content/uploads/downloads/2010/08/Fuentes-Gill.pdf>, accessed 12th April 2015.
221 P.M. Le Noble, *Mémoires sur les opérations militaires des Français: en Galice, en Portugal, et dans la Vallee du Tage, en 1809…* (Paris: Barrois, 1821), p.249; Anon., *Historique du 86e*, p.19–22.
222 Martinien, *Tableaux*, p.299; Oman, *History*, Vol.V, p.587.
223 Muir, *Salamanca*, pp.26–7, 115–116.
224 Oman, *History*, Vol.VI, p.7.
225 Arvers, Brecht, *Historique*, p.123.

66e Ligne: Béchaud mentions newly arrived young soldiers at Villamuriel, these have been estimated at 287 men by comparing returns of 15 October and 1 August, i.e. approximately 29 percent of the men present. The 6/66e Ligne differs in that it filled the vacancy left by the fifth battalion following the reorganisation of the regiment after Salamanca. The 6/66e Ligne served in both the Buçaco and Fuentes de Oñoro campaigns, but the cadre of the battalion was ordered back to France in December 1811, when the battalion had 16 officers and 385 men present under arms, with 14 men detached and 73 in hospital, i.e. a total of 488 effectives.[226] Consequently the 6/66e Ligne missed Salamanca, however it returned to Spain, along with the 6/82e Ligne, as part of the 5e Demi-brigade Provisoire of Aussenac's brigade. The battalions left Bayonne on 8 September 1812 to cover the 266 miles to Villamuriel, a march of 10–15 days. The battalion had certainly re-joined the regiment by 15 October 1812.[227]

82e Ligne: troops who arrived with the sixth battalion in October, approximately 25 percent of the men with the regiment, based on the 15 September return.

86e Ligne: troops who arrived with the third battalion before October, approximately 36 percent of the men with the regiment.

The 15 June 1812 *situation* for the Armée de Portugal shows 12,676 men at Bayonne arriving with the army after Salamanca, making up some 20 percent of the army in October. Thus the 5e Division, with an average of some 30 percent of less-experienced men, had more than the average for army.[228]

However, approximately two thirds of the men with the French infantry regiments at Villamuriel were likely to have been veterans of both the Salamanca and Fuentes de Oñoro campaigns, and significant numbers would have been even more experienced. The numbers of veteran troops have been estimated by comparing the returns for May 1811 with those for March, July and October 1812, which suggest that more than 90 percent of the men at Salamanca were already veterans of Fuentes de Oñoro and earlier battles. Further comparison of the 1812 returns suggests that by the time of Villamuriel approximately 55 percent of the men of the 15e Ligne, 65 percent of the men of the 66e Ligne and 82e Ligne and 70 percent of the men of the 86e Ligne were veterans of the 1811 campaigns. All of these estimates can only be just that, as the levels of sickness must have had a significant influence on the numbers fit for action at any one time. During the period April to June 1812 the Armée de Portugal reported approximately 12 percent of its men in hospital, which had risen to 18 percent in October and November 1812, however the general thrust of the conclusions is probably correct.[229]

Béchaud describes how half of the troops comprising the grenadier company of the 4/66e Ligne were young men, who were seeing the enemy

226 SHD C8 462: *Situation Armées en Espagne,* 15 January 1812.

227 SHD C8 466, 467, 468; *Situations Armées en Espagne*.

228 SHD C8 467, C8 468; Oman, *History*,Vol.V, p.602; Napier, *History*, Vol.V, p.619.

229 Oman, *History*, Vol.IV, p.625, Vol.V, p.602, Vol.VI, p.743; Gill, 'Fuentes', pp.6–7; NAFZIGER, *Portugal 1 March 1812*; Napier, *History*, Vol.V, pp.618–9.

close up for the first time at Villamuriel.[230] This suggests that no attempt was made to bring the grenadier company of the senior battalion of the 66e Ligne up to strength using experienced men. Thus, it appears that the newer recruits were distributed to fill vacancies wherever they occurred. This would appear to be in direct contravention of Imperial decree, as Elting noted 'Napoleon was insistent that only qualified men be assigned to them' [i.e. grenadiers, *carabiniers*, *voltigeurs* and *sapeurs*].[231] Furthermore Crowdy remarks that the 'imperial decree of 18 February [1808] stipulated grenadiers had to be drawn from the tallest men in the regiment and to have served for four years or taken part in two of the four campaigns of Ulm, Austerlitz, Jena or Friedland'.[232]

However, Béchaud believed that the new recruits were of value despite their lack of experience:

> These 10,000 reinforcements are mostly young soldiers, but everyone knows how little time it takes to pick up the customs of their profession, to acquire the valour of old soldiers; it is also known that, mingled with them, they march to the fight as well as them… our young as well as our old soldiers fired so calmly and so well that they destroyed a huge number of the enemy.[233]

On the other hand, Spanish Generals considered that '… any unit in which the proportion of raw recruits amounted to more than one third of the whole was not to be trusted in the slightest'.[234]

However, it would be a mistake to think that the recently arrived men were all new conscripts, just a few weeks from their depots. For example, a study of the *registres matricules* for the recently arrived 6/66e Ligne, shows that only one man at Villamuriel could have joined the battalion within the previous six months. In this study 467 men were identified who could have been at Villamuriel. Although some 301 men joined the battalion in the first quarter of 1812, only 187 them could have served at Villamuriel, the remaining 114 men joined only to be lost to the battalion before October, largely due to desertion (54 percent) and sickness (36 percent). The balance comprised; 'left behind' (four percent), killed in action or died of wounds (two percent), discharged (two percent) or transferred (one percent).

This method is not entirely reliable as the *registres* are not always up to date with regard to battalion attribution, as evidenced by the Villamuriel casualties identified as being with the fifth or seventh battalions which were not present. Furthermore, the *registres* generally only record absence in hospital on occasions when the soldier did not return to the battalion.

These numbers can be compared to 15 October *situation* for the 6/66e Ligne: 450 other ranks were present under arms, 72 men were detached,

230 Colin, 'Béchaud', p.409.

231 J.R. Elting, *Swords around the Throne* (London: Weidenfeld and Nicolson, 1989), p.95.

232 T. Crowdy, *Napoleon's Infantry Handbook* (Barnsley: Pen and Sword Military, 2015), p.34.

233 Colin, 'Béchaud', pp.89, 407.

234 Esdaile, *Spanish Army*, p.95; Similarly in March 1794, Dugommier commanding the Armée des Pyrénées Orientales, preferred to keep his 9,000 untrained conscripts in the rear providing an impression of mass, rather than integrating them within his 18,000 trained and experienced troops (Phipps, *Armies*, Vol.III, pp.172; Chuquet, *Dugommier*, 1904, p.244).

144 in hospital, a total of 684 men. Of these, however, at least 65 men were transferred from the fourth battalion when the regiment was reunited, as evidenced by the *situation* for 15 September, when the sixth battalion had 15 officers and 404 men present under arms.[235]

Furthermore, the *registres matricules* suggest that 60 percent of the men comprising the 6/66e Ligne at Villamuriel in fact had more than 12 months service and 47 percent had more than two years' service. The average age of the 467 other ranks identified as potential Villamuriel men in the 6/66e Ligne was 24 years.

The 222 men from Maucune's infantry, who have been identified by name as casualties of the fighting at Villamuriel, offer another perhaps more direct, albeit smaller-scale, insight into the French infantry's experience with the eagles. Of these men, 41 percent were veterans of more than five years, while 64 percent were veterans with more than two years of experience. At the other end of the scale 23 percent had less than a year and only three percent less than six months. Even for the recently arrived 6/66e Ligne, of the 21 identified casualties, 19 percent had more than five years' experience and 76 percent had more than 2 years, with none less than 6 months. The detail is provided in the following table, based upon their service defined as the time elapsed from first enlistment to 25 October 1812:[236]

Experience	15e Ligne		66e Ligne		82e Ligne		86e Ligne		Total	
> 10 years	21	14%	2	4%	0	0%	0	0%	23	10%
> 5 years	66	43%	17	35%	1	25%	7	50%	91	41%
> 2 years	91	59%	38	78%	3	75%	11	79%	143	64%
> 1 year	112	72%	44	90%	4	100%	11	79%	171	77%
> 6 months	149	96%	48	98%	4	100%	14	100%	215	97%
Total	155		49		4		14		222	

On average these men had 5 years' experience with the eagles. The age of these men varied from 19 to 42 years old with an average age of 26 years old. These data further suggest that the new conscripts were taking longer than six months to reach the war battalions from their depots via Bayonne.[237]

In the words of Elting '... in sum the French infantry was at its height during 1805–6... Its quality remained very high through 1807 and in most veteran regiments, even through 1812'.[238]

235 SHD GR21 YC556, *registre matricule 66e Ligne*, 5 May 1811 to 24 December 1812, available at; <http://www.memoiredeshommes.sga.defense.gouv.fr/fr/arkothequ/inventaires/ead_ir_consult.php?fam=10&ref=23>.

236 This data is taken from the *registres matricules* and *contrôles des officiers* for the four regiments but is skewed towards the units that suffered most casualties. *Registres matricules* SHD GR21YC 133–137 (15e Ligne); SHD GR21YC 551–556 (66e); SHD GR21YC 632–636 (82e); SHD GR21YC 666–669 (86e). *Contrôles des officiers*; SHD 2Yb 157 (15e Ligne); SHD 2Yb 349 (66e); SHD 2Yb 397 (82e); SHD 2Yb 411 (86e).

237 These data are taken from the *registres matricules* for the 215 men whose date or year of birth is recorded. The standard error of this mean is approximately 4 months, so we can conclude that the average age of the French soldiers at Villamuriel was in the range of 25 to 27 years old at 95 percent confidence.

238 Elting, *Swords*, p.224.

There is considerably less readily available data regarding the service of the specific artillery companies engaged at Villamuriel. Although Susane states that the 6/2e Artillerie à Cheval were in Germany in 1808 and then describes them as 'in Portugal' in January 1811, and only describes the deployment of the 11/8e Artillerie à Pied, as in Spain in July 1812, both of these artillery companies had served in the Peninsula since at least 1810.[239] Inspection of the *situations* for 1812 does not indicate any recent influx of new recruits into either of these units, although the horse artillery had been significantly reinforced in February 1812. Thus, it is likely that all the men of the foot artillery were veterans of both the 1812 and 1811 campaigns as were two-thirds of the men of the horse artillery. The remainder of the horse artillerymen would have served throughout the Salamanca and autumn 1812 campaigns.

For Desfossés's light cavalry brigade, the following table shows the battles and engagements which comprise their experience, drawn largely from Martinien's officer casualty data:[240]

Battles of the regiments of Desfossés's light cavalry brigade, 1805-1812				
	3e Hussards, 1er and 2e Escadrons	22e Chasseurs, 1er and 2e Escadrons	26e Chasseurs, 1er and 2e Escadrons	28e Chasseurs, 1er Escadron
1805	Elchingen Ulm	Ulm Wischau Austerlitz	Albeck Ulm Brünn Austerlitz	
1806	Jena	Jena Waren Lubeck		
1807	Hof Eylau Guttstadt Friedland	Hof Eylau Guttstadt Heilsberg	Siege of Stralsund Passarge River	
1808	Madrid Tudela	Medina de Rio Seco Burgos	Roliça Vimeiro	Counter-guerrilla operations
1809	Cacabelos Col de Banos Tamames Alba de Tormes	Benavente	Medellin Talavera d'Almonacid	Counter-guerrilla operations
1810	Almeida Leiria	Astorga	Ciudad Rodrigo	Counter-guerrilla operations
1811	Redinha Fuentes de Oñoro Condeixa	Sabugal El Bodon Aldea da Ponte	El Bodon	Fuentes de Oñoro
1812	Salamanca	Salamanca	Salamanca	Salamanca

239 L.Susane, *Histoire de l'artillerie française* (Paris, J. Hetzel, 1874), pp.348, 361; NAFZIGER, *Artillery of the French Army in Spain, 1 March 1810.*

240 Burnham, *Charging*, pp.297–8, 299–302, 308–309; Smith, *Regiments*, 2000, pp.277, 280, 281, 284; Martinien, *Tableaux*, pp.606, 610–11, 613, 617–8; R. Dupuy, *Historique du 3e Régiment du Hussards de 1664 à 1887* (Paris: Piaget, 1887), pp.45–56; Oman, *History*, Vol.IV, p.564.

The 28e Chasseurs à Cheval were raised in 1808 from the Tuscan Dragoons. Nafziger places the 28e Chasseurs with Bonnet's Asturias division in July 1811, citing Oman who however does not include the 28e Chasseurs. However, Martinien gives a *Capitaine* Ghérardi as wounded at Fuentes de Oñoro in May.[241]

Thus, the French cavalry at Villamuriel had a more distinguished war record than their infantry counterparts. However, similar to the infantry, the returns suggest that the 3e Hussards, the 22e and 26e Chasseurs had, in the autumn of 1812, received new recruits from France, which comprised approximately 30 percent of the regiment. Thus the 1 October 1812 *situation* shows 95 men *en route* to the 3e Hussards. A comparison of 15 October *situation* with that of 1 August 1812 suggests that 33 percent of the 3e Hussards were such new recruits, while the similar number for the 22e Chasseurs à Cheval was 30 percent and that for the 26e Chasseurs à Cheval, 32 percent. Again, similar to the infantry, it is likely that the majority of the remainder of these three regiments would have been veterans of the Salamanca and Fuentes de Oñoro campaigns and indeed many would have served in the earlier campaigns.

Summary

In summary, the British and allied troops at Villamuriel were an experienced force comprising some 75 percent veteran battalions and 25 percent inexperienced or undisciplined battalions. Based on the respective analyses shown above, by individual soldier, the British and allied forces at Villamuriel comprised very approximately of 50 percent veteran, 25 percent experienced and 25 percent inexperienced or undisciplined troops.

On the other hand, the French units were all veteran units, with the possible exception of the 6/66e Ligne, which might have had fewer veterans, although its casualties suggest otherwise. Whereas the French, compared to the British and allied troops, had similar numbers of less experienced men in their ranks, these were incorporated, at an average of approximately 25 percent, into the veteran units, rather than comprising the majority of entire units.

The nature of the battle and campaign experience of the respective sides, however undoubtedly favoured the British and allied army.

241 Oman, *History*, Vol.IV, p.641; NAFZIGER, *French Army in Spain, 15 July 1811*; Martinien, *Tableaux*, p.815.

4

The Battlefield

Villamuriel de Cerrato has significantly changed since 1812 but fortunately much of the development is away from the river and of course the basic geography has not changed. Furthermore, the slopes from which Wellington launched his counterattack are pretty much unchanged. Unusually the riverbanks now boast significantly more trees than they once did. Map 2 has been assembled from a series of 18th and 19th century maps and gazeteers, together with a sketch map provided by Weare. The eyewitness accounts of the action also provide several clues to the nature of the battlefield in October 1812.

Villamuriel de Cerrato: the village of Villamuriel was described in 1828–9 as a 'small borough' with a population of 750, in 181 property owning households.[1] In 1849 the village was described as consisting of 104 houses of poor construction, together with a parish church.[2] Douglas described the village as being in the shape of an 'A' from his elevated position on the slopes of El Miron.[3]

The Monastery at Calabazanos: The Royal Monastery of Our Lady of the Consolation (it was also a convent) is surrounded by a high wall with a main gateway in the southern wall. In the grounds of the monastery was a chapel, an orchard and a parish church with attached cemetery. In 1826, the village of Calabazanos itself comprised 16 property owning households with 75 inhabitants.[4]

The Canal de Castilla was still under construction when the war began, it was consequently dry and two to three metres deep.

1 G.-B. Depping, *Dictionnaire géographique de l'Espagne et du Portugal* (Paris: Masson et Yonet, 1829), p.74; Sebastián de Miñano y Bedoya, *Diccionario geografico-estadistico de España y Portugal* (Madrid: Pierart-Peralta, 1828), Vol.IX, p.404.

2 P. Madoz, *Diccionario geografico estadistico-historico de Espana y sus posesiones de ultramar* (Madrid: Author, 1849), Vol.XV, p.194.

3 Monick (ed.), *Douglas*, p.59.

4 Miñano y Bedoya, *Diccionario*, Vol.II, p.258.

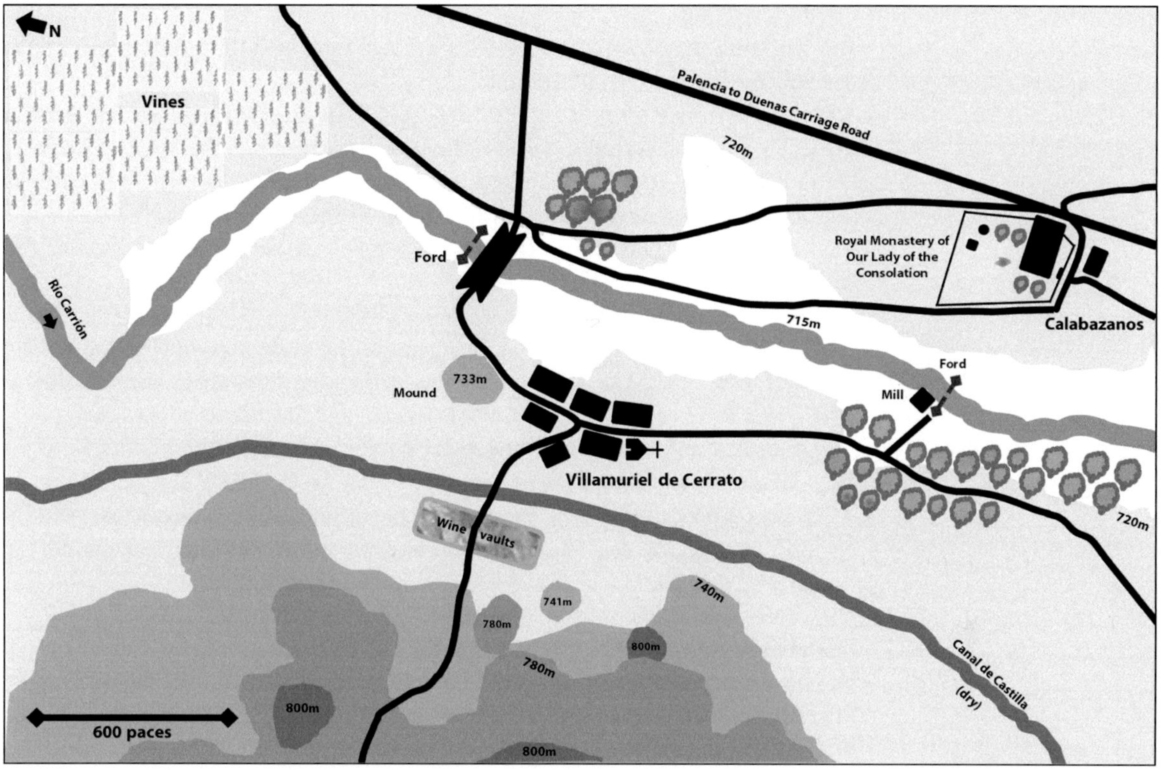

Map 2 Battlefield Terrain.

The Road Network is based on the 1782 map of Palencia province by Tomas Lopez and Simón y Nieto's more local map of 1884, however the Lopez map is prone to inaccuracies since it was not based on a full topographic survey. In the case of Villamuriel, for example, he placed the canal on the wrong side of the river. There is also an 1852 map of the Province by *Teniente Coronel* Don Francisco Coello.[5]

The Mound: to the north west and just outside the village was a mound or small hillock, approximately ten metres high, which features in the sketch map of the battlefield drawn by Captain Thomas Weare (35th Foot, aide de camp to Oswald). The mound was big enough to accommodate Lawson's guns, '... our artillery were firing from a small mound which rose at the end of the street, on our left hand as we stood looking towards the bridge'.[6] Although now within the extended and developed modern day Villamuriel, the 'mound' is still visible, approximately 200m from the bridge.

5 Lopez, *Mapa Geographica de la Provincia de Palencia 1782*, at <http://bibliotecadigital.rah.es/es/consulta/registro.do?id=12660>, accessed 17 July 2015; D. Francisco Simón y Nieto, *Estudio Médico-Topográfico de Villamuriel de Cerrato* (Palencia: Alonso y Z. Menéndez, 1886); M.S.Thompson, *Wellington's Engineers, Military Engineering in the Peninsular War, 1808–1814* (Barnsley: Pen and Sword, 2015), pp.217, 262.

6 TNA, NRA 21704 Oswald, Weare 12 December 1836; *Hart's New Army List*, 1840, p.261; *Army List*, 1813, p.207; CHALLIS.

Fords: Burroughs described the River Carrión near Dueñas as '… narrow and fordable in some places for cavalry; and here and there, the branches of the willow, dangled in its stream'.[7]

In his letters home, Bingham described the heavy rain that fell during the early part of October which affected the rivers in the area.[8] Similarly Daniel recorded in his journal on 12 October that 'for the last three weeks scarcely a night has passed without rain'.[9] Consequently, Ingilby describes the Carrión near Dueñas on the 24th as being '… filled to the banks with the heavy rains…'[10]

Gomm reported how:

> I was also directed to ascertain without delay what fords there were on the Carrion River about Villamuriel and Palencia;– and the defence of the bridge at Villamuriel was pointed out as the object of our particular attention.
>
> These directions were carried into effect and I had already ascertained the question about the fords; of which I have the memorandum by me. There were three between Palencia and Villamuriel and two below. The fords had all been reported difficult.[11]

Pringle's report also states that a ford existed downstream of Calabazanos, but he does not specify where.[12] Taken together with Gomm's comments, Pringle's report suggests that the second ford below Villamuriel was also below Calabazanos and therefore not on this map.

Gomm and Burroughs described how these fords presented some difficulty to infantry attempting to cross. At Calabazanos, the French are reported to have used their light cavalry to help the infantry across; '… then mounting their *voltigeurs* behind their cavalry, they forded the river at some distance below the bridge'.[13] Nevertheless. their casualty lists include five or six men killed by drowning.[14] Girard describes the ford at Calabazanos as being three feet deep, which would generally be considered dangerous for crossing on foot.[15] Girard's three French feet is 38 imperial inches, or waist-deep given the contemporary average height of 65 inches (The French prisoners of war taken at Villamuriel, as identified in the British registers (n=49) and the *registres matricules* (n=122) also had an average height of 65 inches). On the other hand, Béchaud reported no particular difficulty in crossing the ford near the bridge.

At the bridge, the river is approximately 82 paces or 64 yards wide and at the Calabazanos ford it is approximately 43 paces or 33 yards wide.

---

7 Burroughs, *Narrative*, p.21.
8 Glover (ed.), *Bingham*, p.154 (3 October near Burgos), p.159 (17 October near Burgos, rained every day for 7 days).
9 Esdaile, Freeman, *Burgos*, p.196, note 99.
10 Glover (ed.), *Ingilby*, p.55.
11 TNA, NRA 21704 Oswald, Gomm 13 December 1836.
12 UML, GB 133 Eng MSS 1273, item 27.
13 Burroughs, *Narrative*, p.23.
14 Gurwood (ed.), *Dispatches*, Vol.VI, pp.775–6.
15 Desachy, *Girard*, p.205.

The remains of the grist mill. (Author's Photo)

The bodegas today. (Author's Photo)

The rough ground around the bodegas. (Author's Photo)

The Watermill: Béchaud mentions a Calabazanos Mill by the Carrión, which is also described in the 1849 Gazetteer as a flour mill driven by the Carrión. the same Gazetteer does not mention a flour mill associated with Villamuriel. James Hale also mentions a 'grist mill' by the Carrión but is unclear as to where it was, other than to state that it was on the allied side of the river. Both Pringle, in his report to Oswald, and Hill, in his report to Pringle, state that the ford defended by the Caçadores N.8 was near the mill. The mill has subsequently been demolished but its remains can still be identified in the undergrowth near the ford at Calabazanos. These stonework remains are the only such remains identified on either bank of the river below the bridge, therefore it is probable that Hale and Béchaud were referring to the same mill, which was possibly associated with the monastery at Calabazanos.[16]

Vines: these are shown on the 1884 map, which also shows that the hills further out from Villamuriel were also covered in vines.

Bodegas or Wine Vaults: these vaults are underground storage facilities, which are described as being up to 100 steps underground.[17]

16 Madoz, *Diccionario*, Vol.V, p.237, Vol.XV, p.194; Colin, 'Béchaud', p.406; Hale, *Journal*, p.94; UML, GB 133 Eng MSS 1273, item 27; Wellington Papers, Hill to Pringle, 27 October 1812.

17 Green, *Vicissitudes*, p.121; Monick (ed.), *Douglas*, p.60.

Woods: Burroughs described a wood which the French occupied once they were across the Carrión near Calabazanos. Similarly, Gomm stated '... the riverbank below the village was fringed with wood'.[18] This was clearly an open type of wood as Burroughs could observe the effects of the artillery fire on the French defenders from a considerable distance.[19]

Weare described another wood on the left bank of the river near the bridge.[20] Today the banks of the river are more extensively wooded both above and below the bridge. The first edition of Spain's *Mapa Topográfico Nacional*, published in 1918, shows less extensive woods than today, some of which correspond to the contemporary sources.[21]

The Hills: Weare described the high ground to the west of Villamuriel as '... high and naked hills with a gradual but steep slope down to the Canal – but ended before reaching the canal'.[22]

18 TNA, NRA 21704 Oswald, Gomm 13 December 1836.
19 Wellington Papers; Hill to Pringle, 27 October 1812; Burroughs, *Narrative*, p.24.
20 TNA, NRA 21704 Oswald, Weare 12 December 1836.
21 *Mapa Topográfico Nacional, Primeras Ediciones* (MTN), Sheets 311, 312, scale 50,000:1, available via SIGNA at <http://signa.ign.es/signa/>, accessed 4 April 2014.
22 TNA, NRA 21704 Oswald, Weare 12 December 1836.

5

Deployment

The Anglo-Portuguese 5th Division arrived in Villamuriel in the evening of 24 October. Lieutenant Le Mesurier (1/9th Foot) arrived as night fell: 'on our arrival at this place I was ordered on guard in the town to protect the property of the inhabitants and was comfortably lodged in a house that night with plenty of forage for my poney[sic]…'[1] In his journal, the 35-year-old Corporal James Hale (Light Company, 1/9th Foot) described how the remainder of the 1/9th Foot was tasked with guarding the bridge overnight while the engineers began 'boring the bridge' for demolition.[2]

Although he had joined the army on 22 October, at Celada del Camino, and had been with Wellington at Villodrigo on the 23rd and again on the 24th, Major General John Oswald arrived to take command of his division only on the morning of the 25th. In the words of his aide de camp Captain Weare:[3]

> The order was received at Dueñas either very late indeed, on the night of the 24th or early on the morning of the 25th Oct.; you and myself and a groom set out as early as the necessary arrangements would allow us… and reached Villa Muriel, just after the cannonade commenced on the village–and found some of the troops moving into position.[4]

Setting out from Dueñas they had crossed the bridge at San Isidro (where they met Major General Henry Clinton, commander of the 6th Division) intending to reach Villamuriel via the apparently shorter route on the left bank of the Carrión. However, seeing a column of French infantry already on that road, they re-crossed the Carrión at the San Isidro bridge and proceeded to Villamuriel via the safer right bank. The infantry seen by Oswald and

1 Greenwood (ed.), *Le Mesurier*, p.137; letter 2 November 1812, at Tordesillas; sunset on 24 October was at 05:23 p.m.

2 Hale, *Journal*, pp.39, 107.

3 J. Philippart, *Calendar*, 1821. Vol.III, p.50; Wellington (ed.), *Supplementary Despatches*, Vol. XIV, p.146; General Order relating to Oswald's appointment.

4 TNA, NRA 21704 Oswald, Weare 12 December 1836.

Weare was Maucune's 5e Division advancing towards Calabazanos and Villamuriel, as described by *Colonel* Jean-Pierre Béchaud of the 66e Ligne:

> On 25 October, we marched at dawn, we moved on Dueñas by the highway: after two hours of marching the scouts announced that the enemy was massed in great force on the right bank of the Carrión, near to and to the right of Villamuriel.
>
> General Maucune immediately re-directed his columns to the right; he galloped to the Carrión to within half musket range of the enemy, where he soon recognized their strength and formidable position. We arrived at the height of Calabazanos where we found ourselves within musket shot of the enemy, who presented his outposts in the bridgehead and his masses and his artillery on the other side. The General established his infantry behind Calabazanos to shelter them from artillery fire.[5]

When the French arrived and deployed their artillery, Major General Pringle was in the process of moving the 5th Division down from the heights, deploying it in and around the village and in the dry canal bed behind the village, thus masking most of the troops from the French artillery fire. Béchaud described the allied 'masses' as being on the heights, where they had camped, and around the village.[6]

Lieutenant Le Mesurier (1/9th Foot) described the moment of contact:

> About seven o'clock on the morning of the 25th: the Adjt: Genl: of the division [Lieutenant Colonel George Berkeley] passed by the guard and astonish'd me a little by an order to go and support the piquet on the bridge, about 200 yards from this village. On my arrival there I found the picquet lining the bridge and preparations making for blowing it up. We had not been there long when some Spanish dragoons, who had gone out to skirmish, returned, told us the French were coming on with about one thousand cavalry and 600 infantry, but soon found our information was false. Artillery made their appearance, took a position and oppened [sic] a heavy fire of round and grape on the artillery that was supporting the bridge. A short time after, a gun moved to their right and took post in a situation which raked us completely. They then oppened [sic] on the bridge with grape and round[shot], and wounded three of our men.[7]

The 'Spanish dragoons' are unidentified, the 6º Ejército included *Coronel* Conde de Figuelmonte's cavalry division which comprised the Provinciale Cazadores de Galicia, Husares de Cantabria, Husares de Galicia, the Granaderos de Galicia, and Don Juan Sanchez's cavalry. Of these regiments, the Provinciale Cazadores de Galicia were at Dueñas on 25 October.[8]

---

5 Colin, 'Béchaud', p.405.

6 Oswald, 'Affair at Villa Muriele', pp.266–7; Colin, 'Béchaud', p.406.

7 Greenwood (ed.), *Le Mesurier*, p.137; letter 2 November 1812, at Tordesillas.

8 *Estados*, 1822, p.163; Sañudo, *Base*.

Hale's *Journal* continues, 'we remained there very quiet till about nine o'clock the following morning… when we discovered a division of the enemy advancing at a very short distance from us…'[9]

Meanwhile, the 3/1st Foot had marched away from the heights behind Villamuriel on their way to Palencia in order to provide the covering party for the demolition of the bridges there. Campbell wrote that his battalion marched at dawn or approximately 6:15 a.m. and arrived in Palencia between 7:30 a.m. and 8:00 a.m. However, Douglas, although writing perhaps in the 1840's remembered that the order to march only got to the battalion at Villamuriel at 8:00 a.m. and that the battalion only arrived in Palencia when the morning was 'pretty far advanced'. Mackenzie described the 3/1st Foot leaving for Palencia 'early in the morning'. The news of Foy's capture of the bridge at Palencia arrived in Villamuriel around 10:00 to 10:30 a.m., which suggests that Campbell's account is the more accurate, at least with regard to the departure from the heights behind Villamuriel. The march to Palencia is approximately four miles, or 1½ to 2½ hours march.[10]

Captain Weare, writing to Oswald in 1836, in his sketch plan of the village, detailed part of the deployment of the British troops. He shows one battalion in close column on the street at the northern entrance to the village, thus shielded from the fire of the French artillery. He also showed Lawson's artillery deployed on the mound to the west of the village by the road covering the bridge, with a further battalion in close column deployed close to its left rear. The sketch only shows three guns on the mound, but the other accounts suggest that Weare was thereby representing all six of Lawson's guns.[11]

Mackenzie, writing in 1850, confirms that only two of the division's battalions were not deployed in the dry bed of the canal:

> The fifth division took post in the bed of the dry canal, except two battalions, 4th Foot, one of which (the second) was formed in close column, close to the end of the bridge next to the village. Lord Wellington being there in person, ordered the officer commanding to fix bayonets to be ready to charge the enemy, should they attempt to cross, in the event of the mine failing…[12]

Oswald, writing in 1837, stated that:

> [T]he greater portion of the division was admirably disposed of about the village, as also in the dry bed of a canal running in its rear, in some places parallel to the Carrion. Certain of the corps were formed in columns of attack, supported by reserves, ready to fall upon the enemy, if in consequence of the mine failing, he should venture to push a column across the narrow bridge… Lord Wellington entered it [the village], and passed the formed columns, well sheltered from fire

9 Hale, *Journal*, p.94.

10 Wellington Papers, Campbell to Barnes, 28 October 1812; Monick (ed.), *Douglas*, Introduction, p.57; 'McK', 'The Affair of Villa Muriel', p.542.

11 TNA, NRA 21704 Oswald, Weare 12 December 1836.

12 'McK', 'The Affair of Villa Muriel', p.542.

and observation. His Lordship approved the manner in which the post had been occupied, and of the advantage taken of the canal and village to mask the troops.[13]

Although Wellington may have approved the dispositions there were other points of view, Napier cited Lieutenant Elers Pernell Hopkins (1/4th Foot):

> As we approached Villa Muriel the face of the country upon our left flank as we were then retrograding appeared open, in our front ran the river Carrion, and immediately on the opposite side of the river and parallel to it was a broad deep dry canal. On our passing the bridge at Villa Muriel we had the village on our left, from the margin of the canal the ground sloped gradually up into the heights, the summit forming a fine plateau. Villa Muriel was occupied by the brigadier Pringle with a small detachment of infantry but at the time we considered that it required a larger force, as its maintenance appeared of the utmost importance to the army.[14]

Together, these accounts suggest that the 1/9th Foot was the battalion closest to the bridge while the 2/4th Foot held the entrance to the village. Although Mackenzie suggests that the 1/4th Foot was one of these two battalions, this is not consistent with Hopkins's account.

According to Béchaud and Gomm, the British and Brunswick light infantry were initially, at least in part, deployed across the river. Weare's sketch map also shows a 'battalion' across the river at the bridgehead. Gomm describes outposts deployed across the river but in 1836 he remembered them being driven in by the French at a very early 8:00 a.m.[15]

In his journal, despite being in the light company of the 1/9th Foot, Hale makes no mention of being across the river, so this suggests that Pringle had sent the combined light companies of his own brigade, together with the 10th company, Duke of Brunswick Oels Light Infantry across the bridge, commanded by Major Alured Faunce (2/4th Foot). Instead Hale tells us that when alerted to the presence of the French, 200 of his battalion (1/9th Foot) were 'placed very convenient to the bridge' with the rest of the battalion, approximately 100 men, 'extended along the river'.[16]

Pringle confirmed that the combined light companies of Barnes's Brigade together with the 2nd company, Duke of Brunswick Oels Light Infantry, under the command of Captain Thomas Willshire (1/38th Foot),[17] together with the 1/9th Foot, were close to the river, covering the ford. Le Mesurier wrote that Barnes's combined light companies were with the 1/9th Foot throughout the day; 'A captn: of the 38th [Willshire] commanded the picquet on the bridge at Muriel and honorable [sic] mention was made of his name

13 Oswald, 'Affair at Villa Muriele', pp.266–7.

14 Napier, *History*, 1840, Vol.VI, p.xvii; *Army List*, 1812.

15 Colin, 'Béchaud', p.405; TNA, NRA 21704 Oswald, Gomm 13 December 1836.

16 Hale, *Journal*, pp.94–95.

17 C.R. Low, 'Memoir of General Sir Thomas Willshire', pp.69, 75.

by Col Crawfurd [1/9th foot] in his report of the business, as the picquet was attached to our regt: during the whole of the day'.[18]

The 18-year-old Ensign George Freer described Willshire as 'a grave man'.[19] He later, as a general in India, built a reputation as a 'first rate commander' and an 'admirable' and 'rigid disciplinarian' with the soubriquet 'Tiger Tom'.[20]

Major William F.B. Loftus (2/38th Foot) was the over-all commander of the two light 'battalions' of the 5th Division and was present at Villamuriel.[21]

The two battalions of the 38th Foot, and presumably Barnes himself, spent at least the first part of the morning in the canal bed.[22]

Hale's account further states that one company of the 1/9th Foot, commanded by Lieutenant James Whitley was 'convenient to a grist mill'. Whitley's company was detached from the battalion by order of Lieutenant Colonel William Maynard Gomm, Assistant Quartermaster Master General, himself an officer of the 9th Foot. Whitley's company was the 8th Company and was 30 to 34 men of all ranks strong (Le Mesurier states that only four men returned to the regiment from Whitley's company giving it a strength of 30, whereas 34 is a tenth of the regimental strength in the monthly return for October). Le Mesurier described Whitley as a 'gentleman preacher'.[23]

Major Dudley Hill, with the Caçadores N.8, was detached from Spry's Brigade by Pringle and placed under the latter's own orders. Pringle deployed Hill's men forwards towards the river, where they defended the ford near Calabazanos. Hill subsequently described his orders as; '... to protect the ford (near the mill) over the river Carrion'.[24]

The Portuguese line battalions were initially deployed sitting down in the bed of the dry canal where a British officer serving with the Portuguese 'was killed among his men by a cannon shot rolling over upon his head', while reading a newspaper.[25] This officer is variously identified in the sources as 'Evens' of the 38th Foot (Freer), 'Hovens' (Gomm), while Mackenzie

18 Greenwood (ed.), *Le Mesurier*, p.138.

19 W.J. Freer, 'The Thirty-Eighth Regiment of Foot, now the First Battalion of the South Staffordshire Regiment', *British Numismatic Journal*, Vol.XI, 1915, p.303; TNA, WO17/148, September monthly return 1/38th; Freer served in the grenadier company. During the siege of Burgos, he was absent sick in Salamanca having been wounded in the battle. He re-joined the retreating army at Torquemada with his travelling companion Willshire, who had also been absent, while escorting French prisoners of war.

20 C.R. Low, *Soldiers of the Victorian Age*, Vol.I, p.103; Hall, *History*, p.601.

21 *Hart's New Army List*, 1850, p.20; CHALLIS; TNA, October monthly return; Loftus held the MGSM clasp for Fuentes de Oñoro, again perhaps pointing to his role in command of the light companies in 1811.

22 Oswald, 'Affair at Villa Muriele', pp.266–7.

23 TNA, WO17/110; 9th Foot 1803–1812, November 1812 monthly return; Greenwood (ed.), *Le Mesurier*, pp.60, 98, 138; G. Glover (ed.), *Personal Adventures of a Young Officer during Walcheren and the Peninsular War* (Godmanchester: Ken Trotman, 2017), pp.46–51, 59; the memoirs of Whitley's religious mentor, Ensign Edward Watson.

24 Wellington Papers, Hill to Pringle, 27 October 1812; in this letter Hill repeatedly emphasised the fact that he reported to Pringle on this day as Spry was not present with his battalion.

25 Alves, *História*, p.71; positions the RI N.15 'between Dueñas and Villamuriel'.

identifies the officer as serving in RI N.15. The correct officer was *Major* Edward Ovens, attached from the 2/38th Foot to RI N.3.[26]

The Spaniards of Liñan's brigade were deployed on the left wing, as described by Le Mesurier: 'the Spaniards were taking their position on the heights in the rear of Villa Muriel and appeared to us to be in great confusion, everyone trying who could reach the top first, but formed on the hill as soon as the whole had got up.'[27]

The deployment outlined above is in part inferred from Muir's guidance on 'customary battle array'.[28] Thus, Barnes's brigade takes its precedence from Andrew Hay, its incumbent or permanent commander, and occupies the left-hand post of honour of this left-most division of the British Army.[29] The Spanish would be expected to be posted on the left in the first post of honour for the left wing, based on international precedence as the action is in Spain. The Portuguese brigade was posted to the right of the division.

Burroughs tells us that the weather was initially foggy in the plains, but that the sun dispersed the fog by 8:00 a.m.,[30] when part of the French army was seen advancing down the road from Burgos, having begun their advance at daybreak.[31] Leaving at first light, just after 6:00 a.m., the six-mile march from Magaz de Pisuerga would have taken approximately 2½ hours, consequently the French 5e Division arrived at Calabazanos at approximately 9:00 a.m.[32] According to *Général de Brigade* Thomas Mignot, Baron de Lamartinière, Souham's chief of staff, Maucune managed to deploy his artillery quickly without being observed and these guns caused casualties amongst those allied troops defending the river bank and the village of Villamuriel itself.[33] *Colonel* Béchaud does not mention the surprise appearance of the French guns in his account, instead he says the artillery were deployed at the gallop. Burgoyne describes the French guns as being deployed in a 'hollow way'.[34] Béchaud's account continues:

> The infantry having been rested a few minutes during this first fire, the general [Maucune] came to direct the action; a third of the division was distributed along the river bank as skirmishers, from Calabazanos Mill towards the left; the enemy immediately deployed on the opposite bank an equal amount of skirmishers and from one side to the other a very strong fire was initiated, in the which we killed many English.[35]

26 'McK', 'The Affair of Villa Muriel', pp.542–544; Freer, 'Thirty-Eighth', p.298; Divall, *Scrape*, p.112; TNA, NRA 21704 Oswald, Gomm 13 December 1836, Weare, 12 December 1836; Hall, *History*, p.454; TNA, WO17/148, November monthly return, 2/38th Foot.

27 Greenwood (ed.), *Le Mesurier*, p.138.

28 Muir, *Peninsular Army*, pp.90, 99, 131, 136–7, 141.

29 Wellington (ed.), *Supplementary Despatches*, Vol.XIV, p.146.

30 Burroughs, *Narrative*, p.20.

31 United States Naval Observatory (USNO) at <http://aa.usno.navy.mil/>, accessed 8 May 2016; coordinates: 41°57'N, 04°31'W; dawn (civil twilight) was at 6:12 a.m. and sunrise at 6:40 a.m. in local time.

32 Hale, *Journal*, p.94; Crowdy, *Handbook*, p.247.

33 Gurwood (ed.), *Dispatches*, Vol.VI, p.775; Colin, 'Béchaud', p.405.

34 Wrottesley, *Burgoyne*, p.241.

35 Colin, 'Béchaud', p.406.

It is difficult to be precise about what Béchaud meant by 'a third of the division' (*le tiers de la division*), but he was probably referring to the third division of each of the eight battalions, specifically the *voltigeurs* and the fifth platoon, i.e. the second company, according to Heffmeyer, or perhaps the *voltigeurs* with the grenadiers or the fourth company, according to Bardin. Crowdy highlights the difference between Bardin's and Heffmeyer's deployments of the battalion, and the greater popularity of the latter. Under Bardin's preferred arrangement, the *voltigeurs* and grenadiers each constitute an un-numbered division, but they may be ordered to form a single division. Béchaud later describes the contribution of d'Arnauld's brigade as eight companies '*en tirailleurs*', of which four would have been *voltigeur* companies. This suggests that Maucune deployed his eight companies of *voltigeurs* and a further eight companies of fusiliers or grenadiers from his division as skirmishers to contest the riverbanks and crossings. Although Béchaud implies that the grenadiers of the 66e Ligne were not used as skirmishers, as he later mentions them deployed in line as a reserve and he describes Sergeant Bousquet of the grenadiers (albeit of the fifth battalion, according to the *registre matricule*) receiving his mortal wound while with the main body, *Sous-Lieutenant* Magnan's involvement demonstrates that at least one of the two grenadier companies of the 66e Ligne was part of Montfort's later crossing of the river near Calabazanos. The distribution of casualties suffered by the two battalions of the 86e Ligne suggest that the *voltigeur* and fourth companies of this regiment were deployed as skirmishers (nine of the 11 men identified as casualties in the *registres matricules* were from these companies).[36]

In his report to Pringle, Hill described the response of his battalion, the Caçadores N.8, 'I advanced with the right wing of my battn close to the banks under cover of some trees where I kept up a brisk fire against a very superior enemy for 4 hours. This wing having expended all its ammunition I relieved them with the others…'[37]

The Caçadores N.8 would thus have approximately 96 two-man files deployed at intervals of two to six paces, according to the regulations for a unit supported by another close order unit. Whitley's nearby company of the 1/9th Foot would have either sent forward eight files of skirmishers at two to six pace intervals or 'formed a chain' of six double files (groups of four men) at 10-pace intervals. Together, Whitley's men and the skirmishers of the right wing of the Caçadores N.8 would occupy a maximum frontage of approximately 700 paces.[38]

36 Crowdy, *Handbook*, pp.166–7 (citing Heffmeyer, 1815; Anon, *Livret du commandements, ou Tableaux Synoptiques des manoeuvres d'infanterie, Ecole de Bataillon*, pp.1–2); E. Bardin, *Manuel de l'Infanterie* (Paris: Magimel, 1813), Vol.I, pp.438–40; J.S. Vivien, *Souvenirs de ma Vie Militaire, 1792–1822* (Paris: Hachette, 1907), p.244; *Chef de Bataillon* Jean Stanislas Vivien (82e Ligne) who joined Maucune's division in April 1813 reports being on a reconnaissance with eight companies of *voltigeurs* and grenadiers in June 1813.

37 Wellington Papers, Hill to Pringle, 27 October 1812.

38 T.H. Cooper, *A Practical Guide for the Light Infantry Officer* (London: T. Egerton, 1806), p.76; The War Office, *Regulations for the exercise of riflemen and light infantry* (London: T. Egerton, 1814), pp.16–17, 21–2, 25–6.

One third of the division initially deployed as skirmishers, as per Béchaud's account, would amount to 16 companies of which eight would have been *voltigeurs*. On average each of these companies would have deployed 20 or 22 two-rank files of skirmishers (Reille's and Morand's instructions differ in that, for the average company at Villamuriel, Reille's model deploys 22 two-man files while Morand's model deploys 20 two man files).[39] It is often stated that French skirmishers deployed with 15 pace intervals between files, which would have meant that the 16 companies would have covered a frontage of from 3,700 to 4,300 paces, assuming three companies were retained as local reserves, based on Husson's description of whole battalions retaining one of their six companies in close order, when sent to skirmish. However, Husson also describes different file intervals for French infantry when skirmishing:

> When moving forward or retreating, the most appropriate interval from one *tirailleur* to another in the same line, in closed country, is eight to ten paces, and in open countryside, fifteen to twenty paces. The intervals, whether advancing or withdrawing, must depend also on the movements made by the column *that* they are covering, accidents in the field, and unforeseen circumstances.[40]

Even at intervals of eight paces per file, the French skirmishers would have extended from 2,000 to 2,300 paces. Béchaud states that these companies were deployed along the river to the left of Calabazanos Mill, which Hill confirmed was by the ford. With these frontages of between 2,000 and 4,300 paces, it seems very unlikely that all 16 companies of French skirmishers would have been deployed to the left of Calabazanos Mill, otherwise they would have discovered the ford used by the French cavalry later in the day, in the bend of the river near Los Carriones, 2,500 paces south of the mill. Furthermore, Béchaud described how the skirmishers of the first brigade led the assault across the Carrión in the afternoon.[41] With only eight companies deployed the French skirmishers would, at eight paces per file, cover a frontage of approximately 1,300 – 1,400 paces. The casualties suffered by the French battalions also supports this interpretation: for example, the *voltigeurs* of the first brigade suffered six times the casualties of those of the second brigade.

Given the available evidence, it is likely that only the eight companies of skirmishers from d'Arnauld's first brigade were deployed as skirmishers against the Caçadores N.8. Those of the second brigade were probably retained as a general reserve.[42]

---

39 Morand's instructions, 1811 from Anon., 'Skirmishing in I army corps under command of Marshal Davout in 1811', available at <http://www.demi-brigade.org/tirdaven.htm>, accessed 4 June 2017, citing V.I. Charkevitscha, *Materials from the Military (Training) Archives of the General Staff. The 1812 Patriotic War. Part II: Documents Seized from the Enemy. Vol.I: Outgoing Correspondence of Marshal Davout (from 14 October to 31 December 1811)* (St. Petersburg: publisher unknown, 1903), pp.6–11.

40 E.A. Husson, *Instruction pour les Voltigeurs de l'infanterie légère et de ligne* (Paris: Cordier, 1822), pp.13, 44; Husson, who was a *capitaine* in the 1er Légère and served at Quatre Bras, includes a description of Reille's 1815 Instructions.

41 Colin, 'Béchaud', p.407.

42 Husson, *Instruction*, p.23; given either Reille's or Morand's instructions, which differ in the detail of the creation of the local close order reserves, a company of *voltigeurs* can cover

At the beginning of the day, Wellington was further south near Dueñas.[43]

At Palencia, events were unfolding quickly, as reported by Lieutenant Colonel Campbell:

> I proceeded with the regt under my command at daybreak on the morning of the 25th inst. from the camp near Villa morel [sic] but from the extreme fatigue the regt had suffered the day before did not arrive at Palencia until ½ past seven or eight o'clock a.m.
>
> I found Lt. Read [First Lieutenant William Reid] of the Royl Engineers beginning to open a mine on both of the bridges over the River Carrion, he informed me that he had previously posted sentinels at the different gates of the town and a look out party in the steeple. I formed my regt one hundred yards in rear of the bridges and the two Spanish 4-pounders twenty yards in my front.[44]
>
> Before I had time for barrickading [sic] or taking other means for the defence of the bridges, the enemy commenced a fire of musketry from the town in which they had been concealed before our arrival. I at the same time saw a party of cavalry coming out of a wood a little higher up than Palencia, I found also that the enemy's cavalry were on the same side of the river as me below the town, both of these parties the numbers of which I could not ascertain, must have crossed the bridges the preceding night or have forded the river unseen by me.
>
> Under the circumstances I considered it best to send a strong party to each bridge and I formed the remainder of the battn at first only 220 strong into a square as the best means of defence against their cavalry. At this time Major Prescott of the 5th Dn. Guards appeared on the canal. The enemy had now at least six pieces of artillery playing upon me from different points on the opposite side of the river and close to the bridges. As the parties on the bridges were now completely overpowered by numbers and driven off, and I could see in addition to the enemy on my side of the river, strong columns of cavalry and infantry filing thru' the town to be on passing from 4 to 5,000 strong, from six to eight hundred of whom were cavalry, an immediate retreat appeared to me the only mode of saving my battn from being made prisoners, which I with difficulty executed until the remainder of the brigade under your command came to my assistance.[45]

Douglas adds some colour to this account:

> By this time the enemy were moving down the hills which overlooked the town, keeping up a desultory fire… all in a hurry our leather merchants [the company shoemakers] came running down the lines and spread alarm of the enemy being in the town. Scarcely had they reached the column when some close firing took place on the bridge, and the enemy got possession of it. The Engineer Officer [Lt.

---

the frontage of its parent battalion by deploying its files of two *tirailleurs* at intervals of approximately 10 paces.

43 Glover (ed.), *Eyewitness*, p.97.

44 *Army List*, 1812, p.476.

45 Wellington Papers; Campbell to Barnes, 28 October 1812; Monick (ed.), *Douglas*, p.58; the two guns were presumably the two Spanish 'grasshopper guns' referred to by Douglas. The 4-pounders would have been from the Gribeauval system. It is unclear who manned these guns.

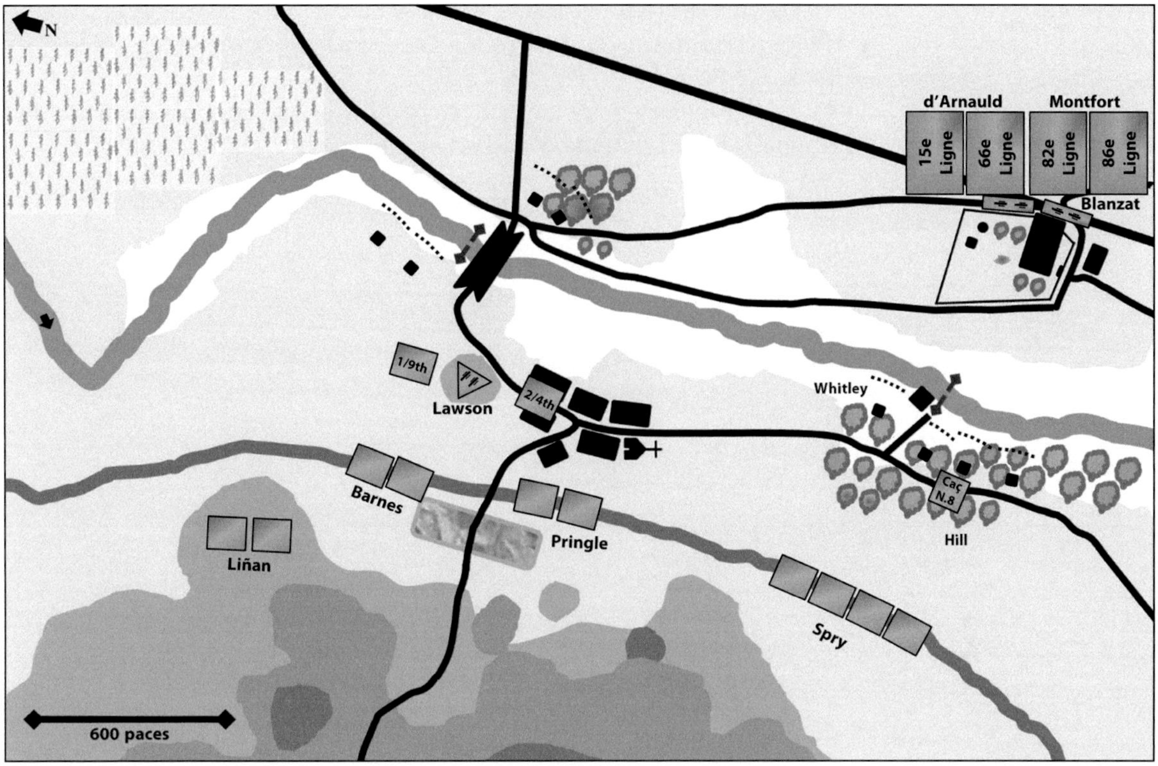

Map 3 Initial Deployment.

> Reid] comes running to Col. Campbell and says "Col. Campbell the bridge is taken. You are at liberty to act as you please with your battalion".[46]

Burgoyne also described the taking of the bridge at Palencia:

> At Palencia, Lieutenant Reid proceeded to destroy the bridges with a working party and 100 men covering party, whom he posted at the gates of the town (Palencia is a walled town); these men were surprised at one of the gates, and were nearly all taken. The officer commanding the Royals who had been sent there with his regiment and two guns did not think it prudent to remain, and the bridges fell entire into the enemy's hands.[47]

Campbell's report was written at the direct request of the Marquis of Wellington, as recorded in the final paragraph of Oswald's letter to Wellington:

> The circumstances respecting the retreat of the Royals shall be the subject according to your Ldship's direction of a separate report… Notwithstanding the

---

46 Monick (ed.), *Douglas*, p.57.

47 Wrottesley, *Burgoyne*, p.241. For other accounts of the action at Palencia, see N. Marcel, *Campagnes du Capitaine Marcel, du 69e de ligne, en Espagne et en Portugal (1808–1814)* (Paris: Plon-Nourrit, 1913), pp.179–180; Ardenne, *Bergische Lanziers*, pp.73–5.

> foregoing I do myself the honour to forward Lt. Col. Campbell's report which yr Lship will perhaps deem of a nature to supersede the necessity of further inquiry.[48]

This clearly reflected Wellington's irritation at the loss of Palencia, and Campbell's report should be read accordingly.

48 Wellington Papers; Oswald, 1 November 1812.

6

The Demolition of the Bridge

Back at Villamuriel, after an hour, Pringle's skirmish screen retired across the bridge over the Carrión.[1] Captain James Ward (1/4th Foot) is described by Mackenzie as having '…returned with his party untouched, just when the French attacked the bridge over the Carrion close to Villamuriel'.[2] Mackenzie is hereby implying that Ward was in command of the light company of the 1/4th Foot, but this has proved difficult to directly verify. The muster roll for the six months to the 24 December 1812 shows Ward in command of the 9th company and Captain Kipping in command of the 10th company. Kipping is described as commanding the grenadier company in the Waterloo medal roll. Conversely, Private George Hatton of the light company was promoted following his exploits at the storming of Badajoz, where he captured the colours of the Hesse-Darmstadt Gross und Erbprinz regiment (Private John Kelton, also from the light company, was rewarded with a regimental medal, together with Hatton, for his part in the capture of the colours).[3] However, the pay-lists for April and October 1812 both show that Hatton was paid in the third company, commanded by Captain William Leighton Wood, the second most junior captain. Mackenzie also describes the man promoted following Badajoz as being in the light company, but names him as Smith and describes him as being killed at San Sebastian.[4]

Having received the order to mine the bridges at 09:00 p.m. on the 24th, Burgoyne began the preparations immediately:

1 Colin, 'Béchaud', p.406.

2 'McK', 'The Affair of Villa Muriel', p.542; TNA, WO12/2206.

3 Cannon, *Fourth*, p.102; Cowper, *King's Own*, p.390; King's Own Royal Regiment Museum, Lancaster, Acc. No. KO2004/01, KO1875/01; the regimental medals awarded to the two men available at <http://www.kingsownmuseum.com/mus03medsregt.htm>, accessed 22 September 2019.

4 'McK', 'The Affair of Villa Muriel', p.544; the pay-list for October 1812 suggests that he is referring to Private Robert Smith who was paid in Ward's ninth company, but this Smith died on 19 October 1812 at Celorico.

> H. Qrs. Dueñas, October 24th, 1812
> My Dear Colonel [Dickson],
> Certain bridges are to be mined tonight. Therefore it will be necessary that you send in upon mules 10 barrels of gunpowder, 30 portfires and some slow match. The bearer, Corporal Fryer, will conduct the mules to Colonel Burgoyne's quarters.
> L.[ieutenant] Woodyear, B. Major[5]

The mine at Villamuriel was prepared under the supervision of assistant engineer Brevet Major Alexander Thompson, 74th (Highland) Foot.[6] Burgoyne recorded the difficulties that Thompson had faced:

> Major Thompson, assistant-engineer, went off at 2 p.m. [sic, 2:00 a.m.] to Villa Muriel, and arrived and set to work at four. The powder had gone so far to the rear that it did not return to Dueñas till 6 a.m. and I immediately sent it off. Thompson received his at eight and commenced loading. The enemy approached before he had finished and brought guns to bear on the bridge and village; he succeeded, however, in destroying one arch completely, having a line of least resistance, (including the arch stone) below of four feet and above to the road of four feet also, which he increased by heavy stones on the summit.[7]

Weare described Wellington arriving in the village of Villamuriel just as the French were advancing towards the bridge:

> The Duke of Wellington came to us at this time – dismounted at the head of the street column, and several times most anxiously enquired of the acting engineer (a Capt. Thompson I think) if he thought the mine would explode – he looked at his watch more than once and expressed his doubts to the engineer; and at last turning to you [Oswald], his Grace remarked, 'be ready with the bayonets!' The men stood ready to rush on the enemy in case they forced the bridge, – the mine was certainly a long time before it exploded.[8]

Wellington's anxiety regarding the successful detonation of the mine was presumably based on the poor success rate of the engineers in the early stages of the Peninsular War. For example, during the Corunna Campaign, due to a lack of practical training, the only successful bridge demolition killed the engineer involved, Lieutenant Henry Davy.[9]

Béchaud's account continues:

> At the end of an hour, with the enemy crossing the bridge to the other bank and pretending to evacuate Villamuriel, the rest of the first brigade came out from behind the walls of Calabazanos, marched in column at full distance, in the

5 Leslie, *Dickson*, Vol.IV, p.777.
6 J. Keltie, *A History of the Scottish Highlands, Highland Clans and Highland Regiments* (Edinburgh: A. Fullerton, 1875), Vol.VIII, p.614; *Army List*, 1813, p.301.
7 Wrottesley, *Burgoyne*, p.241.
8 TNA, NRA 21704 Oswald, Weare 12 December 1836.
9 Thompson, *Engineers*, pp.27, 247.

> direction of the evacuated bridge; it was taken in flank by the enemy artillery that had remained in position; although hit by this fire at half range, the column did not lessen its march, with General d'Arnauld at its head… we had not marched further than 2 to 300 paces in this direction, when we saw an arch of the bridge explode.[10]

Mackenzie also has Wellington present at the bridge, giving the command for the mine to be detonated, before 'riding off'.[11] At this point the French were perhaps 4–500 paces from the bridge, although Oswald and Weare later remembered them being much closer. The former wrote, 'The French supported by a heavy and superior fire rushed gallantly onto the bridge, the mine not exploding and destroying the arch till the leading section had almost reached the spot',[12] and the latter '…but at last up went one of the arches, just as the head of the French column reached it'.[13]

Béchaud suggests that many casualties may have been caused if the bridge was blown just 15 minutes later, when the brigade was crossing the bridge. However, advancing at 100 paces per minute (*pas accéléré*), the French infantry would, in 15 minutes, have covered almost the entire distance from the walls of Calabazanos to the bridge.

Together, the accounts suggest that French skirmishers, advancing ahead of the main columns were close to the bridge when it exploded. Lamartinière's report notes, 'some companies of skirmishers immediately raced to seize the bridge, it exploded in their faces, but not one man was wounded'.[14] Two or three companies of d'Arnauld's eight companies of tirailleurs could have been redeployed without compromising the duel at Calabazanos with Whitley and Hill's Caçadores N.8. The bridge and its approaches are approximately 350 paces long, with the main arch approximately halfway across.

Lieutenant Peter Le Mesurier described the actions of the 1/9th Foot at this time:

> The 9th were on the left of the bridge when we were ordered to leave it as the mine was ready. It blew up very shortly after we left it, and the principal arch was completely destroyed. We joined the 9th with the picket and extended along the banks of [the] river to the left of the bridge, in light infantry order. In the course of a quarter of an hour four officers were carried off the field wounded.[15]

Lieutenants Ackland, Taylor, Curzon and Ford were the four severely wounded officers from the 1/9th Foot.

10 Colin, 'Béchaud', p.406.
11 'McK', 'The Affair of Villa Muriel', p.542.
12 Oswald, 'Affair at Villa Muriele', pp.266–7.
13 TNA, NRA 21704 Oswald, Weare 12 December 1836.
14 Gurwood (ed.), *Dispatches* (1845), Vol.VI, p.775
15 Greenwood (ed.), *Le Mesurier*, p.138.

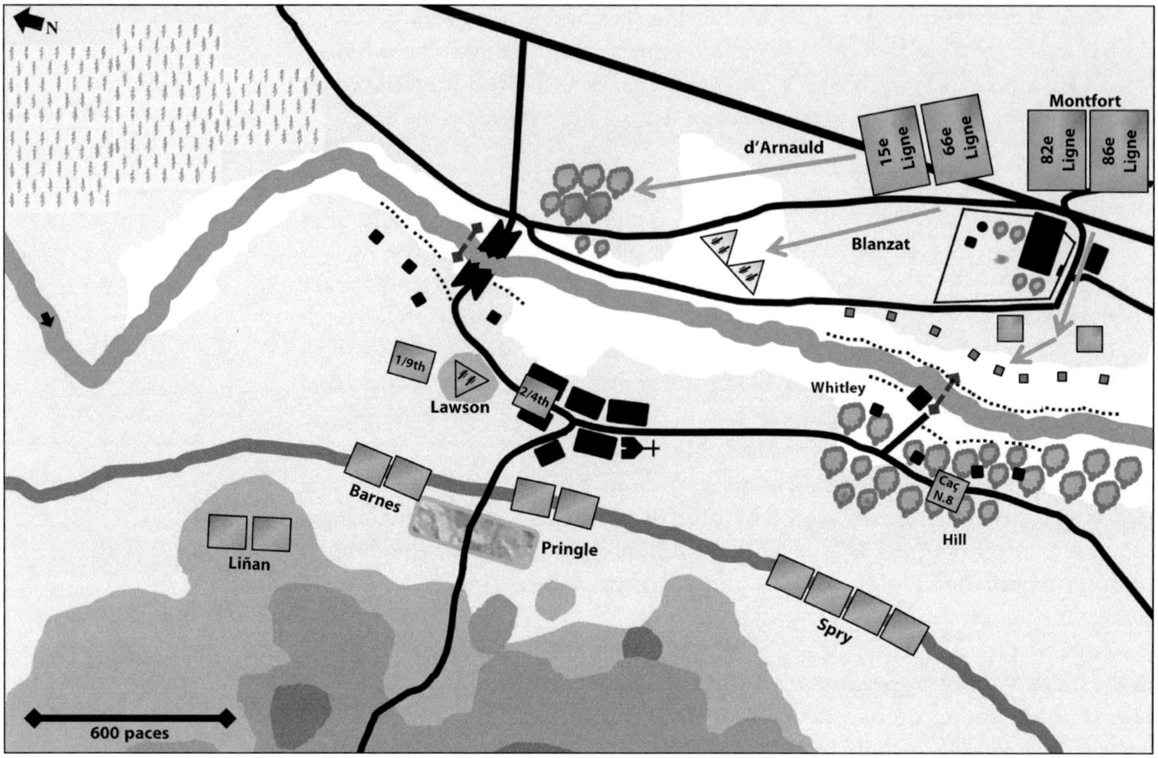

Map 4 Opening Moves.

Ensign George Young (2/38th Foot) described the French attack as follows:

> The next morning being Sunday, 25th, the enemy advanced to force the passage and commenced a heavy cannonade upon us and the bridge… with a large park of howitzers. The fire was returned on our side with effect. We have seen the guns when fired together actually cut lanes through their columns…

To another correspondent, he wrote:

> The morning after we crossed the river the enemy advanced to force the passage of a bridge and a ford where our division were placed to defend; they made a desperate push to force their way, but our artillery being advantageously placed played on their columns in such style that they thought proper to retire for a while.[16]

In response to the British artillery fire, d'Arnauld marched his brigade across the main Palencia–Dueñas road and deployed in line in the fields beyond.[17]

It is most likely that it was during this exchange of fire that one of Lawson's guns was disabled and his casualties inflicted. Mackenzie stated that two of

16 Younge, 'Some Peninsular Letters', pp.512–13; two letters written on 10 and 26 December 1812 respectively.

17 Colin, 'Béchaud', p.406.

Lawson's guns were disabled by the 'superior' French artillery fire; however, Lawson's diary refers to only 'one gun carriage disabled'.[18] As Weare later described to Oswald:

> [Y]ou may remember that someone told Genl Pringle that all the artillery officers were killed or wounded, which the general stated to the Duke [Wellington], who replied 'let the gunners fight the guns'; but in a few minutes he mentioned the mistake to the chief (which arose I think from one artillery officer being wounded).[19]

The wounded officer was Lieutenant James William Johnston. Lawson's brigade was subsequently withdrawn to a dominant position on the heights.[20]

---

18 Leslie, *Dickson*, Vol.IV, p.712; 'McK', 'The Affair of Villa Muriel', p.542.

19 TNA, NRA 21704 Oswald, Weare 12 December 1836.

20 Colin, 'Béchaud', p.409.

7

Wellington sends Oswald towards Palencia

At this time Wellington received word that Foy's troops had already crossed the river at Palencia. Weare, Oswald's aide de camp, remembered that:

> ... the Duke, yourself [Oswald] and others, were standing at the head of the street column, with the men's hands on the bayonet hilts, before the arch of the bridge had taken flight... an officer of heavy dragoons galloping into the mouth of the street, with intelligence that the troops had been obliged to retire from the bridges at Palencia before they were [destroyed]. As he leant back in pulling his horse in, a pace or two before he came amongst us, with the artillery mound close to his right hand, a cannon ball struck into the mound close to his head, I was surprised at the moment in finding him not hurt.[1]

Consequently, Oswald received orders to withdraw part of his division onto the heights with the intention of moving along them towards Palencia.[2] In Wellington's words 'I directed Major General Oswald to throw back our left and the Spanish troops upon the heights and to maintain the Carrion with the right of the 5th Division'.[3] Weare further remembered Wellington concluding his orders, referring to Foy's troops from Palencia, '"... however strong they maybe you must drive them back!" – you [Oswald] as shortly replied "I will my Lord"'.[4]

When the bridge exploded, Gomm remembered Wellington saying, 'now they'll be off for Palencia',[5] before setting off in that direction, as also witnessed by Weare:

1 Gurwood (ed.), *Dispatches*, Vol.VI, p.776; TNA, NRA 21704 Oswald, Weare 12 December 1836; separately Weare stated that Wellington may have received a second notification from Palencia but he could not remember the details.
2 Oswald, 'Affair at Villa Muriele', pp.266–7.
3 Gurwood (ed.), *Dispatches*, Vol.IX, p.512.
4 TNA, NRA 21704 Oswald, Weare 12 December 1836.
5 TNA, NRA 21704 Oswald, Gomm 13 December 1836.

> [T]he Duke rode some little distance along the river side [of] the canal towards Palencia – and as the Carion [sic] twisted about a good deal at this spot, a few French horse then rode into one of the inner bends and appeared to be on our side of the river. I know not now what brought me there, but I was close behind the Duke and he said "these men have got across the river" – immediately some infantry from out of the canal, lower down, were brought up and their muskets drove them back to some distance.[6]

Meanwhile back at the broken bridge, Napier's account includes the following somewhat controversial story of the discovery, by the French, of the ford near the bridge:

> [S]uddenly a horseman darting out at full speed from the column, rode down under a flight of bullets, to the bridge, calling out that he was a deserter; he reached the edge of the chasm made by the explosion, and then violently checking his foaming horse, held up his hands, exclaiming that he was a lost man, and with hurried accents asked if there was no ford near. The good-natured soldiers pointed to one a little way off and the gallant fellow having looked earnestly for a few moments as if to fix the exact point, wheeled his horse round, kissed his hand in derision, and bending over his saddle-bow dashed back to his own comrades, amidst showers of shot, and shouts of laughter from both sides.[7]

Oman describes this as a 'romantic tale' for which he could find no corroborating authority, and indeed neither Gomm, Hale, Hopkins, Lawson, Béchaud (who separately describes the finding of the fords), Mackenzie nor Pringle mention it.[8] The letters from both George Murray and Oswald's aide de camp, Weare, in Oswald's correspondence however do refer to this incident. Murray, writing on 14 February 1837, was at the very least sceptical of Napier's horseman story, but was not with the army in October 1812.[9]

Weare, writing on 12 December 1836, on the other hand, was present at Villamuriel and is clear that he did not recollect Napier's horseman as having approached the bridge, 'I can only say that while I was there I observed no incident ever to form the ground work of such a farce or romance'.[10] The key phrase here is 'while I was there' since Weare left the village initially with Wellington and then again later with Oswald, when they moved part of the division up onto the heights, sometime after the arch of the bridge was destroyed. Furthermore, the bridge was approximately 400 paces from the village, thus the originator of the story is likely to have been a member of the light companies of the 5th Division. The memoir of Lieutenant Peter Bowlby (2/4th Foot) includes the following clue as to Napier's possible source:

6 TNA, NRA 21704 Oswald, Weare 12 December 1836.
7 Napier, *History*, Vol.V, p.301.
8 Oman, *History*, Vol.VI, p.80.
9 TNA, NRA 21704 Oswald, Murray, 14 February 1837.
10 TNA, NRA 21704 Oswald, Weare 12 December 1836.

> We halted one day after crossing the Pensuaga [sic, Carrión], then the 5th Division had the rearguard and were hotly engaged all day. This will be found in detail in Col. Napier's narrative. I met him at dinner at Bath some years afterwards, and on his telling me he was not up in that day's work I gave him the full details.[11]

Clearly Bowlby is endorsing Napier's version and indeed claiming some authorship. It is difficult to confirm whether or not Bowlby was in the light company of his battalion and therefore a witness at the bridge. However, the family tradition that he was the first officer into Badajoz, during the storming of the San Vincente bastion in April 1812, is indicative, as it was the light companies of Walker's Brigade of the 5th Division that led this assault.[12]

Given that the behaviour of the French officer described by Napier is not untypical of the French aides de camp on this day, as reported by Béchaud and Girard, the anecdote does seem credible. Napier may well have given the tale a more romantic and exaggerated tone, but it seems unlikely to have been completely made up, at least by him. Finally, Gomm probably summed up the situation well, in his letter to Oswald of 13 December 1836, when he wrote 'with regard to his facetious "horseman"; I am with yourself, somewhat incredulous; although a great deal passes, on all these occasions, known only to a few'.[13] Incredulous or not, Oswald did not challenge this element of Napier's account during their discussion in 1837.[14]

Oswald recorded that the news of the fall of Palencia arrived just prior to the advance of the French towards the bridge and that his redeployment had begun before the Caçadores N.8 had been driven back from the river, around 1:00 p.m. Thus, in accordance with his new orders, sometime between 11:00 a.m. and noon, Oswald led part of his division away from the village onto the heights.[15]

On 27 October, when at Cabezón, Pringle wrote a report for Oswald regarding the events of the morning of the 25th, which includes his description of the force left to defend Villamuriel:

> As my brigade was detached from you on the 25th and was a good deal engaged, I think it right to report to you the occurrences of that day. My brigade with the exception of one regt. (the 2nd battn. of the 4th), which was sent up the hill by your order, was posted to defend the passage of the bridge at Villamuriel, the 9th Regt also with the piquets of the Royals and the 38th were also under my command to defend the passage of the fords near the bridge, and before your

11 NAM, Acc. No. 2002-02-729, pp.12–13.

12 Cowper, *King's Own*, p.389; F. Haslewood, *The genealogy of the family of Haslewood, Staffordshire and Warwickshire branches* (London: Author, 1881), p.9; Bowlby was in the 1/4th Foot at this time.

13 TNA, NRA 21704 Oswald; a similar instance of deception at a ford is retold by William Hay regarding the advance to Vitoria; see W. Hay (ed. A. Bamford), *Reminiscences 1808–1815 under Wellington* (Solihull: Helion and Company, 2017), p.62.

14 TNA, NRA 21704 Oswald, Napier 9 January 1837.

15 Monick (ed.), *Douglas*, pp.56–7; Oswald, 'Affair at Villa Muriele', p.267.

> arrival in the morning I had detached the *caçadores* from the Portuguese brigade to defend the fords near the mill…[16]

The detachment of the 2/4th Foot therefore left Pringle with the 1/4th Foot, the 2/30th Foot and the 2/44th Foot, together with the light companies of his brigade, to defend the bridge and village, while the 1/9th Foot and the light companies of Barnes's Brigade were defending the ford near the bridge. The 2/30th and 2/44th Foot appear to have served as a single battalion on this day due to the weakness of the 2/44th Foot. In this situation Hamilton of the 30th would have commanded. This arrangement was made official at the end of the campaign, on 6 December 1812.[17]

Although Oswald described himself as moving with the 'main body of the division', Wellington described the right of the 5th Division as being employed in maintaining the line of the Carrión, while Weare refers to Oswald's detachment as 'half the division'. Spry's Portuguese brigade remained on the slopes above Calabazanos and Liñan's infantry also remained at Villamuriel.[18] This therefore left the 1/38th Foot and the 2/38th Foot, from Barnes's Brigade and the 2/4th Foot, from Pringle's Brigade, moving off up onto the heights with Oswald.

In the ranks of Oswald's detachment Ensign Young (2/38th Foot) saw the redeployment a little differently, 'about ten o'clock they brought down about forty pieces of cannon with a great number of howitzers that they [sic] forced us to retire'.[19]

Meanwhile, Wellington, believing that Souham was moving the bulk of his army via Palencia,[20] '… moved the 5th, 7th and 1st Divisions up the hill opposite to Villamuriel as we saw the French army was manoeuvring by our left towards Palencia'.[21] The 7th Division, however, seems to have moved south.[22]

On the heights above Villamuriel near Dueñas, with the 1st Division, Stanhope reports that at this point Wellington, with his flanks threatened both on his left at Palencia and on his right at Tariego was 'visibly annoyed', which together with the fatigue and anxiety, resulted in him looking 'very haggard'.[23]

However, Oswald then described how he had not proceeded far along the heights before he received a further order to retire and remain on the heights above Villamuriel to the right of Liñan's troops, until further orders.[24] Weare described how:

16 Wellington Papers, Pringle to Oswald; UML, GB 133 Eng MSS 1273, item 27, draft of Pringle's letter to Oswald; the two versions of Pringle's report to Oswald differ in that the initial draft reads 'with you' instead of 'by your order' when referring to the 2/4th Foot.

17 'McK', 'The Affair of Villa Muriel', p.543; Divall, *Redcoats*, p.123.

18 Hale, *Journal*, p.95.

19 Younge, 'Some Peninsular Letters', p.513.

20 Burroughs, *Narrative*, p.22.

21 Glover (ed.), *Eyewitness*, p.97.

22 Kortzfleisch, *Geschichte*, Vol.I, p.241.

23 Glover (ed.), *Eyewitness*, p.97.

24 Oswald, 'Affair at Villa Muriele', p.267.

> … we ascended the hills – moved along their tops which were flat and open without trees or fences until we approached a wooded part – we united with a squadron of the 5 Dr Guards under Capt Prescott[25] which had retired from Palencia – and at last we ascertained that the French had retreated across the bridges of Palencia (and I suppose the Spaniards had again got into their post) for we fell back to the tops of the hills again behind Muriel. The enemy, who before our departure had made no particular attempts to force the river, we found had during our absence succeeded in gaining our banks, and had established himself in the canal…[26]

'Two squadrons from the 5th Dragoon Guards and the 3rd Dragoons',[27] presumably one squadron from each regiment, had been sent from Dueñas to cover the destruction of the bridges at Palencia. Foy, in his report to Souham, describes how his cavalry was sent in pursuit of the retreating Spaniards and the 3/1st Foot, while Douglas suggested that the pursuit did not continue onto the high ground.[28] Weare was incorrect in his assumption that the Spaniards had reoccupied Palencia, as Foy described them retreating onto the high ground.

Weare suggests that Oswald led his troops approximately 1½ to 2 miles, to the west, 'to gain the hills direct in the rear of the village', across the plateau of El Páramo to the wooded ground beyond, before returning to Villamuriel. Béchaud described the going on the plateau as being 'very difficult'. At a rate of march of approximately 2 to the 2½ miles an hour specified by Wellington, Oswald would have been absent from Villamuriel for approximately 2 hours, returning sometime after 2:00 p.m.[29] During this march Oswald met Colonel Campbell who was retiring from Palencia with the 3/1st Foot.[30]

---

25 *Army List*, 1813, p.78; Sergentson Prescott; major from 26 December 1811.

26 TNA, NRA 21704 Oswald, Weare 12 December 1836.

27 R. Cannon, *Historical Record of the Fifth or Princess Charlotte of Wales Dragoon Guards* (London: William Clowes, 1839), p.63.

28 M. Girod de l'Ain, *La Vie Militaire du Général Foy* (Paris: Plon Nourrit, 1900), pp.381–2; Monick (ed.), *Douglas*, p.58.

29 J. Haverfield and H. Hofmann, *Scharnhorst's Military Field Pocket Book* (London: Vogel and Schulze, 1811), Appendix p.7; Gurwood, *General Orders*, p.84; Lopez, *Mapa*; MTN.

30 Wellington Papers, Campbell to Barnes, 28 October 1812.

Corporal James Hale, Light Company, 1/9th Foot, skirmishing near the bridge of Villamuriel.
(Artwork by Christa Hook © Helion and Company)

Soldat Jean Chevalier, 2e Compagnie, 2e Bataillon, 15e Ligne, skirmishing around the dry Canal de Castilla. (Artwork by Christa Hook © Helion and Company)

Soldado, Regimiento 1º Asturias, 1ª Sección, 1ª Division, 6º Ejército (Galicia y Asturias).
(Artwork by Christa Hook © Helion and Company)

Major Dudley St. Leger Hill, formerly of the 95th Rifles, commander of the Caçadores N.8, defending the ford at Calabazanos.
(Artwork by Christa Hook © Helion and Company)

Colonel Jean-Pierre Béchaud, commander of the 66e Ligne, riding across Villamuriel to organise the response to the allied counterattack. (Artwork by Christa Hook © Helion and Company)

Ford at Calabazanos with the monastery in the distance, July 2017. (Author's Photo)

The bridge at Villamuriel viewed from the right or allied bank. (Author's Photo)

Lawson's mound viewed from the bridge. (Author's Photo)

The ford at the bridge. (Author's Photo)

Wellington's counterattack was launched from these heights. (Author's Photo)

Villamuriel from the river. Barnes's Brigade advanced from left to right as they advanced to the bridge. (Author's Photo)

8

Montfort crosses the Carrión at Calabazanos

Presumably having observed the withdrawal of the left wing of the Anglo-Portuguese 5th Division, Maucune ordered the French attacks to be recommenced. At 1:00 p.m., *Colonel* François Desfossés arrived from 'the vicinity of Palencia' with his brigade of light cavalry.[1] More French skirmishers were deployed from d'Arnauld's brigade to line the river bank to their right of the bridge as a diversion, while Maucune ordered Montfort's brigade to cross the river through the ford to their left of Villamuriel, close to Calabazanos.[2] The attack was led by d'Arnauld's eight previously deployed companies of skirmishers. The rest of d'Arnauld's brigade remained deployed in line of battle, so that they could move either to the right or the left, as required. Although Béchaud implied that the crossing of the river at Calabazanos happened before the cavalry arrived, this is not consistent with other sources from either side. Baron de Lamartinière describes how one squadron of Desfossés's cavalry was deployed to assist the skirmishers in crossing the river.[3] Meanwhile Desfossés had led the rest of his cavalry downstream to find a ford to enable them to outflank Hill and his *caçadores*.

Béchaud describes the infantry attack as follows:

> With great élan, staff officers competed in zeal and ardour with the infantry, almost all crossed the water, the brave *Capitaine* Lachapelle, aide de camp to General Maucune, charged and slashed at the enemy sharpshooters, his worthy comrade *Capitaine* Bourgevin [François Basile Burgevin de Lesme], *aide de camp* to General Chauvel, carried away by his courage, went beyond the call of duty to receive a mortal blow. The brave *chef de bataillon* Isambert of the [4/]66e commanded the first skirmishers who crossed and was hit by a bullet that broke his jaw (he is a soldier of great *sang-froid* who enjoys the general esteem of the regiment). *Capitaine* Levistre and *Lieutenant* Magnan were the first officers of the

1 Colin, 'Béchaud', p.407.
2 Colin, 'Béchaud', p.406.
3 Gurwood (ed.), *Dispatches*, Vol.VI, p.775; Dumay, *Historique*, p.60; Burroughs, *Narrative*, p.23.

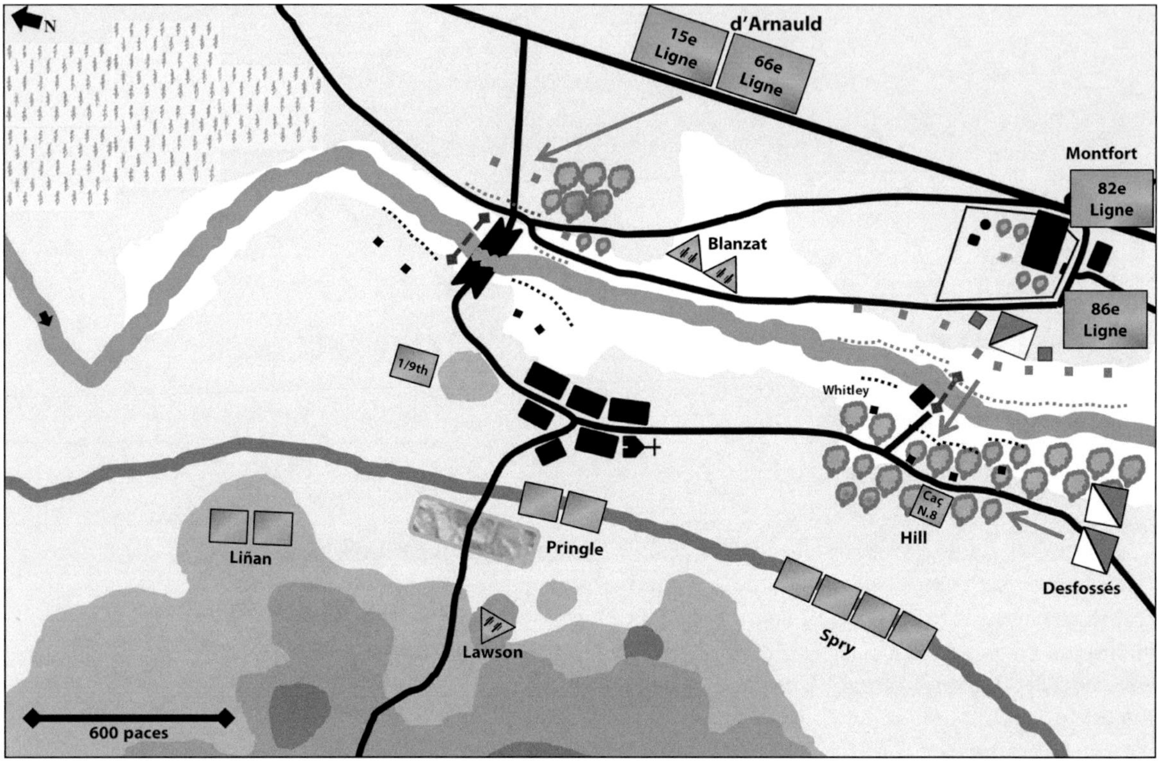

Map 5 Dispositions at 1:00 p.m.

> 66e to have crossed the river; they led their troops to the other side with great valour.[4]

Général de Brigade Chauvel, commander of the 8e Division, Armée de Portugal, was wounded on 23 October at Venta del Pozo and had been replaced by Gauthier.[5] The history of the 15e Ligne describes Lachapelle's exploits in more detail:

> While an *aide de camp* of General Maucune (1) made sure that the Carrion was fordable for the infantry, Lieutenant [F]ouque, at the head of the *voltigeurs* of the 15e (2), threw himself resolutely into water and arrived first on the opposite bank, under the fire of a battalion of British chasseurs…
>
> (1) Mr. Lesueur, known as Lachapelle, who became *chef de battalion* in the 15e on July 4, 1813. Having arrived on opposite bank of the Carrion, followed by only two officers, of whom one was killed, he charged the enemy and took 20 prisoners, including 2 officers.
>
> (2) Lieutenant André [F]ouque was proposed and admitted into the *Legion d'Honneur* in reward for this deed, which is mentioned on his statement of service.[6]

---

4 Colin, 'Béchaud', p.407.

5 Oman, *History*, Vol.VI, p.78; Martinien is less specific about the location.

6 De Tarragon, *Historique*, pp.220, 426; SHD 2Yb 157, *Registre Contrôle des Officiers*, p.146; André François Fouque, born 18 October 1785, is named as Souque by de Tarragon. The

Capitaine Alexandre Lachapelle's record in the archives of the *Legion d'Honneur* also states that his horse received three bayonet wounds during this attack, in which he was supported by the *voltigeurs* of the 15e Ligne.[7]

Capitaine Antoine Levistre (66e Ligne) was named a *Chevalier* of the *Legion d'Honneur* in 1813 and his record in the archives of the *Legion d'Honneur* states 'on 25 October 1812 he forded the River Carrión near Villamuriel at the head of 10 men of the company and, under the fire of 200 English and Portuguese *tirailleurs*, killed and wounded many and took prisoners'.[8]

Sous Lieutenant Bernard Pierre Magnan (66e Ligne) was named a *Chevalier* of the *Legion d'Honneur* in 1814, his record states that as a member of one of the grenadier companies of the 66e Ligne:

> In the affair of Villa Muriel on 25 October 1812 in Spain, he forded the River Carrión near Palencia, under the fire of over 600 English or Portuguese, at the head of the company to which he belonged, he was first to the right bank and took, with some grenadiers that had followed him, a good number of prisoners.[9]

Bernard Pierre Magnan was born on 7 December 1791, in Paris, and volunteered into the 66e Ligne as a *soldat* in December 1809. He was a *sergent* in January 1810 and was promoted to *sergent major* in October of the same year, becoming *sous lieutenant* of grenadiers on 21 July 1811. After Villamuriel, in February 1813, he was promoted to *lieutenant* in a *voltigeur* company. He then served in the 13e Tirailleurs de la Garde Impériale and was wounded at Croanne in 1814. Magnan's career continued after Napoleon's fall and he was appointed *Maréchal de France* in December 1852, before his death in 1865. A baton in his knapsack perhaps?[10]

In his report to the Minister of War, Souham's chief of staff, Baron de Lamartinière, also recognised the valour of *Capitaine* Pierre Abraham Lafont (another aide de camp to General Maucune) whose dossier in the archives of the *Legion d'Honneur* records his actions, 'on 25 October 1812 he was the first to cross the Carrion at the head of the tirailleurs and alone took one officer and ten English soldiers'.[11]

Burroughs described Montfort's attack as follows: 'then mounting the *voltigeurs* behind their cavalry, they forded the river some distance below the bridge, and formed themselves under the cover of a wood'.[12]

---

contrôle des officiers records that Fouque was promoted to *capitaine* in December 1811 and his service at Villamuriel, although dated to 25 October 1809, and that he was appointed to the *Legion d'Honneur* in January 1813.

7 LEONORE LH/1618/55; *Capitaine* Alexandre Jean François Lesueur La Chapelle.

8 LEONORE LH/1628/40; Levistre born 13 October 1779, joined as *soldat*, served with the Armée du Nord and the Armée du Rhin, 1792–1799; *lieutenant*, 1808; in the colonies until 1809; Spain with the 82e Ligne in 1810 and the 66e Ligne in 1811; Dumay, *Historique*, p.60.

9 LEONORE LH/1685/37.

10 SHD 2Yc 555, p.25, *Registre Matricule*; LEONORE LH/1685/37.

11 Gurwood (ed.), *Dispatches*, Vol.VI, pp.773–7; LEONORE LH/1436/67; Lamartinière spells his name Lafond.

12 Burroughs, *Narrative*, pp.23–4.

It was this attack that finally forced Hill's Caçadores N.8 back from the river, which they had defended for several hours, after they ran low on ammunition, as subsequently described by Hill in his report to Pringle:

> The enemy not being able to cross the ford at the mill I protected, a body of cavalry was sent to cross the river lower down which forded and came rapidly on my right flank. This I reported immediately to you by an officer, and advanced my reserve to support the wing of the battn in advance not having a round of ammunition in the battn and almost all my officers wounded and half the battn, I deemed proper to retire and also reporting to you which I did regularly and showing a front to the enemy's cavalry, some of whom, with an officer we bayoneted and took prisoners until your arrival with the British support.[13]

The French officer referred to here by Hill, is not identifiable amongst the French cavalry present that day and therefore it is likely that he is referring to the mortal wounding of *Capitaine* Burgevin, aide de camp to Chauvel, who would also have been mounted.

The Caçadores N.8 were very roughly handled by the French: Hill and up to nine other officers were wounded and Hill later stated that nearly his whole unit was rendered *hors de combat*.[14] Indeed, Beresford later reported that the battalion lost half its numbers.[15] Furthermore, Hill was briefly captured but he managed to escape and rally the remainder of his men. Hill states that the skirmishing lasted eight hours although Oswald's account has Hill's men forced back from the ford to 'rough ground' in the middle of the day.[16] Hill concluded his report to Pringle with the following words of praise for his men:

> It is impossible to say too much in praise of the officers and men, whose conduct was conspicuously gallant in sight of the Division during the whole of the morning. I however should be wanting in justice to the two British officers of the Battn (Captn Western and Adjt Leche) if I did not particularly mention them to you and who are both wounded.[17]

Although not mentioned by Major Hill, the French cavalry also used the watermill or 'gristmill' as a screen, to enable them to surprise the detachment from Barnes's Brigade, capturing Lieutenant James Whitley and 25 men of his company of the 1/9th Foot,[18] as described by Hale: 'while they were busy skirmishing with the infantry that was on the opposite side of the river, a troop of the French cavalry rushed out from behind the mill, quite unawares

13 Wellington Papers, Hill to Pringle, 27 October 1812.

14 AHM, PT/AHM/DIV/3/12/09/7 *Combate de Carrion– 25 de Outubro de 1812, Minuta de oficiais mortos ou feridos*.

15 Santos, *Ordens*, 1813, p.12.

16 Philippart, *Calendar*, 1815, Vol.III, p.308; Oswald, 'Affair at Villa Muriele', p.267.

17 Wellington Papers, Hill to Pringle, 27 October 1812.

18 Greenwood (ed.), *Le Mesurier*, p.138.

to us, and swept away the whole company as prisoners of war before we could give them any assistance.'[19]

Lieutenant Peter Le Mesurier reported that of Whitley's whole company only four men managed to return to the regiment.[20] Le Mesurier was given command of Whitley's company (No. 8) in his absence. In January 1813 Le Mesurier wrote 'we have heard nothing of Whitley who was missing; tis generally supposed he is dead of his wounds'.[21] In fact, Lieutenant Whitley not only survived the war but lived long enough to receive the Military General Service Medal with clasps for Roliça, Vimeiro, Corunna, Buçaco and Salamanca.[22]

Pringle described the consequences in his report to Oswald:

> [A]bout 2o/c I was informed that the *caçadores* were obliged to retire from the fords near the mill by the enemy's cavalry having crossed the river lower down and come on their flank in force, in consequence of this movement our right flank was left totally unprotected and the enemy had already got in the rear of the village before I was made acquainted with the circumstances, e.g. the *caçadores* having retired, I was therefore obliged to withdraw the troops in the village up the hill and I am happy to acquaint you that they retired in the most perfect order, under a very heavy fire of musquetry and artillery, the *caçadores* also retired in very good order...[23]

The 1/4th Foot covered Pringle's withdrawal from the river and village, its commander Lieutenant Colonel John Piper described being '... warmly engaged... in a severe affair that lasted the whole day... while commanding a party that was ordered to cover the retirement of part of that force, received a [slight] wound in the neck'.[24]

Back at the bridge, after four hours of skirmishing, the 9th Foot was withdrawn to rest, being replaced by Liñan's brigade.[25] One account describes how the 9th Foot had its ammunition replenished twice on this day.[26] In Pringle's words '... these troops [the 1/9th, 2/30th, 2/44th, 1/4th Foot and Caçadores N.8 together with the light companies of both brigades] continued to defend the different posts allotted to them for above four hours...'[27]

---

19 Hale, *Journal*, p.94; TNA, WO17/110, 9th Foot 1803–1812; November monthly return.

20 Greenwood (ed.), *Le Mesurier*, p.138.

21 Greenwood (ed.), *Le Mesurier*, pp.141–2, 151; NAM, Accession no. NAM. 1968–07–362–1, Whitley's parole pass at Verdun, 30 December 1812; this describes Whitley as 21 years old, 1.78m tall with black hair and blue eyes.

22 MGSMR.

23 UML, GB 133 Eng MSS 1273, item 27; this is the version in his own papers, in the copy sent to Oswald, (Wellington Papers) he omitted the words 'up the hill'.

24 Hall, *History*, p.470; Philippart, *Calendar*, 1815, Vol.III, pp.282–3; TNA, WO17/101, October monthly return, first battalion; lieutenant colonel was his army rank, which he received in August 1812, in the regiment he was a major.

25 Hale, *Journal*, p.95.

26 Cannon, *Ninth*, pp.62–3; F.L. Petre, *The History of the Norfolk Regiment, 1685–1918* (Norwich: Jarrold, 1924), Vol.I, p.242.

27 UML, GB 133 Eng MSS 1273, item 27.

9

D'Arnauld Captures the Village

At 2:00 p.m., d'Arnauld was ordered to cross the river via the ford to his right of the bridge at Villamuriel, which the main body of his brigade did in close column screened by skirmishers drawn from further companies of the 15e Ligne. Having already deployed the four *voltigeur* and four other companies from d'Arnauld's four battalions, fusilier companies would have provided these skirmishers.[1] Oswald confirms that at this time the Spanish troops were providing the skirmish line before Villamuriel, although Giron's report of Liñan's account does not mention this skirmishing phase.[2]

Chef de Bataillon Edouard Beaufort-d'Hautpoul, chief of staff to the Armée de Portugal's chief engineer, *Colonel* Éléonor Bertrand Anne Christophe Zoa Dufriche de Valazé, had managed to make a partial repair to the bridge, using ladders, to facilitate this attack.[3] Napier mentions the use of ladders based on Hopkins' memoir but this was later challenged by Weare in his correspondence with Oswald. Weare, however, was not present at this time.[4]

Béchaud again provides the narrative:

> At two o'clock, d'Arnault [sic] received the order to seek a ford to the right of the bridge and to cross the river; he did not hesitate, he went at the gallop to the river with the two senior officers [presumably Béchaud himself and *Major* Dornier, commander of the 15e Ligne], several men were sent to search for the passage, which was soon found very near on the right side of the bridge, *Général* d'Arnault crossed first. He was followed by the skirmishers who spread along the right bank, the enemy harassed this passage with some harmless howitzer shells, *Colonel* Béchaud picking up the rest of the brigade, directed them through the water in closed column, and the masses were soon behind the first houses of Villa-muriel.[5]

1 Colin, 'Béchaud', p.407.

2 Oswald, 'Affair at Villa Muriele', p.267; AHNM, *Diversos/Colecciones*/101/n63.

3 Anon., *Biographie universelle et portative des contemporains, ou Dictionnaire historique des hommes vivants et des hommes morts depuis 1788 jusqu'à nos jours* (Paris: Levrault, 1834), Vol.I, pp.285–6; *Capitaine* Génot, 5e Division's chief engineer (SHD C8 468) was presumably also involved.

4 Napier, *History*, 1840, Vol.VI, p.xvii.

5 Colin, 'Béchaud', p.407.

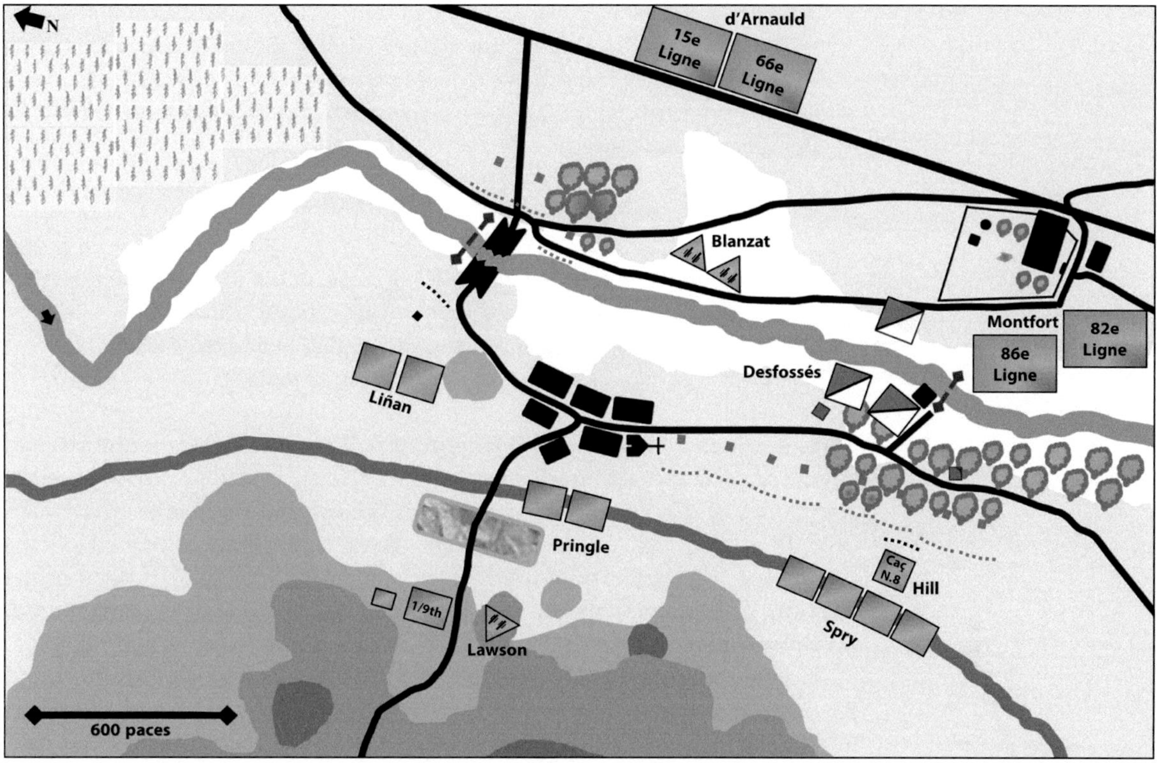

Map 6 Dispositions at 1:30 p.m.

Douglas has the French cavalry also helping the French infantry through this ford, but it is unlikely that he directly witnessed this as he states that the French had already lined the canal before he and the 3/1st Foot returned to the battlefield.[6]

According to Hale, when d'Arnauld's brigade advanced to drive the outnumbered defenders from Liñan's brigade away from the village, the Spanish infantry were 'retreating in an unsoldier-like manner'.[7]

Béchaud described how the main body of d'Arnauld's brigade, gathered behind the first houses of Villamuriel, was covered by 'several platoons' of skirmishers, under the command of *Chef de Bataillon* Alexandre François Frémin (2/15e Ligne). The skirmishers were deployed in front and to the right of the village, along the line of the dry canal and in the area of the bodegas beyond.[8]

Lieutenant Hopkins (1/4th Foot) described the French attack on the bridge and village:

> We were aware that the enemy had passed the Carrion with cavalry and also that Hill's *caçadores* had given way at another part of the river. Our engineers had partly destroyed the bridge of Villa Muriel, the enemy attacked the village,

6 Monick (ed.), *Douglas*, p.59.

7 Hale, *Journal*, p.94; Fortescue, *History*, Vol.VIII, p.603; 'the Spaniards opposed to him [Maucune] at once gave way'.

8 Hale, *Journal*, p.95; Colin, 'Béchaud', p.408.

> at the time that the brigadier and his staff were there, passing the ruins of the bridge by means of ladders, etc. The enemy in driving the detachment from the village made some prisoners. We retired to the plateau of the heights, under a fire of musquetry and artillery, where we halted in close column; the enemy strengthened the village.[9]

Arriving back at the battlefield at the end of this assault, Weare recounts:

> I perfectly remember from the top of the hill seeing D. Hill with the 8 Cacadores coming away from the ford, in a little column covered with flankers, in the direction of the canal. I remember also his coming to us enquiring about his wounded men which he had previously sent from the ford.[10]

Thus, between 2:00 p.m. and 3:00 p.m., the French were across the river in strength, with the advanced guard of Montfort's brigade and six to eight companies of d'Arnauld's skirmishers on the left and the rest of d'Arnauld's brigade on the right, near the bridge. The French guns remained on the left bank of the river, while the cavalry crossed back to the left bank of the Carrión, as explained by Weare: 'the cavalry which passed the fords retired, not appearing to like their precarious post with the stream in their rear'.[11]

It appears however that only d'Arnauld's advance was seriously pressed beyond the river towards the dry canal bed. Béchaud's account and Martinien both make it clear that Montfort's brigade was significantly less involved than d'Arnauld's.[12] This is also supported by the British observers, Wellington remarked that 'the fire upon the left had been very severe throughout the day from which we suffered a great deal'.[13]

Gordon recorded that '… the enemy soon crossed over about 2,000 men immediately under our position'.[14]

Chef de Bataillon Étienne-François Girard, Maucune's chief of staff, has also left us an account of these attacks, in which he perhaps explains Montfort's relative inactivity:

> [T]his passage took place under the protection of the 2nd brigade [d'Arnauld's] and a battery of ten pieces. General Monfort covered the ford and waited for new instructions, while the 2nd brigade [i.e. d'Arnauld's] and the battery, ordered to move to protect the crossing at another point, left him to look after himself.[15]

Montfort thus seems to have been aware of, and concerned by, the fact that Spry's Brigade was well positioned to receive any attack which he might venture. The relative strengths of the two brigades were similar and although

---

9 Napier, *History*, 1840, Vol.VI, p.xvii.

10 TNA, NRA 21704 Oswald, Weare 12 December 1836.

11 Oswald, 'Affair at Villa Muriele', p.267; Gurwood (ed.), *Dispatches*, Vol.VI, p.776; TNA, NRA 21704 Oswald, Weare 12 December 1836.

12 Colin, 'Béchaud', p.407; Martinien, *Tableaux*, pp.152–3, 271, 293, *Supplément*, p.47.

13 Gurwood (ed.), *Dispatches*, Vol.IX, p.512.

14 Muir (ed.), *Gordon*, p.334.

15 Desachy, *Girard*, p.205.

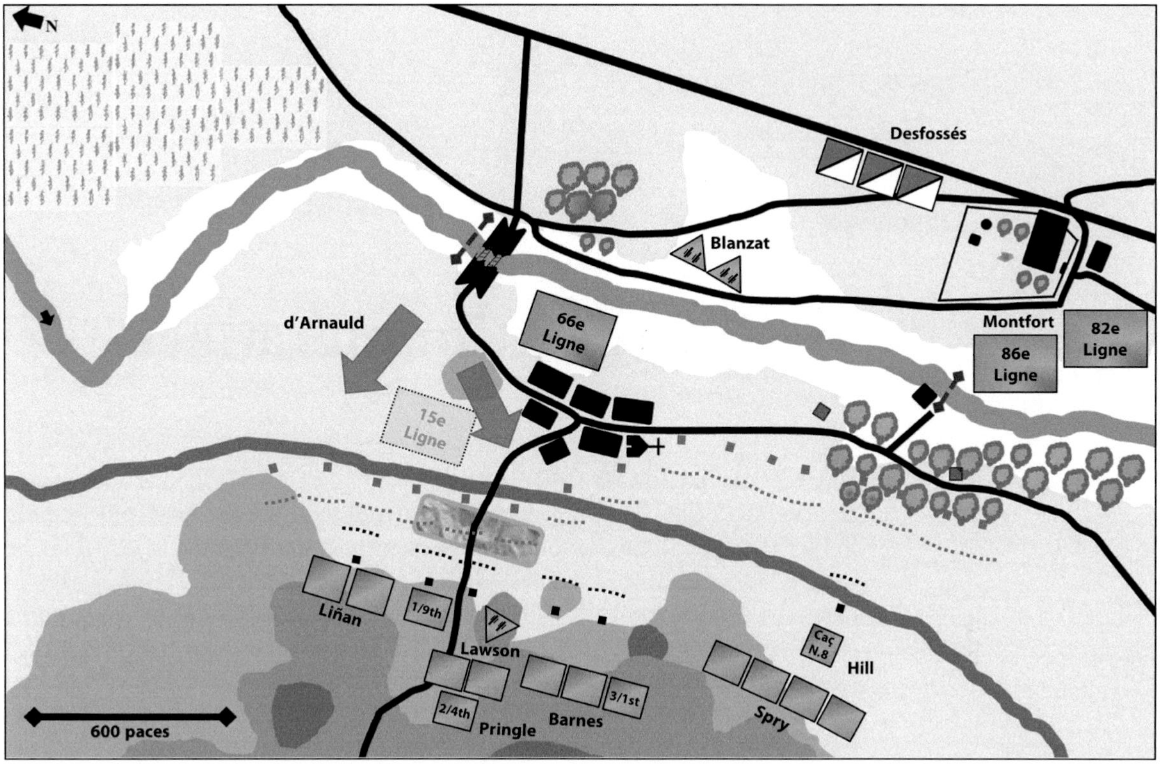

Map 7 Dispositions at 2:00–3:00 p.m.

the force ratio was in Montfort's favour by approximately 10 percent (Spry 1,870 men; Montfort 2,015), it would have been insufficient to guarantee success in an unsupported assault.

Returning to the heights above Villamuriel with Barnes's brigade, Douglas reported that:

> [S]ince our departure in the morning the face of affairs had considerably changed. The enemy had now occupied the dry canal in great numbers, which General Oswald ought to have done. The bridge over the Carrion was blown (or rather down)… In this manner was the dry canal lined with French infantry, under the protection of a crossfire from the opposite side of the town… To let them remain in this situation would have been next to madness, as they were increasing every minute, and not likely to be agreeable companions during the night.[16]

16 Monick (ed.), *Douglas*, p.59.

10

Wellington's Counterattack

Having satisfied himself that all was quiet at Palencia and Dueñas, Wellington returned to Villamuriel but was not prepared to allow the French to remain in the village or along the canal. Consequently, at approximately 4:00 p.m., he ordered Oswald to lead Barnes's and Pringle's Brigades in a counterattack to drive the French from the right bank of the river. There are various accounts of this conversation. Oswald stated that Wellington ordered that the French be driven from the right bank, Oswald then asked if, once the village had been cleared, his division should stay there, to which Wellington replied that the village was to be held in force until the 5th Division was withdrawn, probably in the early morning.[1] Napier, however, stated that Oswald was concerned that the village and canal could not be held. When challenged by Oswald, Napier cited the recollections of Lieutenant Hopkins (1/4th Foot). Hopkins recalled Wellington saying 'Oswald, you will get the division under arms and drive the enemy from the village and retain possession of it...' Oswald replied, 'My lord, if the village should be taken, I do not consider that it is tenable' to which Wellington responded, 'it is my orders, general'. Oswald then concluded, 'my Lord, as it is your orders they shall be obeyed'.[2] However, having read Napier's account, Weare remarked to Oswald in 1836, that 'I never heard you doubt the results of the intended attack on our part or of the occupation of the village for the night'.[3]

Hopkins described Wellington's tactical orders as, '... that he should take the second brigade of the division and attack in line, that the first brigade should in column descend the heights on the right of the second, enter the canal and assist in clearing it of the enemy'.[4] This arrangement reverted to the normal battle array with the first brigade on the right. In conclusion, Wellington said; 'I will tell you what I will do Oswald. I will give you the

---

1 Oswald, 'Affair at Villa Muriele', pp.266–7; Gurwood (ed.), *Dispatches*, Vol.VI, p.*775*; both Baron de Lamartinière and Le Mesurier described the counterattack starting at 4:00 p.m.

2 Napier, *History*, Vol.V, p.301; Vol.VI, 1840, p.xviii.

3 TNA, NRA 21704 Oswald, Weare 12 December 1836.

4 Napier, *History*, Vol.VI, 1840, p.xviii

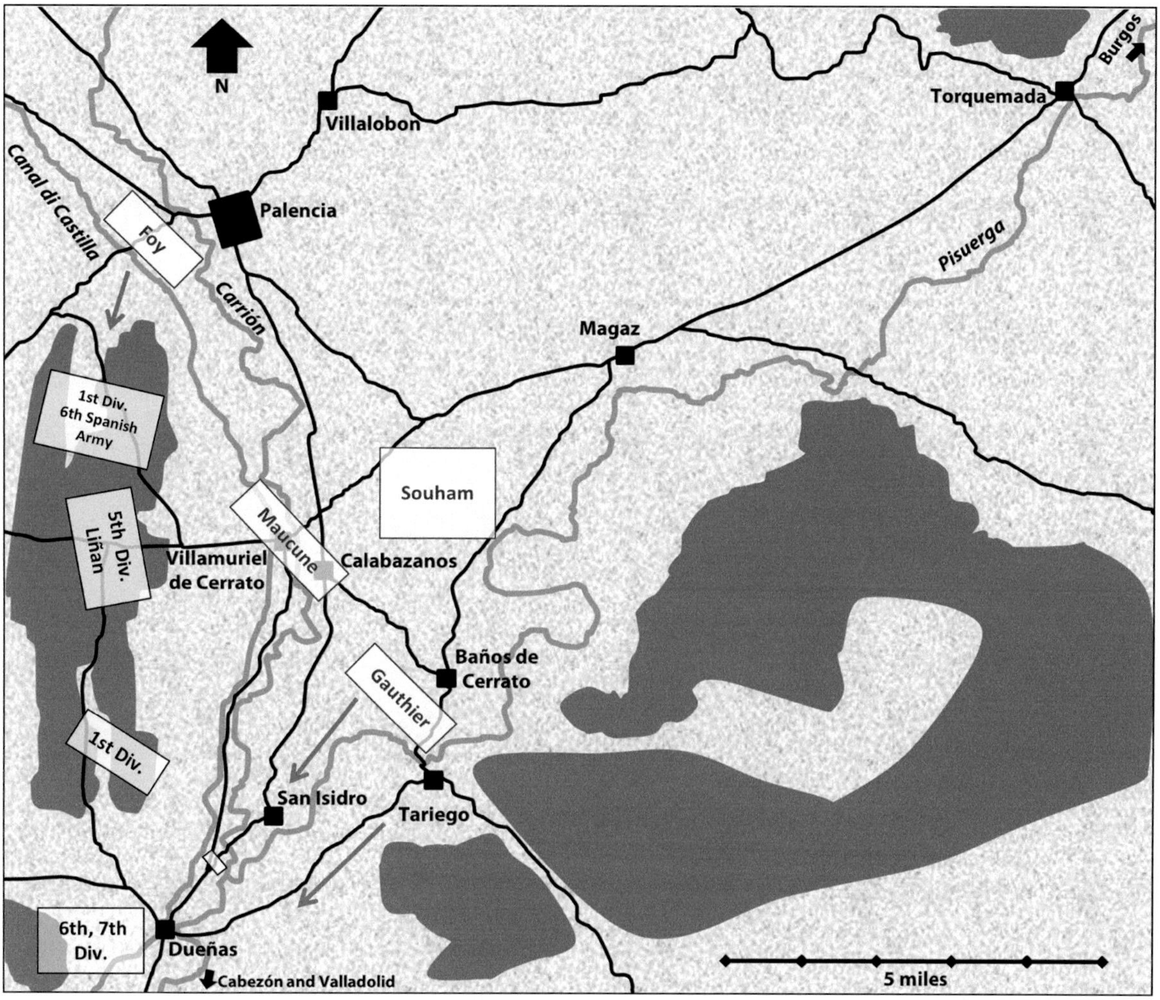

Map 8 Campaign Map – Afternoon.

Spaniards together with Álava into the bargain, headed by a company of the Ninth Regiment upon your left'.[5]

Meanwhile Ensign George Freer (1/38th Foot) has Wellington saying, 'they are coming too far forward and must be driven back', to which Barnes replied, 'My Lord, I will take care of that!'[6]

According to Oswald's own account, Oswald then led the 5th Division in an attack, which was subtly different to Hopkins's description of Wellington's orders; Barnes's Brigade attacked the left flank of the French troops in and around Villamuriel, while Pringle's Brigade advanced in support, extending to their left to support Liñan's brigade.[7] During the counterattack the 2/4th

5 Napier, *History*, Vol.VI, 1840, p.xviii.
6 Freer, 'Thirty-Eighth', p.299; i.e. a similar quote but in a different context to Weare's recollection.
7 Oswald, 'Affair at Villa Muriele', p.267.

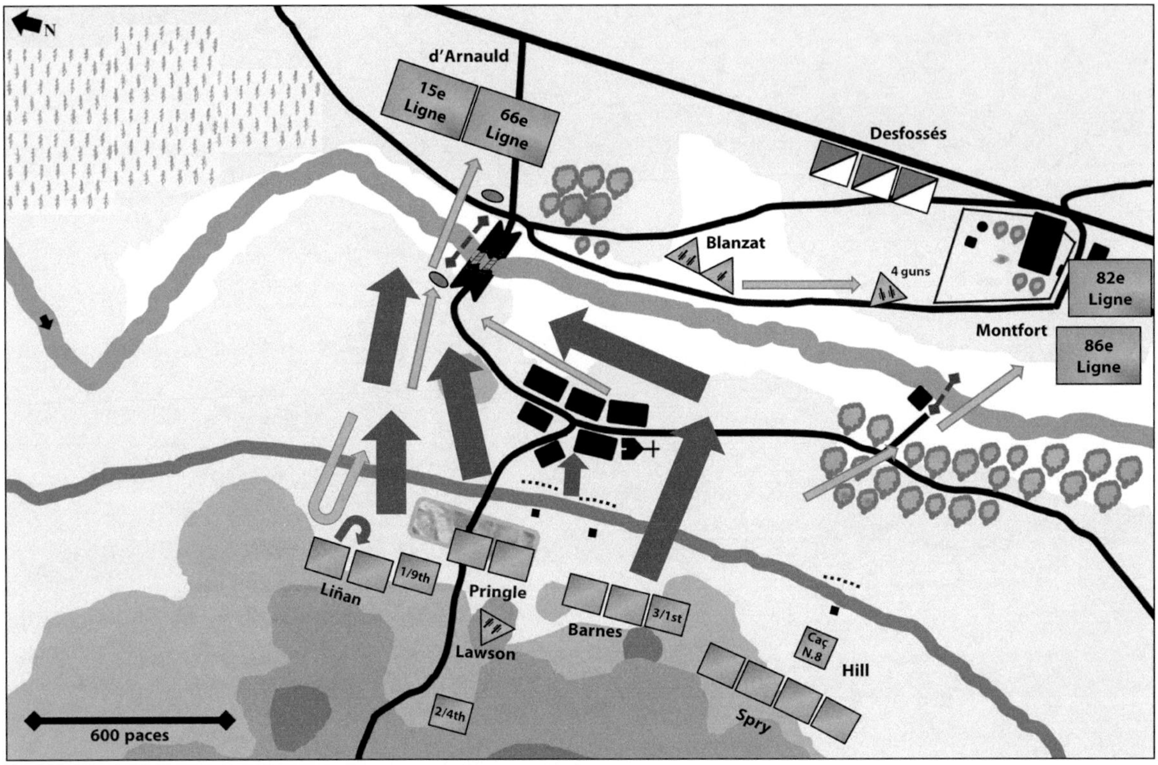

Map 9 Allied Counterattack, 4:00 p.m.

Foot (Pringle's Brigade) remained in reserve in column on the slopes of the heights.[8]

Mackenzie described the formation of the counterattack as comprising:

> [T]he 1st brigade [Barnes] consisting of the three battalions 1st, 9th, and 38th regiments, in contiguous columns at given distance; and the second brigade [Pringle] consisting of the two battalions the 4th, 2nd battalion, the 30th and the 44th [i.e. the 1/4th and the 2/30th and 2/44th Foot acting together, but not the 2/4th Foot], in line, were ordered to march down the hill and retake the village and the canal.[9]

Mackenzie has omitted the 2/38th Foot from his battalion count for Barnes's Brigade and given the other sources he seems to have included the 1/9th Foot in error.

Oman has another version of the counterattack, with Barnes's Brigade replacing the shaken Spaniards and attacking in tandem with Pringle's Brigade,[10] however neither the Spanish sources nor Napier support this version and Wellington's dispatch clearly stated that the Spanish co-operated in the attack and pursued the French.[11]

8 Napier, *History*, 1840, Vol.VI, p.xviii.
9 'McK', 'The Affair of Villa Muriel', p.543.
10 Oman, *History*, Vol.VI, p.80.
11 *London Gazette*, 16,669, 17 November 1812, p.2321; Napier, *History*, Vol.V, p.301.

Oman further mentions that Spry's Brigada N.3 supported the counterattack, but this is not mentioned in any of the eyewitness accounts of the counterattack. Weare described Spry's Brigade as remaining on the hill in reserve and Hill's subsequent report confirms that the line infantry of the brigade was not engaged.[12]

Béchaud gives a vivid account of the counterattack from the French perspective. He described occupying the canal and the bodegas, to the right of the village, for about an hour in a state of quiet tension, while taking measures to prevent the soldiers drinking the wine, which was abundantly available in the houses of Villamuriel. He then heard a resumption of the firing on the far side or left (from the French perspective) of the village. There the skirmishers screening the advance elements of Montfort's brigade fired at the attacking British at point blank range, 'causing many casualties' before quickly and completely withdrawing to the left bank of the river.[13]

Girard's account also describes these events:

> Wellington brought down three columns of infantry [3/1st, 1/38th and 2/38th] to envelop him [Montfort]. I saw the danger and was going to report this to General Maucune when, not fifteen paces from him, a cannonball carried away my epaulette, a piece of clothing and scorched my shirt.
>
> Go quickly to get your wound dressed, he cried to me.
>
> Yes, later. But your 1st brigade [i.e. Montfort] is lost if it does not re-cross the river.
>
> It has its general, he will advise.
>
> And if he cannot see the threatening movement? And if he waits for your orders?
>
> He is a general! He must act for the best.
>
> I was not satisfied with that answer. I joined General Montfort and told him to immediately withdraw the two wings back on the centre and back to the positions that he had quit on the other side. This movement was then on-going as the centre began already to experience the fire of one of the enemy columns while the other deployed, when half of the battery of *Commandant* Blanzat, which I had asked to follow me, fired his four pieces so successfully that they turned back the first of these columns.
>
> I took this opportunity to get the last platoons, with which I had stayed, to the ford. The pain I felt in my shoulder and arm did not allow me to delay taking advantage of the necessary care; I went to give an account to General Maucune of the movement of Montfort's brigade, and then went to get my wound dressed.[14]

Although Girard's account seems particularly self-serving, his superiors clearly viewed him as credible, as this extract from Baron de La Martinière's report of 4 November shows; '*Chef de Bataillon*, Girard, chief of the general staff of the 5e Division received at the combat of Villamuriel a strong contusion

12 TNA, NRA 21704 Oswald, Weare 12 December 1836; Wellington Papers, Hill to Pringle, 27 October 1812.

13 Colin, 'Béchaud', p.408.

14 Desachy, *Girard*, p.206.

in the shoulder and did not want to leave the field of battle. This is an action where this brave officer again justified the interest that his leaders take in his advancement'.[15] Furthermore, a decree of 8 February 1813 appointed Girard *colonel d'état-major*. It would appear from this account that Girard perceived that Montfort's brigade, on the French left, was the main target of Barnes's attack, whereas Maucune seems to have understood that d'Arnauld's more advanced brigade was in greater peril.

Having crossed the village to investigate, *Colonel* Béchaud posted the company of *Capitaine* Jean Sempé and the *voltigeurs* of the 4/66e Ligne at the left-hand entrance to the village and behind a parapet of the canal.[16] Their orders were to hold this position to the last extremity: they were subsequently involved in a 30 minute musketry duel at short range, before being forced back by greater numbers.[17] Weare described how Oswald was leading on Pringle's Brigade at this point:

> I have a most perfect recollection of the movements of the two brigades which attacked and drove the enemy from the canal into the river, where many were drowned. The Duke came to us. – General Pringle's brigade moved in line down the hill to attack the front of the troops in the canal – Genl Barnes's brigade moved in open column across the canal and the enemy's left flank when they wheeled into line – by these two movements, and attacks, the enemy were quickly driven from the position – their right attempted [to] stand in the village you know best the result of the severe struggle there, because you were there in person – the left of the enemy attempted the ford of Dudley Hill, where many, as well as in the rear of the village, were drowned. When Genl Barnes's brigade had gone halfway down the hill, the column suffered much from the roundshot from the opposite side of the river, and you sent me to desire him to move on quicker, by which I lost sight of you, as you got with the attack on the village. The other brigade [i.e. Spry's] remained on the side of the hill in reserve I think.[18]

Béchaud's account continues:

> *Colonel* Béchaud, after this troop placement, crossed the village at a gallop, to General d'Arnauld who was in the field to the right where he had made his deployments to receive the enemy, and said to him 'my General, I have just come from the left, our companies of skirmishers and the second brigade have re-crossed the river, I have placed two companies to the left of the village, they are firing, you see, at columns that descend from all sides of the mountain to assail us, I advise you to move our eagles and a reserve to the other bank.' The general replied, 'We'll see what they will do', and continued to bring out the 15e [Ligne]

15 Desachy, *Girard*, p.206, the second sentence is not reproduced in Gurwood's *Dispatches*, Vol. VI, pp.773–7.

16 LEONORE LH/2499/48; Sempé was born 10 September 1776, joined as a *soldat* 1792 serving in the Pyrenees and Italy before joining the 66e Ligne in 1807 as a *sous-lieutenant*. He was promoted to *capitaine* on 17 December 1811 and named *Chevalier* of the *Legion d'Honneur* in November 1813.

17 Colin, 'Béchaud', p.408.

18 TNA, NRA 21704 Oswald, Weare 12 December 1836.

> from behind the houses. … At this moment, we were assailed on all sides by a six fold strength, this force is supported in its movement from the hills above us, the two companies on the left are holding on for a while longer, from the bodegas *Chef de Bataillon* Frémin delivered a heavy fire on the columns coming to force this point, the rest of the 15e Ligne were deployed as skirmishers, General d'Arnauld went to those on the right, the fire becomes general and very heavy, the result hung in the balance for a moment, the skirmishers took the opportunity to advance too far on the right, pushing up to the third mound that supports the enemy line, no leader's voice can be heard anymore, each soldier is alert and fights as he sees fit.[19]

Béchaud's assessment of the odds he faced was incorrect. It was, in fact, approximately a four to three force ratio; at the beginning of the day d'Arnauld's brigade was approximately 2,600 men strong while Barnes's, Pringle's and Liñan's brigades were together approximately 3,500 men strong. Béchaud then relates that he did indeed move his eagle to the other bank of the Carrión and recommended to *Major* Dornier, commanding the 15e Ligne, that he did the same.

Thus, when the allied counterattack began, all companies of the two battalions of the 15e Ligne had been deployed to skirmish. In total d'Arnauld's brigade had deployed 16 companies as skirmishers, which together with perhaps four companies from Montfort's brigade covered the French front. These skirmishers covered a frontage of approximately 3,000 paces, with perhaps three to six of the 20 companies held back as formed supports and the skirmish files at eight to ten pace intervals. The use of skirmishers in this way was clearly deliberate as the frontage could have been covered, at 15 to 20 paces per file, by only the eight companies originally deployed in the morning.[20] This left, in d'Arnauld's brigade, only two battalions of the 66e Ligne, each of four companies, formed in close order to provide a formed response to the allied counterattack.[21]

Under the general and heavy fire opened on the allied columns, the contest was, according to Béchaud, in doubt for some 25 minutes, with the French skirmishers, personally led by d'Arnauld himself, making good progress on their right, against Liñan's infantry.[22]

According to Stanhope, Liñan's Brigade had advanced crying '*Vamos, adelante, carajo, carajo, carajo*'.[23] However, early in their advance, the 1° Asturias, on the left, were outflanked and pushed back by d'Arnauld's advancing skirmishers, when their 'courageous' commander *Coronel* Pedro Dejoui was badly wounded by a musket shot.[24] Dejoui's successor, *Teniente Coronel* Miramon, apparently 'a man of lesser merit', could not stop his

19 Colin, 'Béchaud', p.408.

20 Husson, *Instruction*, pp.13, 44.

21 Colin, 'Béchaud', p.408.

22 Colin, 'Béchaud', p.409.

23 Glover (ed.), *Eyewitness*, p.97; 'Go forward, shit, shit, shit!'

24 Martinez, *Diccionario*, p.257; G.S. Urrecha, *El general Álava y Wellington: de Trafalgar a Waterloo* (Legardeta: Foro para el Estudio de la Historia Militar de España, 2015), p.242.

men retiring who, according to Stanhope 'ran away as hard as they could'.[25] Watching the development of the attack with Wellington, *Mariscal de Campo* Miguel Ricardo de Álava y Esquivel, Wellington's Spanish liaison officer and one of his aides de camp,[26] dashed down the hill to take personal command of the two remaining formed companies and led the battalion back into the attack.[27] Gomm accompanied Álava and described the initial retirement of the Spanish as 'unnecessary'.[28] Meanwhile Liñan was on the right of the brigade leading on the 2º Voluntarios de la Corona.

Álava was popular with the British, for example Napier described him as a:

> brave, generous, and disinterested Spaniard… Attached to British headquarters, as the military correspondent of the Junta, he was too sagacious not to perceive the necessity of zealously seconding the English general. But in the manner of doing it, he never forgot the dignity of his own country, and, as he was too frank and honest for intrigues, his intercourse was always honourable to himself and advantageous to both nations.

During the subsequent advance *Mariscal de Campo* Álava was severely wounded in the groin while leading the Spanish infantry forward. Stanhope also provides us with some examples of the black humour occasioned by Álava's wound, for example 'they say that he will sing better for his wound'.[29] On 31 October, Wellington mentioned Álava's wound in a letter to Beresford; 'Alava's [wound] was in a bad way this morning. Bleeding came on and Gunning [Staff Surgeon John Gunning attached to H.Q.] was not to be found; he soon stopped it, however, and he is now doing well'.[30]

Stanhope contradicts Hale's account in stating that the Spanish were the first units engaged by the French: however, he starts his account 'towards the afternoon'.[31] Stanhope was with Wellington both in the early morning and at some time in the middle of the day, but Wellington sent him with 'two battalions of Germans' to cover the withdrawal of the cavalry retiring from Tariego and 'to destroy a wooden bridge near Dueñas'.[32] It is therefore unlikely that Stanhope was a witness to the skirmishing at Villamuriel in the morning.

Once the British brigades were fully committed, they were able to force the French left and enter the village, thereby threatening the retreat of the more advanced French right. Consequently, d'Arnauld's brigade now retreated

---

25 Glover (ed.), *Eyewitness*, p.97; Toreno, *Historia*, 1838, Vol.III, pp.155–6; the descriptors of the senior officers of the 1º Asturias are attributed to Álava in Urrecha, *Álava*, pp.248–9, citing the *Archivo General Militar de Segovia, Exposición de la guerra que acaba de concluir del general Álava a Su Majestad. AGM Segovia. Expediente General Álava. Carpeta 7.*

26 Napier, *History*, Vol.III, p.273.

27 AHNM, *Diversos/Colecciones*/101/n63; Urrecha, *Álava*, p.248.

28 TNA, NRA 21704 Oswald, Gomm 13 December 1836.

29 Glover (ed.), *Eyewitness*, pp.97, 223, 250 note 42.

30 Gurwood (ed.), *Dispatches*, Vol.IX, p.523; CHALLIS.

31 Glover (ed.), *Eyewitness*, p.97.

32 Glover (ed.), *Eyewitness*, p.97.

rapidly towards the bridge and ford in order to cross the Carrión to safety. The Duke of Brunswick Oels Light Infantry companies, acting together, were instrumental in the success of the counterattack, capturing the village itself 'without firing a shot'. The Brunswick companies lost three officers in this attack, which resulted in Lieutenant Friedrich S. Häusler, the only remaining officer of the second company, having to command both companies, due to the lack of fit officers in the tenth company.[33]

Kortzfleisch is clear that the two Brunswick companies acted together in this attack. Liñan is specific that it was the Brunswick infantry that took the village. However, it is less clear whether the converged light companies of the two British brigades were acting together in advancing through the village or whether the British light companies had been returned to their parent battalions for the close order counter-attack against the more numerous dispersed French skirmishers. In his report, Oswald singled out the two Brunswick companies for praise.[34] On the other hand, Le Mesurier wrote that the 'picket' of Barnes's brigade served with the 1/9th Foot 'throughout the day'.[35]

Gomm described how 'our two British Brigades had very little trouble in gaining their point'.[36] The other British and Allied eyewitness accounts of the counterattack are, individually, not so detailed but together give a good picture of the allied perspective;

The Left Wing – Liñan's *Sección*

Liñan's report to *Mariscal de Campo* Don Pedro Augustín Girón, chief of staff of the 6º Ejército,[37] did not dwell on the disorder amongst his men, which was perhaps not visible to him given the broken nature of the terrain:

> I have the satisfaction of addressing to your lordship the report that was sent to me from the regiments therein mentioned that belong to my *sección*, and that under my orders had the glory yesterday afternoon to contribute to the eviction of the enemy defenders from the parapets on the left of the canal and from the village of Villamuriel in full view of their army, and while their cavalry was threatening to cross the ford, which they did not do, in view of the resolution of our troops and the courage of two English battalions who attacked to our right in line of battle, disregarding not only the lively musket fire, but the very heavy cannon fire and even grapeshot, directed by the enemy towards their front and right flank, so that according to what I saw they suffered many casualties, a German detachment contributed decisively to the success by managing to overrun their position. I have been told that General Álava, while on the height with his Excellency the Duke of Ciudad Rodrigo [i.e. Wellington], perhaps seeing that I was in the centre,

33 Kortzfleisch, *Geschichte*, Vol.I, pp.240, 242.
34 Wellington Papers, Oswald to Wellington, 1st November 1812.
35 Greenwood (ed.), *Le Mesurier*, p.158.
36 TNA, NRA 21704 Oswald, Gomm 13 December 1836.
37 Martinez, *Diccionario*, p.377.

directed the attack on the left contributing much with his presence and drive to that battalion's [1° Asturias] fulfilment of its duties; but unfortunately he was wounded by a musket shot. I must not forget to point out to your Lordship that I saw your assistant, *Sargento* [i.e. *Sargento Mayor*, Major] Josef Antonio Pravia, attached to the Corona regiment, who assured me he had come down with the permission of your Lordship, at the head of the cazadores with sword in hand encouraging them, and making several prisoners, so that I find him worthy of a recommendation. The chiefs, officers and troops fulfilled their duties very well such that I cannot point out anyone in particular.[38]

Lieutenant Colonel Alexander Gordon, another of Wellington's *aides de camp*, accompanied Álava and has left us this account of the action:

In this attack we had an opportunity of witnessing what we were to expect from our Spanish Army. I went to lead on two battalions and after much difficulty got them to follow me, but like a flock of sheep. I do not think altogether that the men want spirit, but their state of discipline is so terrible that one can do little or nothing with them, and they absolutely could not stand against the French light infantry, and still less is it to be expected they will ever make head against their columns. One regiment who was following me pretty well, upon seeing the French run upon their right who had been attacked by us, immediately set up a sort of yell and every fellow ran forward and let fly his piece and it was impossible ever to get them in order again.[39]

This suggests that Gordon was accompanying the 2° Voluntarios de la Corona with Liñan.

Although apparently unnoticed by Gordon, Álava's heroics were reported to Henry Wellesley by Thomas Sydenham:

Our friend Miguel Alava behaved with great spirit and resolution at Dueñas, in rallying his countrymen and leading them on against the French. The moment he saw the Spaniards give way, he drew his sword and put himself at the head of them, abusing them and licking them till he got them to turn and re-attack the French.[40]

Daniel tells us that Wellington called up his own carriage to take the injured Álava to Salamanca.[41]

Le Mesurier described how the 1/9th Foot supported Liñan's advance:

At four the Spanish light infantry advanced to skirmish with the French who had crossed the river (about two thousand in number), but the Spaniards would, I believe, have made a bad hand of it if English troops had not been at hand. As we were an independent Battn: we seized a favourable opportunity, gave the Spaniards three cheers, and rushed down the hill. This had a capital effect the

38 AHNM, *Diversos/Colecciones*/101/n63.
39 Muir (ed.), *Gordon*, p.334.
40 Wellington (ed.), *Supplementary Despatches*, Vol.VII, p.465.
41 Daniel, *Journal*, p.176.

> Spaniards pushed forward and took some prisoners. Others (of the French) attempted to cross the ford near the bridge but, being closely pressed, leaped into the river and never reached the opposite banks.

In running down the hill, Le Mesurier had 'a tumble' and sprained his knee, becoming 'completely lame'.[42] Hale describes the 1/9th Foot charging with 'great vigour' capturing 400 prisoners 'in a few minutes'.[43] Hale's account differs from Le Mesurier's in that while the latter describes his battalion being 'independent' attacking in support of the Spaniards, Hale refers to 'our brigade' being stood to arms and charging the enemy. Hale does not make it clear which brigade he was referring to, his original brigade, Barnes's, or that to which the 1/9th had been attached to throughout the day, i.e. Pringle's. His account suggests the latter.

Burgoyne also described the advance of Liñan's men:

> The enemy however crossed by a ford and gained the village; the Spaniards would not retake it till a company of the Brunswick Corps advanced at double quick time, with their arms trailed into the village; the Spaniards then advanced and entered with them, while on the right, two British regiments drove off at least an equal number of the enemy, though they were protected by a cannonade of ten guns from a hollow way near the village.[44]

Wellington later commented to Henry Wellesley that the Spanish infantry 'manifested a desire to close with the enemy' but they could 'neither advance nor retreat in order', with all their movements made '*à la débandade*'. In the same letter, Wellington went on to say, '… if I had not ordered a movement on the enemy's flank by the British troops, not only [sic] the enemy would not have been driven across the Carrion, but they would have carried the heights above Villa-muriel, on which the Spanish troops were posted…'[45]

Burroughs remarked that 'the Spaniards are reported to have acquitted themselves well'.[46] Lieutenant and Captain John Aitchison (3rd Foot Guards) similarly remarked that the 'Spanish infantry… behaved well' in his letter home on 31 October, presumably reporting the view prevailing in the army at the time.[47] Indeed the *Royal Military Chronicle* in March 1813, reported that the Spanish had behaved with 'extraordinary gallantry'.[48]

Mackenzie described how 'the Spanish soldiery delighted at having assisted in the recapturing the lost position, singing patriotic songs and also in praise of their leader Alava who was wounded at their head'.[49]

---

42 Greenwood (ed.), *Le Mesurier*, p.138–9.
43 Hale, *Journal*, p.95.
44 Wrottesley, *Burgoyne*, p.241.
45 Gurwood (ed.), *Dispatches*, Vol.IX, p.528.
46 Burroughs, *Narrative*, p.23.
47 W.F.K. Thompson, *An Ensign in the Peninsular War* (London: Michael Joseph, 1981), p.216; see also Daniel's account (pp.175–6), although he confuses Cabeçon with Villamuriel.
48 *Royal Military Chronicle*, March 1813, Vol.V, pp.353–4.
49 'McK', 'The Affair of Villa Muriel', p.543.

During the retreat of the French infantry, Liñan reported that the infantry of his brigade killed 89 men and captured a further 104, while clearing the canal and during the ensuing pursuit.[50] They were also later reported to have captured the band of one of the French regiments, and although this does not feature in the French accounts, the *registres matricules* confirm that bandsmen Arnould and Chandellier together with *Tambours* Dudoux and Laye, all of the 15e Ligne, were indeed taken prisoner. Arnould and Chandellier are identified as members of the '*petit état major*', which included the regulation eight musicians of the regimental band.[51]

The Centre – Pringle's Brigade

Weare remembered 'General Pringle's brigade moved in line down the hill to attack the front of the troops in the canal.'[52] Lieutenant Hopkins (1/4th Foot) adds further details:

> [T]he attack was made accordingly, the second battalion of the fourth regiment being left in reserve in column on the slope of the hill exposed to a severe cannonade which for a short time caused them some confusion. The enemy were driven from the canal and village, and the prisoners which they made in the morning were retaken. The enemy lost some men in this affair, but General Alava was wounded, the officer commanding the company of Brunswickers killed, and several of the division killed and wounded. During the attack Lord Wellington sent the Prince of Orange under a heavy fire for the purpose of preventing the troops exposing themselves at the canal, two companies defended the bridge with a detachment [of the 30th Foot] just arrived from England.[53]

It was presumably during this counterattack that Ensign Henry Beere was wounded while carrying one of the colours of the 2/30th Foot. In his history of the 30th, Bannatyne speculates that Madden and Tincombe were also wounded while carrying colours, although as already mentioned, in the case of Madden it would have been at the end of the action. Beere was later killed in action at Waterloo.[54]

The Right Wing – Barnes's Brigade

In his response to Napier, Oswald described the counterattack by Barnes's brigade as follows:

50 AHNM, *Diversos/Colecciones*/101/n63.

51 Pérez, *Liñan*, p.23; SHD, *registres matricules*, 15e Ligne; SHD GR 21 YC 133, p.310; SHD GR 21 YC 135, p.96; SHD GR 21 YC 136, pp.265, 276; page numbers refer to the online records; Elting, *Swords*, p.335; Crowdy, *Handbook*, pp.18–21.

52 TNA, NRA 21704 Oswald, Weare 12 December 1836.

53 Napier, *History*, 1840, Vol.VI, p.xvii.

54 Hall, *History*, p.50; Bannatyne, *Thirtieth*, p.288; CHALLIS.

> [T]he casualties in the division were not numerous especially when the fire it was exposed to is considered. The enemy sustained a comparative heavy loss. The troops [i.e. the French] were by a rapid advance of the first brigade cut off from the bridge and forced into the river where many were drowned.[55]

Brigadier General Barnes's report to Oswald, written on 31 October from Tordesillas, describes his actions during the counterattack:

> It is unnecessary to enter into any minute detail of the operation of my brigade in the share assigned to it in driving the enemy from the post he had assumed on the canal at Villamuriel as they were performed under the immediate attentions of his Lordship the Commander of the Forces and yourself.
>
> But it may however be proper to account for a slight deviation in the first instance from the orders I received from the Marquis of Wellington, which were to cross the canal in column and wheel into line on the enemy's left flank and advance in that manner.
>
> Just as I had myself crossed the canal I perceived the enemy's left to give way and therefore considered that every object had been answered that was in the first instance expected from my Brigade, and consequently ordered it into the canal to protect it from the enemy's artillery; but on proceeding further along the canal I found that the French still maintained their position, I therefore formed line in the direction originally designed. This of necessity presented my right flank to much fire from the enemy's guns but the brigade continued to advance in the most steady manner until the enemy was effectually driven across the ford and as soon as the Major General Pringle directed his brigade to retire I ordered mine also to take shelter in the canal…[56]

In his letters home in December, Ensign George Young (2/38th Foot) described the counterattack:

> In the meantime they [the French] crossed in force both infantry and cavalry and for a time were masters of the ground we occupied, but his Lordship ordered us to charge with the bayonet, which we did in a most gallant style, not that I boast. Our brave fellows advanced not firing a shot till they came within forty yards of them, we all cheered them and rushed on with the bayonet, which the fellows did not like to stand, they were nearly all killed, wounded or drowned in re-crossing the river. We suffered severely in killed and wounded and I unfortunately got wounded by the bursting of a shell, a splinter of which struck me in the right side and arm. It took me a little above the wrist and broke it…

In a separate letter he added:

> [H]is Lordship ordered a second attack by flanking, which succeeded in killing, wounding or drowning nearly the whole, not without severe loss on our side, they

55 Napier, *History*, 1840, Vol.VI, p.xvi.

56 Wellington Papers, Barnes to Oswald, 31 October 1812 from Tordesillas.

> being covered by their artillery which played on us the whole time, yet our brave fellows charged them to the water's edge.[57]

Ensign George Freer (1/38th Foot) also described the pursuit of the French:

> The French had crossed a river and were advancing up the hill on which we were posted. A dry canal ran parallel to the river at the foot, further than which orders were given not to drive the French, of six fold number; but the impetuosity of the men charging downhill could not be suppressed, and we drove them through the river up to the mouths of their guns, within 50 yards of which we had a captain, Forster, killed, being actually cut in two parts by a cannon ball [Although severe, Matthew Forster survived this wound]. In retiring through the river we suffered considerably, but gaining the dry canal we kept the enemy from advancing for more than two hours.[58]

Thus, both Béchaud and Freer simultaneously claimed to have been outnumbered by six to one. Freer was presumably only counting Barnes's brigade (1,292 men) but counting both French brigades (4,573 men).

Douglas describes the 3/1st Foot and the 38th Foot advancing to the attack together:

> The Royals and the 38th went, which was none of the easiest jobs, as it was very steep and broken. The fire of the enemy slackened on seeing us move down, until we came on a level with their guns, and then the play began. Our first fire and advancing with the bayonet cleared the canal and here, if Lord Wellington's orders had been obeyed, our loss would have been trifling as we were to halt and keep possession of it, and then it would have been impossible for those dispossessed of their lodging to have escaped, as they became exposed to the two fires. But, instead of occupying this post, we were ordered to follow the fugitives to the river's brink, exposed to a front and flanking fire of round and grapeshot with occasional shells. One of the latter fell close to Lieut. [John] McKillegan, and he very wisely threw himself on the ground when it exploded, killed 5 and wounded a great many more.[59] The enemy were driven to the river's brink and were all either killed, wounded or made prisoners. Indeed there were very few of the latter class. We now fell back to the canal under a cloud of bullets. On the bank Col. Campbell's horse received a bullet between the shoe and hoof which caused it to kick most unmercifully. Dismounting and looking to see where the animal was hurt, he exclaimed (while his eyes flashed like fire), 'What ails the bugger…'[60]

---

57 Younge, 'Some Peninsular Letters', pp.512–3; letters written on the 26 and 10 December 1812, respectively. In the latter he also remarks that he had fully recovered from his wound.

58 Freer, 'Thirty-Eighth', p.299.

59 The Gazette gives the 3/1st casualties as 8 killed and 8 men wounded.

60 Monick (ed.), *Douglas*, p.59.

Thus, Douglas and Freer both stated that Wellington only wanted the canal cleared. However, we know that Wellington wanted his troops to cross the canal and retake the village. Consequently, it is likely that the comments of Douglas and Freer relate more to the losses incurred as the battalions pursued the French to the riverbank. Burroughs's account states that Barnes's horse was killed while he was commanding the 3/1st Foot at Palencia, but Wellington is clear, in his dispatch to Bathurst, that Lieutenant Colonel Colin Campbell commanded the battalion at Palencia.[61] Perhaps unsurprisingly Barnes does not mention his horse being killed in his report to Oswald and it remains a possibility that Burroughs confused Barnes and Campbell.[62]

61 Burroughs, *Narrative*, p.23.

62 Wellington Papers, Barnes to Oswald, 31 October 1812 from Tordesillas.

11

The End of the Action

As the allied counterattack got within striking distance of the river, the two grenadier companies of the 66e Ligne were stationed behind the mound near the village. Béchaud deployed them to cover the withdrawal of the skirmishers by positioning them at either end of the broken bridge. Béchaud ordered the grenadiers of the 6/66e Ligne to go to the right bank, close to the bridge. Meanwhile, the grenadiers of the 4/66e Ligne were sent back across the river to provide support from the left bank. However, the grenadiers of the 4/66e Ligne, 'half of them young men', were initially shaken and recoiled from their task, 'seeing the enemy closely for the first time', but the colonel and their officers steadied the company and got them into position. The grenadiers were then able to keep the approaching allied skirmishers at bay, while the rest of the brigade crossed the river and reformed into line of battle on the plain beyond.[1] Béchaud continues, 'in this moment of crisis, brave *Capitaine* Lafit[t]e, commander of a battalion [the first] of the 15e, was killed while inspiring some soldiers of the 15e to protect those who were re-crossing the river'.[2]

During the withdrawal of the French, Lawson's guns continued to bombard them as they re-crossed the river. Béchaud reports the effect on d'Arnauld's brigade as it retreated across the river close to the bridge 'during this critical time, the enemy artillery, posted on a point of rock that dominates Villamuriel fired shells incessantly on the ford, on the bridge, on the men who were very hurriedly re-crossing the river and on those who defended the crossing'.[3]

Meanwhile Burroughs observed the effect of the spherical case shot on Montfort's men as they crossed the river close to Calabazanos:

> The artillery on our heights now began to open on them, and the execution of the shrapnell [sic] shells soon became visible. The wood did not less feel the effects of that all-destructive shot, than those, to whom it offered a cover; and after the trees

1 Colin, 'Béchaud', p.409.
2 Colin, 'Béchaud', p.410.
3 Colin, 'Béchaud', p.409.

> had been pretty well stripped of their branches, the enemy re-crossed the river, having sustained much loss.[4]

The ford at Calabazanos is approximately 1,500 paces from Lawson's likely position on the hills above Villamuriel. This would have been at long range for his guns and certainly Montfort's brigade was less affected than Burroughs thought.

Meanwhile, at Palencia, Foy reported to Souham that the 6º Ejército had retired west, up onto the heathland on their way towards Valladolid. The 6º Ejército was at Cabezón on 26 October.[5]

On Wellington's right flank in the early morning, Gauthier personally led the 118e Ligne against the bridge across the Pisuerga at Tariego and his accompanying cavalry successfully rushed the bridge,[6] capturing it intact together with its covering party of 50 men, led by Captain Adam Ferguson, 58th Foot, as described by Burroughs:

> This party had lain the train, and put everything in order for the destruction of the bridge, and left it only a few moments before the enemy began to pass over; and while witnessing their approach, expecting every instant to see them blown in the air, they could not be more surprised than disappointed, at finding themselves made prisoners.[7]

Oman gives the covering party as 40 strong but describes them as being from the 4th, 30th and 44th Foot (Pringle's Brigade, 5th Division). However, Burroughs, Vane (i.e. Charles Stewart, Wellington's Adjutant General, 1809 – February 1812) and Mackenzie name Ferguson. Ferguson, a friend of Sir Walter Scott, was later knighted, and became Deputy Keeper of the Regalia at Edinburgh Castle. Mackenzie has Ferguson at Palencia, together with a covering force 'drawn from the second brigade [of the 5th Division]', and not Tariego. However, along with Burroughs, Stanhope is clear that the party of 50 men at Tariego was from the much closer 1st Division, to which he was attached as Deputy Assistant Quartermaster General. Ferguson and his men are not listed in the official casualty lists published in the *London Gazette*. Stanhope seems to blame Ferguson for the bridge not being blown on the evening of the 24th, however, as we have seen, Ferguson's party was delayed by a false report that the French had already crossed at Tariego.[8]

4 Burroughs, *Narrative*, p.24.
5 Girod, *Foy*, pp.381–2; AHNM, *Diversos/Colecciones*/101/n63.
6 Anon., *Historique du 118e régiment d'infanterie* (Paris: Charles-Lavauzelle, 1893), p.62.
7 Burroughs, *Narrative*, p.24.
8 C.W. Vane (Marquess of Londonderry), *Story of the Peninsular War* (London: Henry Colburn, 1848), p.343; *Army List*, 1812, pp.128, 252; 'McK', 'The Affair of Villa Muriel', p.542; Glover (ed.), *Eyewitness*, p.97; Oman, *History,* Vol.VI, p.79; J.T. Jones, *Journals of the Sieges Undertaken by the Allies in Spain: In the Years 1811 and 1812, with Notes* (London: T. Egerton, 1814), p.222.

Burgoyne gives further detail:

> It was found in the morning that the enemy were not at Tariego, and Pitts went off again to mine it; the enemy, however, were very close, and he was consequently hurried; and the enemy advancing against him, the mine was sprung, and failed, the enemy immediately crossed the bridge and made most of his working and covering parties (sixty two men) prisoners.[9]

After this success, the French cavalry moved on to the monastery at San Isidro. Captain Harry (Henry) Ross-Lewin (32nd Foot) describes what happened:

> Some of our troops occupied a large convent before the town, and we had some guns masked there, which were intended to open on the enemy as soon as they should approach sufficiently near. With better management this battery would have done much execution, but, very foolishly, the guns were discharged on the first appearance of the first few dragoons that came within range, and consequently the ruse failed of its desired effect.[10]

Presumably, Ross-Lewin is referring to Second Captain W. Greene's Brigade of six 6-pounders attached to the Sixth Division.

Having captured the bridge at Tariego intact, Gauthier did not press his advantage any further.[11]

During the action at Villamuriel, the main body of the Armée de Portugal arrived and deployed on the plain on the left bank of the Carrión, impressing Hale, who remarked that 'their numbers were so great, that the fields appeared to our view almost black'.[12] Looking on from the heights above Dueñas, Ross-Lewin described the sight:

> An uncommonly level plain, extending before our position to a considerable distance in every direction, afforded us an opportunity of viewing the whole French army, and so great did their numbers appear to be, that report makes Lord Wellington declare, on this occasion, that he had never seen so many Frenchmen in his front. They showed a splendid body of cavalry, and a formidable array of infantry formed in contiguous columns, and certainly they presented a most imposing military spectacle.[13]

Souham, clearly satisfied with having turned Wellington's position by both Foy's capture of Palencia and the capture of the Tariego bridge on the opposite flank, chose not to risk a further attack at Villamuriel on this day. Meanwhile, Wellington was satisfied with repulsing Maucune's attack and the fighting ended. The sun set at 5:20 p.m. and dusk was at 5:48 p.m.[14] Béchaud reported that:

---

9 Wrottesley, *Burgoyne*, pp.241–2; CHALLIS; *Army List*, 1813, pp.503–4.
10 Ross-Lewin, *With the 32nd*, pp.202–3; Leslie, *Dickson*, Vol.IV, pp.685–7.
11 Glover (ed.), *Bingham*, p.162.
12 Hale, *Journal*, p.95.
13 Ross-Lewin, *With the 32nd*, p.203.
14 USNO; times in local time.

> The two regiments [15e and 66e Ligne] promptly rallied in the plain, reordered in line of battle, and maintained some skirmishers along the river during the rest of the evening. The night was spent very quietly, we saw early the evacuation of the British, and at midnight parties were sent to search for biscuit in Palencia and others to mend the bridge at Villamuriel.[15]

De Tarragon describes the 15e Ligne and part of the Pinoteau's brigade being in Villamuriel until nightfall on 25 October, but no other source supports this. At this time, *Général de Brigade* Pierre Armand Pinoteau commanded the 6e Division, however in mid-1813 he became the commander of Maucune's first brigade, in place of d'Arnauld.[16]

Douglas recorded the British perspective:

> We took up our lodgings here [at the canal] for the night but were greatly annoyed with shells as long as light remained. At dusk we threw out our pickets, having sentries close to the river to prevent surprise, and dare not so much as light a pipe while the boys on the other side were making themselves quite at home. The night was very cold, and having no means of keeping ourselves warm, it set sore on the old ague men from Walcheren. Before night we could hear the guns and baggage on the move, and as day began to dawn our pickets were called in and we resumed our march to the front.[17]

Lawson's diary for this day reveals perhaps a greater concern for the behaviour of his men overnight than during battle itself:

> 25. Remain in position at Villamuriel and were attacked by the enemy, the 5th Division only having care of that post. My brigade losses 3 killed, 6 wounded. One officer wounded and a gun carriage disabled with one horse and one mule wounded. Most of the men again drunk and in the morning of the 26th Gunner [Joseph] Reed so mutinous that I was obliged to send him away to the provost guard. Gunner Jones deserts.[18]

Lieutenant Peter Bowlby (2/4th Foot) was equally sanguine, 'having blown up the bridges and driven the French back across the fords [we] gave the remainder of the army a day's rest.'[19]

Around 3:00 a.m. on the 26th, Wellington broke camp and continued his retreat.[20] Hale has them leaving at 4:00 a.m.

---

15 Colin, 'Béchaud', p.410.

16 De Tarragon, *Historique*, p.220.

17 Monick (ed.), *Douglas*, p.60.

18 Leslie, *Dickson*, Vol.IV, p.712; The muster roll indicates that Jones is likely to be Gunner John Jones.

19 NAM, Acc. No. 2002-02-729, p.13.

20 J. Gurwood (ed.), *Selections from the Dispatches and General Orders of Field Marshall the Duke of Wellington* (London: John Murray, 1851), p.635; Glover (ed.), *Eyewitness*, p.98; Hale, *Journal*, p.95.

Béchaud tells us that in advancing on Dueñas:

> On the 26th the vanguard crossed the Carrion at the ford near Villamuriel bridge, in which village they found many wounded English and even some others who were uninjured, who were taken prisoner; the different arms crossed the old line of the English, and reaching the top, they found a huge, uncultivated plateau covered with rocks or ferns, which made marching very difficult.[21]

An account in the regimental history of the 44th Foot gives a British perspective:

> All the wounded were left on the ground, the baggage and women of the fifth division falling into the hands of the enemy. Assistant Surgeon [John] Collins of the 44th was sent on the following morning to take care of the wounded, and had a rouleau of doubloons given to him by the Commissary General; a drunken trumpeter of the French army, however, was the first person that met him after starting, and robbed him of the money. The poor doctor was then marched to the rear, and never saw the ill-fated wounded soldiers, who were left to the mercies of the enemy's surgeons.[22]

This is confirmed by the monthly return of the battalion, 'Assistant Surgeon J Collins was absent on command with [the] wounded in the enemies [sic] hands.'[23]

Le Mesurier (1/9th Foot) gave further insights into the circumstances of the retreat:

> Seven men that had been severely wounded at the hospital station which was on the top of a hill in rear of the village, and were left there by the waggon train, are returned missing instead of wounded and missing, but it would not have looked well in a dispatch to have said that our wounded were left on the field.[24]

In a subsequent letter, he added further detail:

> A corporal of ours that was taken at the bridge of Muriel, having been wounded, has joined us. He made his escape from Palencia. He says that, after being there 3 or 4 days, the French retired in consequence of a Spanish force advancing, and left all their sick and wounded behind. The Spaniards immediately collected as many mules and horses as could be found and sent the English away.[25]

The monthly return for the battalion confirms that '1 serjeant and 7 rank and file were wounded and left on the field.'[26]

---

21 Colin, 'Béchaud', p.89.
22 Carter, *Forty-fourth*, p.69.
23 TNA, WO17/156; 44th Foot 1808–1812, monthly return for second battalion, November 1812.
24 Greenwood (ed.), *Le Mesurier*, p.146; letter written 29 December 1812.
25 Greenwood (ed.), *Le Mesurier*, pp.150–1; letter written 11 January 1813.
26 TNA,WO17/110; monthly return, 9th Foot 1803–12, first battalion for November 1812.

12

The Aftermath

Wellington described the action at Villamuriel in his dispatch to the Earl Bathurst, Secretary of State for War and the Colonies, from Cabezón de Pisuerga on 26 October:

> The army continued its march on the 24th, and took up its ground on the Carrion, with its right at Dueñas, and left at Villa-muriel; and the 1st batt. 1st Guards joined us from Coruña. I halted there on the 25th, and the enemy attacked our left at Villa Muriel. They were repulsed, however, by the 5th division of infantry, under the command of Major General Oswald, in the absence of Lieut. General Leith, on account of indisposition.
>
> I had directed the 3rd batt. of the Royals to march to Palencia, to protect the destruction of the bridges over the Carrion at that place; but it appears that the enemy assembled in such force at that point, that Lieut. Colonel Campbell thought it necessary to retire upon Villa Muriel, and the enemy passed the Carrion at Palencia.
>
> This rendered it necessary to change our front, and I directed Major General Oswald to throw back our left, and the Spanish troops upon the heights, and to maintain the Carrion with the right of the 5th division. The bridge of Villa Muriel was destroyed, but the enemy discovered a ford, and passed over a considerable body of cavalry and infantry. I made Major General Pringle and Brig. General Barnes attack these troops, under the orders of Major General Oswald; in which attack the Spanish troops co-operated, and they were driven across the river with considerable loss. The fire upon the left had been very severe throughout the day, from which we suffered a good deal; and Major General Don M. de Alava was unfortunately wounded while urging on the Spanish infantry in the pursuit of the enemy.
>
> I broke up this morning from the Carrion, and marched upon Cabezón del Campo [sic], where I have crossed the Pisuerga. The enemy appear to be moving in this direction from Dueñas. I propose to halt here tomorrow.[1]

1 *London Gazette*, 16,669, 17 November 1812, p.2321; TNA, WO1/256 War department in letters and papers, pp.117–119.

However, Le Mesurier pointed out that Wellington's dispatch was incomplete, 'General Hay told Coll: Craufurd that Genl: Oswald's report of our conduct at Villa Muriel had been sent in too late for any of his Lordship's observation in the dispatch'.[2] In that report to Wellington, dated 1 November at Tordesillas, Oswald wrote:

> I have the honour to transmit for your Lordship's information the reports made to me by the Genl and Comg Officers of corps respecting the affair of the 25th ult. As your Lordship superintended, I directed the principal attack for the recovery of the bridge and village of Villa Muriel. It is superfluous for me to enter into details respecting the conduct of the troops. Still however I much value the gallant manner in which the Brunswick Light Comps supported by the 2nd Brigade under M. Gl Pringle led into the village whilst occupied by a big defence force a great portion of which was then driven into the Carrion and destroyed in the attempt to re-cross that river. Mr Lawson's brigade of artillery particularly distinguished itself supporting for a long time an unequal contest against the enemy. The circumstances respecting the retreat of the Royals shall be the subject, according to your Ldship's direction, of a separate report.
>
> I am sorry to say that considering the numbers engaged our loss has been considerable…[3]

However, in his later response to Napier, Oswald qualified his statement, stating that '… the casualties in the division were not numerous especially when the fire it was exposed to is considered'.[4]

Lieutenant Colonel Alexander Gordon, writing on 29 October to Lord Aberdeen, described the proceedings at Villamuriel as follows:

> In the meantime he [the enemy] opened a very heavy cannonade upon the village of Cabazanca [Villamuriel de Cerrato] in our centre held by the 5th Division and where there was also a bridge over the Carrion which however, we had blown up. In consequence of our left being turned we were obliged to move our army to the heights above the Carrion and to throw back our left, holding at the same time our post upon the river particularly at the village in the centre where there was a ford; by some mistake or other this village was given up and the enemy soon crossed over about 2,000 men immediately under our position. As soon as we saw this, we ordered them to be attacked, which was done by part of the 5th Division and two regiments of Spaniards. We soon drove them across the river with great loss and made some prisoners…[5]

Pringle concluded his report to Oswald by acknowledging the conduct of his men:

> [T]o inform that the conduct of the officers and men under my command was such as to merit my highest approbation and I must beg to call to your observation, for the information of the Com[mander] of the Forces, the gallant

2 Greenwood, *Le Mesurier*, p.146; letter written 29 December 1812.

3 Wellington Papers, Oswald to Wellington, 1 November 1812.

> conduct of Lt. Colonel [Francis] Brooke commanding the 1st battalion of the 4th Regt. and Colonel [Alexander] Hamilton commanding the 30th Regt., Lt. Col. [George] Harding (who was wounded early in the action) commanding the 44th Regt. and of Captain [John Cleland] Guthrie, who succeeded to the command of the regt. on Colonel Harding being obliged to leave the field and I must also beg to mention to you the very gallant conduct of the 9th Regiment under the command of Lt Col [Henry] Crawford [sic] who also commanded the picquets of the 1st Brigade who were engaged during the whole of the day and repulsed every attempt of the enemy to cross the fords, Lieutenant Häusler of the Brunswick Light Infantry also particularly distinguished himself and was the only officer of that corps with us who was not killed or wounded. I received every assistance from my own personal staff during the day.[6]

There are two versions of this report, the one in the Wellington Papers and the other in Pringle's own papers. This is the one sent to Wellington via Oswald. The differences between the two copies are not large: for example, Pringle specifies 'my brigade major and my aide de camp' when referring to 'my own personal staff' in his own copy.

In contrast to what he confided to his diary, Lawson was sure to complement his men in his report to Oswald written from Cabezón on 27 October 1812:

> I have the honour to acquaint you that my returns of killed wounded and missing of the brigade under my command in the affair of the 25th inst, are already transmitted to Lt. Col. Berkely.[sic] These numbers you will perceive are for my strength considerable, but I trust that its contents will have met with your approbation; – I beg leave to express to you my sense of the exertions and good conduct of my two only [sic] officers present, Lts Johnstone and Sinclair, as well as the generality of my gunners and drivers.[7]

On 17 January 1813, in his order of the day, Marshal William Carr Beresford, commander in chief of the Portuguese Army, recognised the gallantry and losses of the Caçadores N.8 at Villamuriel.[8] On 8 February 1813, Beresford promoted Hill (*tenente-coronel*), Western (*major*), Pereira de Macedo (*capitão*) and Salustiano da Costa e Sá (*tenente*) specifically for their conduct at Villamuriel on 25 October.

Souham's chief of staff, Baron de Lamartinière, wrote a report on the operations of the Armée de Portugal between 17 and 31 October 1812, which contains the following description of Villamuriel:

> The army marched on Magaz, spent the night and began moving on the 25th at daybreak.
>
> The enemy was already covered by the Carrion, along which he guarded all of the bridges; he took positions on the steep hills of Dueñas and occupied the

6 Wellington Papers, Pringle to Oswald; UML, GB 133 Eng MSS 1273, item 27.
7 Wellington Papers, Lawson to Oswald, 27 October 1812.
8 Santos, *Ordens*, 1813, p.12.

convent of San Isidro, near the confluence of that river with the Pisuerga, with many infantry and cannon, which also protected the batteries on the right bank. General Maucune approached them with the 5e Division and the light cavalry. His artillery, deployed before being seen, brought havoc and disorder in the masses who sought safety in the hills that dominate the Carrion. Some companies of skirmishers immediately raced to seize the bridge, it exploded in their faces, but not one man was wounded. Several hours passed in exchanges of cannon fire and skirmishing. A squadron was ordered to cross the ford, each rider taking a *voltigeur* behind him. This movement was too slow for the impatience of the *voltigeurs*; they rushed into the river; they drove back the enemy with loss; the foot of the whole position was cleared.

The commander in chief of the British army, concerned for the fate of some cannon thus exposed, decided at 4 o'clock in the afternoon to attack this division with an immense superiority of force. So he ordered 4 very deep infantry columns to descend from the plateau. The light cavalry brigade retreated across a ford. The 5e Division re-crossed at that of Villamuriel, leaving on the right bank part of its 1st brigade stationed in the village, and a good line of skirmishers. These troops fought with great courage; their fire was very deadly. Our artillery, in support from the left bank, kept up an incessant and vigorous fire and dispersed the columns of attack; the enemy could no longer maintain the fight as skirmishers... In the evening we gave them possession of the village of Villamuriel, which it was not possible to hold overnight...[9]

Souham himself wrote to the Minister of War:

In the morning of the 25th, General Maucune sent a reconnaissance along the road to Dueñas, and confirmed that the English army occupied the heights beyond this town, its front covered by the Carrion, and having strong detachments responsible for defending the approaches to the bridges at both San Isidro and Villamuriel. General Maucune strongly attacked the bridgehead of Villamuriel with the 5e Division. The enemy was overthrown and thrown back in an instant to the other side of the river. As our troops dashed to the bridge, the explosion of a mine, which had been prepared, destroyed one of the arches, and stopped the march of the column that was going to take it. I felt the need to promptly force the enemy to evacuate the bridge of San Isidro, which was also mined, and I had given the order to cross the bridge over the Pisuerga below Baños [de Cerrato]; but this bridge exploded at the time when this movement was going to be carried out. However, the mine was not entirely successful and the portion of the arch which had only been partly destroyed allowed a few squadrons of dragoons to cross onto the left bank, who ardently pursued the English infantry that guarded the bridge, who in turn, although supported by cavalry, were surrounded and taken prisoner. The enemy, seeing that we were masters of the left bank of the Pisuerga, was quick to accelerate his retirement, and blew up the bridge of San Isidro, on the great road of Torquemada to Dueñas.

---

9 Gurwood (ed.), *Dispatches*, Vol.VI, pp.775–6.

> We were immediately engaged with the repair of bridges. These works were protected by the 5e Division and the artillery placed on the left bank of the Carrion, who cannonaded the enemy masses…[10]

The claims for casualties inevitably varied between the participants. Stanhope wrote that 'the French suffered severely. I think we must have lost between 2 and 300 men'.[11] Assistant Quartermaster General Lieutenant Colonel William Gomm described 'a heavy day the 5th Division passed at the bridge of Villamuriel on the 25th. We lost nearly 600 men but did all that was expected of us'.[12] Souham's chief of staff, Baron de Lamartinière concluded his report:

> This affair has cost them 1,000–1,200 men; an English General and the Spanish General Alava were also wounded… Our loss was 30 killed, 5 or 6 drowned, 180 wounded, and 30 prisoners. Mr. Burgevin, General Chauvel's *aide de camp*, was killed in the midst of the English ranks. *Capitaine*s Lafond and Lachapelle, *aides de camp* to General Maucune, behaved with brilliant bravery in fighting with our skirmishers, leading them and plunging into the middle of those of the enemy, making them prisoners. *Chef de Bataillon* Girard, chief of staff of the 5e Division, received a severe contusion in the shoulder, but did not want to leave the battlefield… At end of this day, 1,000 prisoners were gathered at headquarters…[13]

Similarly Souham concluded his report with a reference to 'enemy masses, who had lost 1,000 men, including killed, wounded, and prisoners, on this day.' Deducting the prisoners captured at and near Palencia and Tariego, this suggests that Souham believed that the British and allied army lost some 450 men, from all causes, at Villamuriel itself.[14] On the other hand, Lamartinière's figure of 1,000 prisoners included the 100 men taken by Foy at Palencia and the 50 captured at Tariego, together with the 400 men captured by the Berg Lancers near Palencia.[15] Consequently, he is suggesting that approximately 450 British and allied men were captured at Villamuriel.

Consistent with these reports, Béchaud also estimated British and Allied losses at 1,200 men.[16] Finally, *France Militaire* reported the casualties as 1,200 Anglo-Portuguese and 250 French.[17]

Likewise, the British and allied estimates of the French casualties vary from account to account. As already reported, Wellington described their loss as 'considerable'. Liñan reported that his brigade killed three officers and 86 other ranks as well as taking 104 prisoners.[18] Other British eyewitnesses

10 Wellington (ed.), *Supplementary Despatches*, Vol.XIV, pp.149–151.

11 Glover (ed.), *Eyewitness*, p.97.

12 Carr-Gomm, *Gomm*, p.289.

13 Gurwood (ed.), *Dispatches*, Vol.VI, pp.775–6.

14 Wellington (ed.), *Supplementary Despatches*, Vol.XIV, pp.149–151.

15 Girod, *Foy*, p.381; Wellington (ed.), *Supplementary Despatches*, Vol.XIV, p.147; Ardenne, *Bergische Lanziers*, p.74.

16 Colin, 'Béchaud', p.407.

17 A. Hugo, *France militaire: histoire des armées françaises de terre et de mer, de 1792 à 1833* (Paris: Delloye, 1837), Vol.V, pp.30–32.

18 AHNM, *Diversos/Colecciones*/101/n63.

push this total of captured Frenchmen to over 700. Oman gives the casualties as approximately 500 for each side, with the British and Portuguese losing, at Villamuriel and Palencia, 440 men, killed and wounded. Oman further states that Oswald's 5th Division casualties included 150 men captured by the French on 25 October.[19] Gates gives the casualties at Villamuriel as more than 800 Allied compared with 350 French.[20]

British and Allied Casualties

The following table summarises the losses of Oswald's 5th Division incurred between 22 and 29 October, as reported in the *London Gazette*.[21]

	Officers				Other Ranks						
Unit	Killed	Wounded	Missing	Total	Killed	Wounded	Missing	Total	Total	Strength, 25 Oct.	% Loss, 22–29 Oct.
3/1st Foot	0	0	0	0	8	8	27	43	43	418	10
1/9th Foot	0	5	1	6	7	37	33	77	83	338	25
1/38th Foot	1	0	1	2	3	21	0	24	26	316	8
2/38th Foot	0	3	0	3	1	20	3	24	27	175	15
1/4th Foot	0	2	0	2	5	44	3	52	54	395	14
2/4th Foot	0	0	0	0	1	5	18	24	24	335	7
2/30th Foot	0	7	0	7	4	25	10	39	46	229	20
2/44th Foot	1	3	0	4	4	22	0	26	30	165	18
Royal Artillery	0	2	0	2	3	4	8	15	17		
Brunswick Oels Light Infantry	2	1	0	3	7	26	20	53	56		
Portuguese	0	10	0	10	38	136	17	191	201	1,807	11
Totals	5	32	2	39	81	348	130	559	598	4,178	13

Note:

Strength is 'Present under arms at headquarters' excluding staff: the eight British battalions had 21 staff between them.

These casualty figures have been compared to the regimental casualty returns, pay-lists, monthly returns and other sources.

3/1st Foot: Douglas describes how five men were killed by one shell in the counterattack at Villamuriel but mentions no fatalities at Palencia. The pay-list for the battalion confirms that seven men, one sergeant, one corporal and five privates, were 'killed in action' specifically on 25 October, the remaining *Gazette* casualty, a sergeant, is unidentified. The pay-list suggests that the

19 Oman, *History*, Vol.VI, pp.81, 153, 747.

20 D. Gates, *The Spanish Ulcer, A History of the Peninsular War* (London: Allen and Unwin, 1986), pp.372–3.

21 *London Gazette*, 16,675, 3 December 1812, pp.2417–8.

missing sergeant was James Allen who was sick in hospital at Salamanca and died on the 13 October, but this is outside of the reporting window of the *Gazette*.[22] Oman states that the missing men, one sergeant and 26 rank and file, were captured at the bridge in Palencia rather than at Villamuriel. However, the pay-list shows a greater number of men missing, 35 divided into two groups, 27 men 'missing' and eight men 'prisoners of war', while the casualty return has one of these missing recorded as a prisoner of war. Douglas confirms that the men left behind at Palencia were those so badly wounded that they couldn't get away, including some of the ten men hit by the same round shot.[23] Nicholas Marcel also perhaps described the same incident; 'The 2/69e Ligne arrived at the bridge that the English had mined; their sappers were going to ignite the fuse when a well-fitting cannonball threw seven of them on the ground'.[24]

Interestingly the 'prisoners of war' from the pay-list are distributed one or two from each of the five even numbered companies, suggesting, the difference between platoons and companies notwithstanding, that they were inflicted by Douglas's and Marcel's single cannonball striking the battalion while formed in column of grand divisions. However, Douglas describes the battalion as being formed in open column of companies rather than of grand divisions.

It is probable that the author of the pay-list distinguished between those he knew were left behind at Palencia, the prisoners of war, from the missing who were of unknown fate, probably divided between the actions at Villamuriel and Palencia. The wounded mentioned in the *Gazette* comprised one sergeant and seven rank and file.

1/9th Foot: The November monthly return includes the following comments, '1 serjeant and 7 rank and file were wounded and left on the field… Of the numbers returned dead, 1 serjeant and 6 rank and file were killed in action on the 25th ultimo [October]' and 'Lieut. James Whitley, with 25 rank and file of the numbers returned missing were detached by order of Lt. Col. Gomm Assistant Quartermaster General on the 25th Ultimo'.[25]

The battalion pay-list names the men killed on 25 October, as Sergeant Thomas Barefot, Corporal Richard Maddox, Privates James Buy, James Clark, Edward Davis, John Kennedy, and William Smith (#757).[26] The pay-list further details seven men as 'wounded left in the field missing', three men as 'missing' and nineteen men 'missing taken in the field' on 25 October and a further man, Corporal John Randle 'missing taken in the field', whom Le Mesurier confirms was taken at the 'Bridge of Muriel' (Le Mesurier does not mention Randle by name but gives his rank and Randle is the only corporal named as 'missing taken in the field', in the pay-list). Le Mesurier added that Randle had been wounded but subsequently escaped and returned to the regiment.[27]

---

22 TNA, WO12/2012, quarterly pay-list of the 3/1st Foot, 25 September to 24 December 1812.

23 TNA, WO25/1506; Oman, *History*, Vol.VI, p.79; Monick (ed.), *Douglas*, pp.56–9.

24 Marcel, *Campagnes*, p.179.

25 TNA, WO17/110, November monthly return, first battalion.

26 TNA, WO12/2665, pay-list 24 December 1812, 1/9th Foot.

27 Greenwood, (ed.) *Le Mesurier*, pp.150–1.

The total of 30 missing men leaves three men unaccounted for, but the pay-list includes four privates, who were missing at the October muster, but the date of their disappearance is not included. One of these men, Private John Thorne was 'wounded, left in the field', presumably at Villamuriel.

Le Mesurier wrote that 'we lost half our battn: on the 25th… having only 168 rank and file in the field'. The total of 83 casualties as given in the Gazette, however, includes only 77 killed, wounded and missing men from the rank and file and these include the men from Whitley's detached company. This number is only a quarter of the 280 rank and file who were 'fit for duty' at headquarters as given in the October monthly return. It is possible that Le Mesurier was referring only to the party that he was with, for example Hale's 'two hundred men… very convenient to the bridge'. Nevertheless, the losses of the 1/9th Foot were approximately double those of the average for the division.[28]

1/38th Foot: The quarterly pay-list and casualty return show that three of the wounded, Privates Joseph Barlow, James Murdock and Thomas Woodhouse, died of their wounds on 27, 26 and 26 October respectively. The battalion also lost one man on 25 October and a further seven on the 26th, who all became prisoners of war, presumably after being wounded.[29]

2/38th Foot: The quarterly pay-list shows that none of the missing were recorded on the 25th but that two men had gone missing on the 23rd and two more on 24 October, with a further man taken prisoner of war on the 26th. Private Joel Ball died on 23 October.[30]

1/4th Foot: The November monthly return includes the following comment, '1 Serjeant and 4 rank and file killed in action 25th October 1812'.[31] The quarterly pay-list includes the names of 11 men (one sergeant, two corporals, one drummer and seven privates) taken prisoner of war on 25 October 1812. These men were Sergeant William Rhoades (wounded), Corporals Charles Moon and Vincent Philpott, Privates Henry Conard, James Duffin, John Ellis and James Whiting. The pay-list also shows that one of the wounded men, Corporal David Hopkins, died of his wounds on 26 October.[32]

2/4th Foot: The quarterly pay-list shows that only 16 men went missing on the 25th, although in the period covered by the Gazette report, 22–29 October, the battalion lost a total of 49 men missing.[33]

2/30th Foot: The November monthly return includes the following comment, '26 rank and file missing on the march from Burgos supposed taken by the

28 Greenwood, (ed.) *Le Mesurier*, p.139; Hale, *Journal*, p.94.
29 TNA, WO12/5184, pay-list 24 December 1812, 1/38th Foot; WO25/1742, casualty return for October to November 1812.
30 TNA, WO12/5245, pay-list 24 December 1812, 2/38th Foot.
31 TNA, WO17/101, November monthly return, first battalion.
32 TNA, WO12/2206, pay-list 24 December 1812, 1/4th Foot.
33 TNA, WO12/2265, pay-list 24 December 1812.

enemy, since last monthly return, 9 of whom were wounded in the action at Villamuriel'.[34]

The pay-list names 16 men as missing on 25 October and another 12 in the period 21–26 October.[35] The regimental history names the men killed as Sergeants James Keith, of Paisley, and John Nightingale, of London, and Private Patrick Shearin of Longford. The regimental history also names Private Morgan Blakeney of Athy as being killed at Villamuriel, presumably based on the pay-list which records him as 'Died 25th Oct'. However, in the casualty return he is described as missing. This man clearly survived and is named as a recipient of the Military General Service Medal. His discharge papers describe him as being born in the Parish of Faryland, Carlow in Ireland (Athy is 13 miles north of Carlow) in 1789 and being discharged in 1817, having also served at Waterloo. His pension records show that he died in 1858 at the age of 73, indicating a different birth year of 1785.[36]

The regimental history also names Private Rodney Tansey as subsequently dying of wounds received at Villamuriel.[37] The pay-list shows that Private Tansey died on 11 November and also records Sergeant Keith and Private Shearin as 'Killed 25 Oct.' and that Sergeant John Nightingale was wounded on the 25th but died of his wounds the next day.[38]

2/44th Foot: Pringle's casualty return for the second brigade lists only two other ranks from the 2/44th Foot as being killed on the 25 October rather than the four reported in the *Gazette*. The pay-list shows that Sergeant Thomas Brooks and Private William Murray were killed in action on the 25th while Corporal Patt [sic] Martin, died of his wounds on 28 October. The other two men counted in the *Gazette* were Sergeant William Davey who died in hospital on the 24th and Private William Reilly who died in hospital on 25 October. Pringle's casualty return covers the period to 26 October and therefore counted Corporal Martin amongst the wounded.[39]

The *Historical Record* of the 44th Foot records that the after the action, 'the strength of the battalion was reduced to only 42 men of all ranks fit for duty at regimental headquarters.' The history also records that Sergeant Farrell was the only man of the seventh company still with the colours. The November monthly return of the battalion confirms that '2 serjeants, 2 drummers and 17 rank and file were taken at the bridge of Placencia [sic] and the village of Villamuriel on the 25th October'.[40] The mention of the bridge at Palencia implies that some of the 2/44th also went to Palencia, but this is not mentioned in other primary accounts including Pringle's own report to

34 TNA, WO17/138, November monthly return, 2/30th Foot.

35 TNA, WO12/4646; pay-list 24 December 1812.

36 TNA, WO12/4646; pay-list 24 December 1812; WO25 1695, casualty return, Oct. to Nov. 1812; WO97/484/77, Discharge papers; WO22/180, p.118, Pension records.

37 Bannatyne, *Thirtieth*, pp.285–289.

38 TNA, WO12/4646, pay-list 24 December 1812.

39 UML, GB 133 Eng MSS 1273, item 26, casualty return for Pringle's brigade; TNA, WO12/5716, pay-list 24 December 1812, 2/44th Foot.

40 Carter, *Forty-Fourth*, p.68; TNA, WO17/156, November monthly return, second battalion.

Oswald. They may however have formed part of Lieutenant Reid's initial 100 strong covering force.[41]

Of these men, the pay-list shows that while the two drummers, seven privates and a 'boy', became prisoners of war on 25 October, the two sergeants, a corporal and nine further privates became prisoners of war during the retreat between 22 and 24 October inclusive.[42]

Royal Artillery: The *Gazette* figures cover the regiment as a whole, in his diary Lawson gave his casualties as; one officer wounded, three other ranks killed, seven wounded and one missing.[43] The muster roll names the three men killed as Gunners John Hardy, Edward Rogers and John Davidson.[44] One of the wounded appears to be Gunner John Chapman who lost his left leg 'on the retreat from Burgos'.[45]

The Duke of Brunswick Oels Light Infantry: these casualties will also include those for the companies with the other Divisions (i.e. one company in the 4th Division and nine in the 7th Division). However, the three officers who were killed or wounded were all at Villamuriel. On 1 November the two companies with the 5th Division had a present under arms strength of 39 (Barnes's Brigade) and 41 (Pringle's Brigade) men compared to 61 and 62 men respectively in July after Salamanca.[46] However, in addition to the officers, Pringle's casualty return shows that the 10th Company suffered 1 rank and file killed, 2 wounded and 5 missing on 25 October. It further shows that this company lost another 5 men 'missing' on the other days in the period 21 to 26 October inclusive.[47] Together these sources suggest that perhaps 20 of the 56 casualties listed here were inflicted at Villamuriel.

Portuguese: All 10 of the officers named in the *Gazette* are from Spry's Brigade, which strongly suggests that all the killed and wounded casualties mentioned were also from Spry's Brigade. Indeed, Beresford recorded that the Caçadores N.8 lost half their men in killed and wounded (i.e. approximately 200 men) on 25 October.[48]

The names of the officer casualties for 25 October 1812, as separately listed in the *London Gazette* are as follows. For the British and Brunswick men, given names have been added, in parenthesis, and surnames corrected using the *Army List* entries for 1812 and 1813:[49]

41 Oman, History, Vol.VI, p.79; Oman was perhaps mistaken in describing a 40-strong covering force from Pringle's brigade at Tariego, when it was at the much closer Palencia.

42 TNA, WO12/5716; pay-list 24 December 1812.

43 Leslie, *Dickson*, Vol.IV, p.712.

44 TNA, WO10/916, Muster Roll, Lawson's company for October 1812.

45 TNA, WO97/1219/061.

46 *Army List*, 1812, pp.414–5; R. Foster, 'Duke of Brunswick Oels (Jäegers)', *Napoleon Series*, at <http://www.napoleon-series.org/military/organization/Britain/Infantry/WellingtonsRegiments/c_BrunswickOels.html>, accessed 15 January 2014.

47 UML, GB 133 Eng MSS 1273, item 26, casualty return for Pringle's Brigade.

48 Santos, *Ordens*, 1813, p.12.

49 *London Gazette*, 16,675, 3 December 1812, p.2418.

Killed

1/38th Foot: Captain [Andrew] Todd

2/44th Foot: Lieutenant [William Fitzmaurice] Lennon

The Duke of Brunswick Oels Light Infantry: Captain [Georg David von] Sternfeld and Lieutenant [Karl] Hartwig. Challis incorrectly identified San Muñoz as the place of Sternfeld's death on 25 October 1812–San Muñoz was fought on 17 November. This error is repeated for all the Brunswick officers.

Wounded

Royal Artillery: Lieutenant [James William] Johnston

1/4th Foot: Lieutenant-Colonel [John] Piper, slightly; Lieutenant [W.B.C.] Edgell, severely.

1/9th Foot: Lieutenants [John] Ackland, [Jeremiah] Taylor, [Honourable William] Curzon and [John Butler] Ford, severely; Lieutentant [Edward] Ross-Lewin, slightly.[50] Ackland lost the use of a hand, for which he received a pension of £100. The return places his wounding at Burgos, but he is not included in the casualty lists for the siege of Burgos.[51] Taylor is given as Jeremiah Taylor in Harts, which records his service at Villamuriel. This is also the case in his obituary, however the 1812, 1813 and the 1815 Army Lists as well as the monthly returns for the 9th Foot record his name as John.[52] Le Mesurier wrote that 'poor Ford was severely wounded in the thigh and leg and had balls through his coat'.[53]

2/30th Foot: Lieutenant [John] Rumley and Ensign [George] Madden, severely;[54] Captain [John] Hitchin, Lieutenant [Matthias] Andrews,[55] Lieutenant [George] Brisac, Ensigns [Henry] Beere and [Francis] Tincombe, slightly.

2/44th Foot: Lieutenant-Colonel [George] Harding, slightly [in the face];[56] Lieutenant [Henry] Elwin, dangerously; Ensign [James] Smith, severely. The battalion monthly return reports that Lieutenant Elwin died of his wounds on 14 November.[57] It also records that Ensign James Smith died of his wounds

50 TNA, WO17/110; Ross-Lewin, *With the 32nd*, p.xv; *Army List*, 1813, p.147 gives his surname as Ross-Lewen but the monthly returns of the 1/9th Foot gives it as Ross-Lewin. Edward was a kinsman of Harry Ross-Lewin.

51 Hall, *History*, p.19; War Office, *Return of the Names of the Officers in the Army* (London: House of Commons, 1818), pp.6–7; *London Gazette*, 3 October (16,654), 10 October (16,657), 13 October (16,658), 17 November 1812 (16,670).

52 *Hart's New Army List*, 1850, p.262; 'Obituary', *USM* (1862), Vol.XCVIII, p.440; CHALLIS.

53 Greenwood, *Le Mesurier*, p.138.

54 TNA, WO17/138; Hall, *History*, p.413; *Army Lists*, 1812 and 1813, spell Madden's surname as Modden, but he appears as Madden in the *Gazette*, the battalion monthly muster rolls and CHALLIS. Hall lists him as Modden.

55 Hall, *History*, pp.27–8.

56 'Obituary', *The Gentleman's Magazine*, July 1829, Vol.XCIX, p.89.

57 TNA, WO17/156, November 1812 monthly return, second battalion.

on 30 October 1812. (Both Carter and Hall incorrectly identify this officer as Ensign Michael Smith, who arrived in the Peninsula only in February 1813).[58]

The Duke of Brunswick Oels Light Infantry: Captain [Ludwig von] Nassau, severely.

The corrected and full Portuguese names are given below in parenthesis based on both Beresford's orders of the day and an archival record of the casualties of the Caçadores N.8.[59]

Regimento de Infantaria N.3: Ensign Joze de Moneada. The best candidate for this officer in RI N.3 is the paymaster, *Tenente* Joaquim Jozé Pereira de Macedo. However, a similarly named officer, *Alferes* José Maria Moncada of the RI N.15 may be the man referred to in the Gazette.[60]

Caçadores N.8: *Major* [Dudley St. Leger] Hill, slightly; *Capitão* [Charles] Western, severely; *Capitão* Manuel Castin [Manoel Caetano Ferraz], slightly;[61] *Tenentes* Antonio Carlos [Antonio Carlos Pereira de Macedo] and Joao Baptist [João Baptista Ferreira], severely; *Tenente* Domingo Fortenha [Domingos de Sá Pereira Farinha], slightly; *Alferes* Joao dos Santos [Jose Fernandes dos Santos], Joao Sebastiano [Joao Saliustiano da Costa e Sá], and Rodrigo Navarre [Rodrigo Navarro de Andrade], and *Ajudante* [James] Leech, severely.[62] Western received a pension of £100 for 'a wound received at the Carrion'.[63] Neither *Capitão* Manoel Caetano Ferraz or *Tenente* João Baptista Ferreira are included in the Caçadores N.8 casualty list from the Lisbon archives. However, Ferreira is separately listed as either killed in action or died of his wounds at the combat on the Carrion. He and Ovens are the only two officers in Portuguese service so listed.[64]

Missing

1/9th Foot: Lieutenant [James] Whitley.

1/38th Foot: Brevet-Major [Thomas] Evans. He was taken prisoner during the night of 24 October when returning from duty in Dueñas.[65]

58 TNA, WO17/156 (monthly return), WO12/5716 (pay-list); Carter, *Forty-Fourth*, pp.41–42, 68; Hall, *History*, p.522, CHALLIS.

59 AHM, PT/AHM/DIV/3/12/09/7; Santos, *Ordens*, 1810, p.105; 1811, pp.134, 223; 1812, pp.42, 84; 1813, p.26.

60 AHM, PT/AHM/G/LM/B-03/09 – *Livro nº 9 – Livro de Registo do Regimento de Infantaria, de 1812 a 1814*; Santos, *Ordens*, 1813, p.181.

61 Soriano, *Peninsula*, Vol.IV, pt.2, p.370; Santos, *Ordens*, 1810, p.105; *Capitão* Manoel Caetano Ferraz was promoted to *capitão* in May 1810 and was killed in action or died of his wounds at the siege of San Sebastian.

62 CHALLIS; *Army List*, 1813; Halliday, *Portugal*, 1812, p.225; Leech was an ensign in the 86th Foot into which he was commissioned on 4 March 1812; Halliday spells his name 'Leitch'.

63 War Office, *Return*, pp.26–27.

64 Soriano, *Peninsula*, Vol.IV, pt.2, p.366.

65 Philippart, *Calendar*, 1821, Vol.V, p.204; TNA, WO17/148, first battalion monthly return for September and October; Evans is entered as 'prisoner of war' in October but not September.

Thus, the list of officer names for 25 October in most respects matches the numbers of officers reported as casualties incurred between 22 and 29 October. The exception is the 2/38th Foot for which the list of names excludes three wounded officers, a captain, a lieutenant and an ensign, who are in the numerical list. The excluded captain is Matthew Forster who, as mentioned above, was severely wounded at Villamuriel.[66] The regimental digest of services also records that Lieutenant William Harrison was wounded at Villamuriel.[67] According to the monthly returns, the only ensign serving with the second battalion on 25 October was George Young and, while neither Challis nor the regimental digest records Young as wounded, his own letters home confirm a wound to his right side and arm due to a shell splinter.[68] Instead the regimental digest names the third wounded officer as Thomas Milward Oliver, who was promoted on 9 September 1812 to lieutenant, before being wounded at Villamuriel. Oliver is listed with Harrison as the two wounded lieutenants in the 38th Foot. This entry in the digest is focussed on the second battalion and only lists those officers of the second battalion who were casualties. Thus, Captain Andrew Todd and Captain Edward Ovens, both members of the second battalion, are named even though they were serving with the first battalion and the RI N.3 respectively, when they were killed, while Ensign George Young, an officer of the first battalion serving with the second battalion, is not.[69]

In summary, the return published in the *Gazette* appears to have understated the number of officers wounded in the 2/38th Foot by one lieutenant. Another name missing from the *Gazette* list and numbers is that of Major Edward Ovens, 2/38th Foot, killed in action while serving with the RI N.3.

The following three men are all excluded from the dispatches published in the *London Gazette*:

- The obituary of Lieutenant Edward Guichard (1/4th Foot, Pringle's Brigade) reports him being slightly wounded at Villamuriel.[70]
- Assistant Surgeon Thomas Bulkeley of the 30th Foot was slightly wounded.[71]

CHALLIS has him captured at Villamuriel and a prisoner of war until 1814. The numerical listing in the *Gazette* records the missing officer in his regimental rank of captain. Evans was promoted to brevet major on 17 August 1812.

66 Archives of the Museum of the Staffordshire Regiment, Lichfield (AMSR), Acc. No. 13, *Digest of the 38th Regiment, 1804–1885*, p.14; CHALLIS; the digest refers to Forster as wounded rather than killed. Forster is not included in Hall, *History*.

67 AMSR, Acc. No. 13, *Digest*, p.14.; while Challis mentions Harrison's service at Villamuriel neither he nor Hall (*History*, p.263) mention the wound received at Villamuriel.

68 Younge, 'Some Peninsular Letters', p.512; CHALLIS.

69 AMSR, Acc. No. 13, *Digest*, p.14; *Army List*, 1813, p.214; Hall, *History*, p.451, describes Oliver as an ensign but records his promotion to lieutenant in September 1812; TNA, WO25/770/57, Oliver's 1828 service return, records his wound at Villamuriel.

70 'Obituary', *The Gentleman's Magazine*, April 1857, Vol.CCII, p.497; Guichard's wound at Villamuriel is also mentioned in *Hart's New Army List*, 1840, p.392, where his name is spelt Gichard.

71 Glover (ed.), *Cameron*, p.32.

- Pringle's casualty return states that Volunteer Cole (1/4th Foot) was severely wounded. This casualty return does not specify that Cole was wounded on the 25th but all the other killed and wounded for this battalion in the return were.[72]

The Quarterly Pay-Lists

The following table is based on an analysis of the quarterly pay-lists for the British battalions at Villamuriel, for the period covered by the *Gazette* report of the casualties in the last week of October 1812. The pay-lists for each battalion describe, for the privates, drummers, fifers and non-commissioned officers, the fates or whereabouts of each man at each of the musters during the quarter. This study highlighted that the pay lists gave a more detailed and complete statement of the battalion losses than the casualty returns. However, for a full picture the two resources need to be used together.[73]

Quarterly Pay-list 25 Sept.–24 Dec. 1812	Killed in Action 25 October	Died of Wounds 25–29 October	Died 25 Oct.	Missing, wounded and left in the field or taken and prisoner of war				
				22–24 October	25–26 October	27–29 October	Total	Gazette
3/1st Foot	7	0	0	10	35	0	45	27
1/4th Foot	5	1	0	19	15	0	34	3
2/4th Foot	0	0	1	26	21	2	49	18
1/9th Foot	7	0	0	3	29	0	32	33
2/30th Foot	2	2	1	7	18	0	25	10
1/38th Foot	3	1	0	6	8	0	14	0
2/38th Foot	1	0	0	4	1	0	5	3
2/44th Foot	2	1	0	12	10	0	22	0
Totals	27	5	2	87	137	2	226	94

Notes

2/4th Foot: four men also went missing on 20 and 21 October, at the beginning of the retreat.

1/9th Foot: excluded here are the two sergeants and six other ranks who went missing on the 23rd with the sick car, of whom all but one (a private) were missing throughout November but managed to re-join the battalion in December.[74] The total excludes four men who missed the October muster, but whose records are undated.

2/30th Foot: three men also went missing on 21 October, the first day of the retreat.

1/38th Foot: one man also went missing on 21 October, the first day of the retreat. The total excludes the five men who missed the October muster, but whose records are undated.

2/38th Foot: the November monthly return states 'one serjeant, one drummer and sixteen rank and file returned sick absent were with the sick cart, and are supposed to be taken by the enemy not having been heard of since 23rd ultimo'.[75] However, the pay-list for 24 December 1812 shows

72 UML, GB 133 Eng MSS 1273, item 26.

73 TNA, pay-lists; WO12/2012 (3/1st Foot); WO12/2206 (1/4th); WO12/2265 (2/4th); WO12/2665 (1/9th); WO12/4646 (2/30th); WO12/5184 (1/38th); WO12/5245 (2/38th); WO12/5716 (2/44th); casualty returns; WO25/1506 (3/1st Foot), WO25/1522 (1/4th), WO25/1527 (2/4th), WO25/1556 (1/9th), WO25/1695 (2/30th), WO25/1742 (1/38th), WO25/1750 (2/38th), WO25/1795 (2/44th).

74 TNA, WO12/2665, December pay-list.

75 TNA, WO17/148.

that a further two sergeants, one corporal and two drummers were with the sick car at this time.[76] These men are all excluded from the total of missing men, and they all re-joined later in the year.

The table demonstrates that the *Gazette* significantly understated the missing for the period 22–29 October, while giving numbers closer to those for 25 October alone.

All 27 of the men described as killed in action were killed on 25 October. The pay-list for the 2/30th Foot used both 'Died' and 'Killed in action' suggesting that the two men who died, did so from sickness or from wounds on the 25th, however the battalion returned four men as killed on the 25th, suggesting the latter. One of the two men reported as died, Private Morgan Blakeney, survived and should have been reported as missing, as he is in the casualty return.

The proportion of men of the 5th Division who went missing before 25 October, during the retreat from Burgos, was in some of the battalions quite significant. While the average for the division between 22 and 24 October was four percent missing of total men present at headquarters, the level in the 2/4th Foot was eight percent and that of the 2/44th Foot was seven percent, approximately three times the average of the other six battalions. Within these figures the number of men that went missing on 23 October, at the time of the drunkenness at Torquemada, was only 50 percent higher than the other days of the retreat (38 men, against an average of 25 men), the 4th Foot suffering the most losses of 11 in the first battalion and 10 in the second. This analysis uses data where the dates are clear on the pay-list, therefore excluded are six privates from the 1/38th Foot who were missing at the October Muster but whose disappearance was not specifically dated.

The quarterly pay-list data thus shows that the 5th Division was only seriously engaged at Villamuriel during the period 22–29 October, and together this body of evidence strongly suggests that all the 'wounded' casualties reported in the *Gazette* for the period are likely to have been incurred on 25 October at Villamuriel.[77] The next significant loss of men in the retreat took place in mid-November, i.e. outside of the 22–29 October window. This is further confirmed by Pringle's casualty return for his brigade for the period 21–26 October inclusive, which shows that 98 percent of his brigade's killed and wounded as listed in the *Gazette* (22–29 October) were inflicted on 25 October.[78] Pringle's return gives figures for the missing which better reflect the pay-list data than those in the *Gazette*. Although the *Gazette* numbers are correct for 25 October only, the numbers of missing for the whole period 21–26 October are much higher, such that only 25 percent of the total missing were lost on 25 October.

76 TNA, WO12/5184.
77 Oman, *History*, Vol.VI, p.154.
78 UML, GB 133 Eng MSS 1273, item 26, casualty return for Pringle's Brigade.

Pringle's Brigade Return	Total Missing 21–26 Oct.	Missing 25 October	Missing 22–29 October (*Gazette*)
1/4th Foot	34	3	3
2/4th Foot	48	18	18
2/30th Foot	31	10	10
2/44th Foot	19	0	0
10th Coy. Brunswick Oels Light Infantry	10	5	20 for the whole regiment

As a final point, this table also highlights that as a proportion of total effectives, the Duke of Brunswick Oels Light Infantry lost at least as many men missing in this period before Villamuriel as the worst of the British battalions. The five men lost from this company before 25 October is either 13 percent of total effectives based on the estimate for the sick absent, or eight percent in the unlikely case of no men being absent sick. Lindau gives us an insight into their plight, writing: 'even worse off than us were the poor Brunswickers, … they froze in their linen trousers even more badly than we did'.[79]

In Barnes's Brigade, a further challenge to the *Gazette* as an accurate statement of casualties on 25 October is provided by the regimental digest of the 38th Foot, which, while giving the names of Captains Ovens and Todd as killed and Captain Forster, Lieutenants Harrison and Oliver as wounded at Villamuriel, also gives the other casualties for the period 24 to 26 October as '1 rank and file killed, 7 rank and file wounded and 1 sergeant, 7 rank and file prisoners of war and missing'.[80] Thus, while the regimental digest of the 38th Foot shows that all four of the officer casualties described in the Gazette for the period 22–29 October, were killed or wounded at Villamuriel, it also records that only 16 of the 48 non-commissioned officers and other ranks, mentioned by the *Gazette*, were lost in the period 24–26 October. This in turns suggests that a fifth of the casualties suffered by the 38th at Villamuriel were officers, an unlikely ratio, which must cast doubt on the statements in the digest with regard to the numbers of killed and wounded men.[81] The pay-lists for the two battalions show that, excluding officers, four men from the two battalions were killed in action on the 25th and a further man died of his wounds on the 26th. The pay-lists also reveal that while Sergeant Thomas Bagley was taken prisoner of war on 24 October, a further fourteen privates were taken prisoner of war in the period referred to by the regimental digest. For the 1/38th the 25 October monthly return records one serjeant and two rank and file missing as having fallen out of the line of march on 24 October and the 25 November monthly return shows that nine other ranks men died in the preceding month; for the 2/38th the 25 November monthly return shows that eight other ranks men died in the preceding month.[82] Taken

79 Lindau, *Hero*, p.95.

80 AMSR, Acc. No. 13, *Digest*, p.14; however the manuscript copy consulted had incorrectly transcribed 'Ovens' name as 'Owens'.

81 Officers comprise 6.5 percent of the total casualties in the data set from the *Gazette* for the Villamuriel period. Ovens is excluded for the casualties in the 38th Foot as he was with the Portuguese brigade.

82 TNA, WO17/148 (monthly returns 38th Foot); WO12/5184 (pay-lists, 1/38th).

together the evidence suggests that the casualties in the digest of the 38th Foot refers to the 2/38th Foot alone.

For his brigade, Liñan reported casualties of six men killed and 30 wounded, including Álava.

In conclusion, the Allied casualties incurred at Villamuriel can be summarised by brigade as follows:

Brigade	Killed	Wounded	Missing	Total	
Barnes	23	97	59	179	14%
Pringle	19	109	59	187	16%
Spry	41	144	17	202	11%
Liñan	6	30	0	36	3%
Lawson (RA)	3	7	1	11	9%
Total	92	387	136	615	12%

Notes

Barnes: the totals include an estimate of ten casualties from the Duke of Brunswick Oels Light Infantry (one killed, five wounded and four missing) but excludes the eight men of the 3/1st Foot captured by the French at Palencia in the morning and half (i.e. 14) of the missing. All the killed and wounded of the 3/1st Foot are assumed to have occurred at Villamuriel. The number of men killed in action from the 3/1st Foot is reduced by one man to reflect the pay-list data. The missing of the 1/9th Foot has been reduced by two. The missing also includes an additional eight men from the 1/38th Foot. The total includes Lieutenant Thomas Milward Oliver amongst the wounded of the 2/38th Foot but reduces the missing of this battalion by one man and excludes Major Ovens from the killed.

Pringle: the totals are based on Pringle's own casualty return and the pay-lists and includes Guichard and Cole of the 1/4th Foot as wounded but reduces both the missing of the 2/4th Foot and those men killed of the 2/44th Foot by one. Also included are the additional 10 men shown as missing from the 2/44th Foot, Surgeon Bulkeley (wounded) and an extra six missing men of the 2/30th Foot, as well as an additional four missing as recorded in the 1/4th Foot pay-list. Morgan Blakeney of the 2/30th Foot is included as missing rather than killed and Private Rodney Tansey is included amongst the killed rather than the wounded.

Spry: the totals include Major Ovens from the 38th Foot and Lieutenant João Baptista Ferreira of the Caçadores N.8 amongst the killed.

Oman gives the total losses of the 5th Division at Villamuriel at 500 men, from which he excludes all 43 men of the 3/1st Foot.[83] The equivalent number from this table, excluding Liñan's brigade, is 550. Allowing for the differing interpretation of the events at Palencia, this leaves a difference of approximately 65 men.

Oman gives the total prisoners of war, lost by the 5th Division on 25 October, as 150.[84] It is not clear which numbers Oman was using but presumably he was including the 27 men missing from the 3/1st Foot, which he described as being captured at Palencia. Furthermore, Oman may have included all the missing men from the Duke of Brunswick Oels Light Infantry, as described in the *Gazette*, this would add an additional 14 men to the numbers given here, a difference of 5 men.

83 Oman, *History*, Vol.VI, p.81.
84 Oman, *History*, Vol.VI, p.747.

In his Journal, the engineer Jones gave the total casualties for Wellington's army in the retreat from Burgos to the Duero as: four officers and 123 men killed, 45 officers and 455 men wounded and eight officers and 235 men prisoners. This total of 870 men emphasises the significance of Villamuriel, where 70 percent of these casualties were incurred, in this first stage of the retreat.[85]

French Casualties

In his dispatch to the Minister of War, Souham gave his own casualties, from the cavalry combats on 23 October until 30 October, as around 300 killed and wounded, but gave no figure for the missing.[86] Souham's chief of staff, Baron de Lamartinière, gave the casualties for the action at Villamuriel as five or six men drowned, 30 men killed, 180 men wounded and 30 men prisoners, a total of 245–6.[87]

To provide detail for Lamartinière's summary, the following is drawn from Martinien, the regimental *registres matricules*, and the *contrôles des officiers*, and comprises the names of the officers and men who were killed, wounded or taken prisoner of war on 25 October 1812. Martinien does not include any officers who were unwounded but taken prisoner. The prisoners of war are therefore taken from the other sources.

Divisional staff, two officers in total:
Killed; *Capitaine* François Basile Burgevin de Lesme.[88]
Wounded; *Chef de Bataillon* Étienne-François Girard, in the left shoulder.[89]

D'Arnauld's Brigade
15e Ligne; five officers in total:[90]
Killed; *Capitaine* Jean Lafitte (commanding officer of the first battalion).[91]
Wounded; *Lieutenant* Pierre Perret,[92] *Sous-Lieutenants* Jean Baptiste Paré[93] and Jacques Innocent Maury.[94]
Prisoner of War; *Lieutenant* Julien Galtier.[95]

85 Jones, *Sieges*, p.224.
86 Wellington (ed.), *Supplementary Despatches*, Vol.XIV, p.155.
87 Gurwood (ed.), *Dispatches*, Vol.VI, p.776.
88 Martinien, *Tableaux*, p.51; Jorge Planas Campos personal communication citing *Liste de membres de la noblesse impériale*, p.33; SHD XEM 270; Burgevin was 30 years old.
89 Desachy, *Girard*, pp.205–6.
90 Martinien, *Tableaux*, pp.152–3.
91 SHD 2Yb157 *Contrôle des Officiers*, p.63; SHD C8 468.
92 Jorge Planas Campos personal communication citing the *registre matricule* of the *Velites des Grenadiers de la Garde*, SHD 20Yc 12, p.26.
93 LEONORE LH/2049/54.
94 SHD 2Yb 157, pp.85, 265; de Tarragon, *Historique*, p.220; the history of the 15e Ligne names a *Sous-Lieutentant* Dazé among the wounded, but this is a misreading of Paré's *contrôle des officiers* entry.
95 SHD 2Yb 157, *contrôle des officiers*, p.224.

Other ranks; eight men killed, three subsequently died of wounds, 27 men wounded, and 112 men lost as prisoners of war.[96] The registers refer to Villamuriel as Villamuriel, Dueñas and variants, near or at Palencia, Montbertrand or simply Spain.

The *registres matricules* name the men killed as *Voltigeur* G. Arodeaux, *Soldats* J. Ré*(*= died of wounds), F. Petit*, P.F. Caillaud, J. Crecy, J.M. Delaporte and J. Escoland, *Grenadiers* J.B. Dubois and J. Bourget (register 137), *Grenadier* J.E. Delafoy and *Voltigeur* C.E. Durand* (134).

The registers name the men wounded as *Grenadier* J. Buron, *Soldats* J. Girard, P. Guillezit, S. Beuilly, G. Galien, J. Gossec and J. Degrave (register 137), *Sergent-major* A. Descoins, *Soldats* A. Debetouille, N. Fratidier and C. Clavier (136) *Grenadier* A. Wecker, *Caporal* J.L. Brisson and *Grenadier* J. Auvray, dated 24 October (134) and *Sergent* N. Perrin (133).

Three further men are identified as wounded at Villamuriel by their entries in the *contrôles des officiers* register, they are *Adjutant* T. Vanniev, *Sergent* F. Courtois and *Caporal* J.J. Prentout, although their entries in the *registres matricules* make no mention of their wounds.[97] A further nine men are described as entering hospital, in seven cases specifically naming the hospital in Palencia, on 25 or 26 October without specifically mentioning a wound at Villamuriel. These men are *Soldat* P.J. Belot (register 137), *Soldat* E. Perrot (136), *Soldats* L. Poirou and L. Rocheteau (135), *Sergent* J.H de Malderée, *Soldats* M.M. Lubin and P.S. Janvier (134), *Grenadier* H. Gerard and *Caporal* F. Pérard (133).

Thus, the registers of the 15e Ligne suggest that the regiment's casualties at Villamuriel included from 18 to 27 wounded non-commissioned officers and rank and file. Assuming that de Tarragon's figure of 28 wounded men includes the four officers he mentions; he is suggesting that in total 24 other ranks were wounded.

A comparison of the British prisoner of war registers with the *registres matricules*, suggests that the 15e Ligne lost one officer and 112 men as prisoners of war on 25 October 1812. Of these men, 44 men feature in both the *registres matricules* and the POW registers. These men, one *lieutenant*. three *sergents* and 40 *soldats*, can be found in the prisoner of war registers of the Forton Depot and the prison ships, *Assistance*, *Crown*, *Guildford*, *Kron Princessa*, *St. Damaso*, *Sophia Frederica*, *Suffolk*, *Veteran*, *Vigilant* and *Waldemar*, at Portsmouth and the depots at Portchester and Perth.[98]

35 of these men were recorded in the POW registers as being captured on 25 October 1812. A further three are recorded as being captured either on 25 September or 25 November but the respective *registre matricule* entries date their capture to the day of Villamuriel. The remaining six men are recorded in the POW registers as being captured in July 1812 at Salamanca (three men) or in August 1812 at Madrid (three men); however, the respective entries in the *registres matricules* date their capture to the day of Villamuriel.

---

96 SHD GR21YC 133–137, *registres matricules*, 15e Ligne.

97 SHD 2Yb 157, pp.286, 355, 391.

98 TNA, ADM 103/8, 86, 165, 216, 264–7, 337–8, 364–8, 391, 408, 443, 448, 454; 100,000 individual records were reviewed from 74 registers of a total of 103 likely to be relevant.

The POW registers never record Villamuriel as the place of capture; instead Dueñas (various spellings all incorrect, e.g. *Doignas and Guigras*), Burgos and Valladolid are mentioned. Four of the men recorded in the POW registers are recorded as taken 'near Sarragossa' but the *registre matricule* entries for these men, all of the first battalion, record them as being taken at Montbertrand (one), Palencia (one) and unspecified (two), but all on 25 October 1812.

The *registre matricule* entries of six of these 44 men do not mention their status as POWs. For a seventh man, although the *registre matricule* entry does not mention his POW status, the *contrôles des officiers* record does. An eighth man is described in the *registre matricule* as being 'left behind on 24 Oct.' although the British register has him taken on the 25th. The *registre matricule* entry for a ninth man describes him as a prisoner of the English, but his date of capture is not given. Finally, of these 44 men, seven men were recorded as being captured by 'Spanish forces'.

A third (38) of the 114 men in the *registres matricules*, while captured on 25 October 1812, are described as being taken at Fort Montbertrand in Spain or simply Montbertrand and sometimes the descriptions states specifically 'by the English'. Of these men, eight also appear in the POW registers, none of whom are described as being taken at Montbertrand. Instead the British registers describe four of these eight men as being captured at Duenas (25 October 1812, spelt variously – Doinas, Dognas, Doignas etc), two at Madrid (14 August 1812), one at Salamanca (18 July 1812) and one 'near Sarragossa' (25 October 1812).

Montbertrand most likely refers to *Mombeltrán* castle, just north of Talavera de la Reina, where two battalions of Maucune's Division (5/82e Ligne and 6/82e Ligne) formed the garrison until January 1812. Brenier's division then formed the garrison until March 1812. Wellington confirmed in July 1812 that the French had evacuated the castle. Although a member of the 82e Ligne died in the castle hospital as late as May 1812, it is thus highly unlikely that any men of Maucune's division were taken there in October 1812. Interestingly *Grenadier* Dubois (2/15 Ligne) who, according to his entry in the *registre matricule*, was 'killed in action in the battle on 25 October 1812 at Montbertrand', *Soldat* Bussac (1/15 Ligne) is described as being 'wounded on 25 October 1812 and taken prisoner on the same day at Montbertrand', and *Soldat* Girard (1/15 Ligne) is described as being 'wounded on 25 October 1812 at Montbertrand to the hospital the next day in Burgos'. Taken together these three records suggest that Montbertrand was a mistaken reference to Villamuriel.[99]

A further man, *Soldat* Charles Claisen, was recorded in the *registre matricule* as being captured on 24 October, although the POW register records his capture as having happened in Madrid in August. If this man was taken on the 25th, the total would be 114.[100]

Thus, in summary, the number of prisoners of war lost by the 15e Ligne at Villamuriel ranges from one officer and 112 other ranks – assuming that

99 SHD GR21 YC137, pp.73, 208, 237.

100 SHD 21 YC133, p.48; TNA, ADM 103/264, p.128.

all of the men whose POW references, in either the British registers or the *registres matricules*, dated 25 October 1812 were taken at Villamuriel – down to one officer and 70 men, excluding all of the 'Montbertrand' men, three of the four men described as being captured 'near Sarragossa' and the man described as 'left behind on the 24th'. Of these alternatives the most likely, given the war record of the 15e Ligne, is the total of one officer and 112 men.

The grand total of casualties for the 15e Ligne, based on the *registres matricules*, is thus nine men killed, three men subsequently died of wounds, 30 men wounded, and 113 taken prisoner, or 155 casualties of all types. The *registres matricules* indicate that these men were divided approximately equally between the first and second battalions. These numbers differ significantly from those given in the regimental history, which states that 65 men were killed and that 28 were wounded, while Béchaud gives the total loss of the regiment as 200, which taken together imply that 107 were missing.[101]

The *registres matricules* are unlikely to have recorded all the wounded, especially those with light wounds, as is demonstrated by the ratio of the killed to wounded given in this data 1:3.5. For the officers, the ratio is one to four which is closer to that expected as given by Hodge. Obviously, de Tarragon's ratio of more than two men killed for every wounded man is far from expected. Using Hodges's ratio of 4.3 wounded men for every man killed, excluding those who subsequently died of their wounds, the total wounded can be estimated at 33 other ranks in addition to the three officers.[102]

Combining all this information the best estimate of the losses of the 15e Ligne is; one officer and eight men killed, three men subsequently died of wounds, three officers and 33 men wounded, and one officer and 112 men lost as prisoners of war. A grand total of 161 men of all types, divided approximately equally between the two battalions.

66e Ligne; six officers in total:[103]
Killed; *Sous Lieutenant* Georges Portenseigne.[104]
Wounded; *Chef de Bataillon* Michel Izambard (commander 4/66e Ligne),[105] *Capitaine* Claude Sausse,[106] *Lieutenant* Pierre Colaert,[107] *Sous Lieutenants* François Alexis Poirier (shot in the left hand) [108] and Nicolas Goirot.[109]
Béchaud names only four officers as casualties; Izambard, Portenseigne, Colaert and Poirier.[110]

101 De Tarragon, *Historique*, p.220; Colin, 'Béchaud', p.410.

102 W.B. Hodge, 'On the Mortality Arising from Military Operations' *Journal of the Royal Statistical Society*, (1856), Vol.XIX, p.233; Hodge studied the British Army, 1793–1815. He concluded that on average for every man killed, 4.3 were wounded. He also reported that 1/12th of the wounded officers and 1/8th of the wounded other ranks subsequently died.

103 Martinien, *Tableaux*, p.271, *Supplément*, p.47.

104 SHD GR21 YC551 p.263, *Registre Matricule 66e Ligne*; Portenseigne joined the regiment on 1 May 1806 as a *soldat*, promoted *sous lieutenant* 31 July 1811, aged 26 in 1812.

105 LEONORE LH/1337/89.

106 Jorge Planas Campos, personal communication citing SHD 2Yb 411, p.170.

107 Colin, 'Béchaud', p.410; spells his name Calaert.

108 LEONORE LH/2188/17; Martinien, *Supplément*, p.178; appends '*de Noisseville*' to his name.

109 SHD 2Yb 349, *Contrôle des Officiers*, p.150.

110 Colin, 'Béchaud', p.410.

Other ranks; 12 men killed, three men subsequently died of wounds, 19 men wounded, and nine men lost as prisoners of war.[111] The *registres matricules* contain the names of the 12 other ranks men who were killed at Villamuriel on 25 October 1812 and the three men who subsequently died of their wounds; *Soldats* J. Moun, G.J.M. Mosteau, T.H. Simonet and *Tambour* J.A. Carbone (register 556); *Soldat* J. Marot (555); *Sergent* J.P. Bousquet and *Soldat* J. Bobineau (554); *Soldat* G. Richard (553); *Sergents Major* J.M. Bosco and A. Mathieu, *Soldat* P.M. Gratarollo (552); *Caporal* F.J. Hubis, *Tambour* J.J. Valery, *Soldats* J. Rivel and J.F. Roussel (551). Roussel died of his wounds on 25 October in the hospital in Palencia. Bousquet also died of his wounds at the hospital in Palencia, his wounding at Villamuriel is confirmed by Béchaud.[112] Mathieu died of his wounds in the hospital at Palencia on 10 November 1812, presumably from wounds incurred at Villamuriel.

The wounded include 12 men who are described in the registers as being wounded at Villamuriel or, in one case, Palencia on 25 October 1812; *Soldats* A. Dupuy and A. Barbesson (register 556); *Soldats* P. Labarthe and L. Durand (555); *Sergent Major* M.R. Lefebure, *Sergent* C.A. Servetti, *Grenadier* F. Genovese and *Soldat* J. Spinelli (552); *Sergent* F.L. Lévêque, *Caporals* J. Peyre, J.B.L. Vanregementes and J.B. Pitau (551). A further man, *Voltigeur* P. Jullian (551), is described as 'wounded… at Dognas on 24 October 1812', when the regiment was still at Magaz.

Another six men are described as 'entering hospital… on 25 October 1812,' five of them specifying the hospital in Palencia (*Soldats* J. Cassot, J. Mansol and M.A. Rossi (556); *Soldat* J. Mora (555); *Tambour* P. Poignard (554); *Soldat* E. Dupuis (553)). In each case, the man's fate is unrecorded, and they are 'written off' after the long absence. Given the date and the fact that sickness is usually recorded only in the case of death, these men have all been assumed to have been wounded for this study.

A comparison of the British POW registers with the regimental *registres matricules*, suggests that the 66e Ligne lost nine men as prisoners of war at Villamuriel on 25 October 1812. These men are described as being taken at 'Dognas', 'Bagnas', 'Palencia' and 'Villamuriel'; *Sergents* J.P.S. Sol and P. Vandoren, *Soldat* J.B. Meyfroidt (register 551); *Voltigeur* J. Lelong and *Soldat* J.B.M. Lemuale (553); *Soldats* J.B. Couterot and P.J. Coquet (554); *Soldats* J.B. Magnano and J. Verlhiac (555).

The *registre matricule* entry for *Sergent* Sol makes no reference to him being taken as a POW. The British POW records for Lemuale and Vandoren are not dated 25 October 1812, but 25 July and 25 September respectively. In both cases the *registres matricules* describes them as killed in action at Villamuriel. Lelong and Verlhiac are also described in the *registres matricules* as having been killed in action at Villamuriel.[113]

As a final point regarding the French prisoners of war taken at Villamuriel, the Forton register includes, amongst the prisoners captured on 25 October, a

111 SHD GR21YC 551–556.

112 Colin, 'Béchaud', p.407.

113 TNA, ADM 103/367, pp.85, 87, 88; ADM 103/391 entry 45968; ADM 103/448, p.82.

Soldat Andre Spilman of the 4e Régiment d'Infanterie Suisse.[114] The fourth, or Göldlin, battalion of this regiment was with Vandermaesen's division.[115] This division is not mentioned in any of the sources for the action at Villamuriel, Baron de Lamartinière places them at Tariego on the 26th. The register for the ship *Veteran* however also includes *Soldat* Spilman but dates his capture by Spanish forces at Dueñas to 28 October.[116] Souham's dispatch to the Minister of War places the Armée du Nord contingent, including Vandermaesen's division, at Cigales opposite Cabezón at this time, 12 miles from Dueñas, which suggests Spilman was a straggler or prisoner escort as Souham moved south in pursuit of Wellington. Meanwhile Giron's dispatch of 26 October was written from the headquarters of the 6º Ejército at Cabezón, which in turn raises the question of who took Spilman prisoner.

Assuming that Béchaud's over-all numbers and the number of wounded are both accurate, given that his account was written only three months after the battle, the best estimate of the losses of the 66e Ligne is one officer and 12 men killed, three men subsequently died of wounds, five officers and 49 men wounded, and nine men lost as prisoners of war. A grand total of 79 men of all types.

The *registres matricules* suggest that these casualties were distributed between the fourth and sixth battalions, in the ratio of one third to two thirds. Approximately a quarter of the total casualties are recorded in the *registres matricules* as still belonging to their original battalion, i.e. the fifth or seventh, and are therefore excluded from this calculation, assuming they were proportionally divided between the fourth and sixth battalions on the day of battle.

Montfort's Brigade

Martinien gives no officer casualties for either the 82e or 86e Ligne on 25 October.[117] Béchaud stated that Montfort's brigade lost 'much less' than d'Arnauld's brigade, because they 'only committed a vanguard'.[118] This is reflected in the *registres matricules* of the two regiments;

82e Ligne; Four men killed, one *sergent* and three *soldats*.[119]

The men 'dead on the field of honour' were *Soldat* J.P. Sudre (register 636), *Soldats* L. Cynard and V. Piger (635) and *Sergent* P. Dupuy (633). However, the registers date the deaths of Dupuy and Piger to 26 October. There are no men identified as wounded, which is typical of these registers, in which only three wounds are recorded amongst a sample of 192 records. However, using Hodges's model, these can be estimated at 17 men. Similarly, no men are identified as having been taken prisoner of war.

114 TNA, ADM 103/367; by coincidence the 66e Ligne was originally created in 1672 under this name.

115 G. Dempsey, *Napoleon's Mercenaries: Foreign Units in the French Army under the Consulate and Empire* (London: Greenhlll, 2002), pp.292–293.

116 TNA, ADM 103/443.

117 Martinien, *Tableaux*, p.293, 299; SHD 2Yb 397, p.1382.

118 Colin, 'Béchaud', p.410.

119 SHD GR21YC 632–636, *registres matricules* 82e Ligne.

The history of the regiment reports only three other ranks killed for the period 18–30 October.[120] These men are named as Gavanie, Damont and Dupuy. *Soldat* S. Gavanie was killed in action on 21 October (register 636) and *Soldat* P. Demont was killed on 29 September at Logroño ('Ogronne', register 635). The same history names a *Lieutenant* Joseph Galpy as wounded in the period 18–30 October, but Galpy was a *sergent* when he was wounded on 20 October at Monasterio. The history also names *Lieutenants* Vernaërt and Zandrino, but Martinien tells us that these two officers were both wounded at the bridge of Tordesillas on 30 October. Martinien also names *Sous-Lieutenant* Daniel Verpraet as wounded on 21 October near Burgos.[121]

86e Ligne; The regimental history records that two *soldat*s were killed, and 11 men wounded, two *caporals*, two *tambours* and seven *soldats*.[122] The *contrôles des officiers* for the 86e Ligne also names *Adjutant Sous Officier* Jean Pierre Thierry as wounded. Thierry was 'shot in the right chest' but survived to be promoted to *sous lieutenant* on 8 February 1813, therefore he is not in Martinien.[123] Together this gives a total of two men killed and 12 men wounded.

The two *soldat*s 'killed before Duenas' were L. Daveau (register 667) and D.-C. Lebbe (666). The wounded men were *Grenadier* J.L. Brasseur, *Soldat*s C. Fondaneyche, J.A. Claux and J. Dory (669); *Caporal* M. Fleury, *Tambour* E.J. Aubern, *Soldat*s S. Coutuzier, J.N. Jamel and F.R.T. Waller (667); *Caporal* J.P. Prevol and *Tambour* N. Fessard (666).

For the 86e Ligne, Martinien identifies *Sous Lieutenant* Prat as wounded on 24 October at the 'combat before Burgos'.[124] However Pierre Jacques Prat was wounded at Monasterio on 20 October.[125]

No men from either regiment are recorded as missing or taken prisoner on 25 October. There are also no prisoners in the British POW registers examined, from either the 82e or 86e Ligne, captured on 25 October 1812.

In summary, the losses for Montfort's brigade can be estimated at six men killed and 29 men wounded.

Artillery

Martinien identifies no officer casualties amongst Maucune's artillery. A comparison of the orders of battle for the Armée de Portugal between 15 October and 15 November confirms this and suggests that Maucune's artillery lost 10 artillerymen from the foot artillery and four members of the artillery train from all causes between these two dates. However, it is unlikely that all these losses occurred at Villamuriel. The casualties amongst the artillery are estimated to have been five men wounded based on the equivalent analysis for the infantry which shows that only a third

120 Arvers, Brecht, *Historique*, p.129.
121 Arvers, Brecht, *Historique*, p.129; SHD 2Yb 397, p.195.
122 SHD GR21YC 666–669, *registres matricules 86e Ligne*.
123 SHD 2Yb 411, p.266.
124 Martinien, *Tableaux*, p.808.
125 SHD GR21YC 666, p.52; LEONORE LH/2220/69; SHD 2Yb 411, p.241.

of the infantry's losses between 15 October and 15 November occurred at Villamuriel.[126]

Cavalry

Again Martinien gives no officer casualties for Desfossés' brigade and only one for Souham's light cavalry on 25 October 1812.[127] A comparison of the orders of battle for the Armée de Portugal between 15 October and 15 November suggests that Desfossés's brigade had a combined net loss of one officer and 35 men from all causes between these dates.[128] However the 3e Hussards received some reinforcements during the same period, their net change being an increase of five officers and 17 men. A detachment of six officers and 10 horses of the 22e Chasseurs à Cheval disappears from the order of battle by 15 November but a similar detachment of five officers and 44 men appears in the 25 November order of battle.

Both Béchaud and Hill suggest that casualties were inflicted on the cavalry; however, it is unlikely that all the losses recorded by the orders of battle occurred at Villamuriel. Hill of the Caçadores N.8 states that his men wounded and took prisoner a French cavalry officer, and the orders of battle suggests that this man was a member of the 26e Chasseurs à Cheval, who were missing one officer by 15 November. However, neither Martinien nor the *contrôle des officiers* for the 3e Hussards, the 22e and 26e Chasseurs à Cheval identify such an officer. Hence, Hill was most probably referring to *Capitaine* Burgevin, aide de camp to Chauvel.

Accounting for the reinforcements and detachments referred to above suggests that the brigade lost at least 58 men during the period 15 October to 15 November. Using the infantry analysis referred to above we can estimate that a third of these losses happened at Villamuriel, i.e. 19 men, who can be allocated between killed and wounded using Hodge's model. Thus, the casualties amongst the cavalry are estimated to have been three men killed and 16 wounded.

In summary for the French forces at Villamuriel, these data and estimates can be totalled as follows:

Brigade	Killed	Drowned	Died of Wounds	Wounded	Missing	Total	%
d'Arnauld	22		6	90	122	240	9
Montfort	6			*29*		*35*	2
Artillery				*5*		*5*	1
Desfossés	*3*			*16*		*19*	2
Total	**31**	**0**	**6**	**140**	**122**	**298**	**5**
Lamartinière's Report	30	5–6		180	30	245–6	

(Italics indicate that estimates are included)

126 Martinien, *Tableaux*, pp.645, 649; SHD C8 468; NAFZIGER, *Portugal*, 15 November.

127 Martinien, *Tableaux*, p.597; *Lieutenant Nicol*, 13e Chasseurs à Cheval, wounded 'near Palencia' but not recorded in the regimental history.

128 SHD C8 468, NAFZIGER, *Portugal, 15 November 1812.*

Thus, there are some significant differences between these estimates of casualties and Baron de Lamartinière's report to the Minister of War, in which he clearly underestimated the missing. The *registres matricules* do not specify drowning as a cause of death. At least three of the men who died of their wounds did so after the report was written, which leaves two men killed and 37 men wounded from Lamartinière's report unaccounted for.[129]

If we assume that Lamartinière's report was accurate with respect to killed and wounded, but inaccurate with regards to the missing, we can estimate the number of French casualties as 36 killed, 180 wounded and 122 missing, a grand total of 338 men. However, in his detailed analysis of the French losses at Salamanca, Rory Muir has concluded that Lamartinière's return for that battle underestimated French casualties by approximately 20 percent, by excluding those men who were lightly wounded or were missing but subsequently returned to the ranks by the time the report was submitted, in this case 10 days after the action, on 4 November 1812. Applying Muir's conclusions to this analysis suggests that the French casualties at Villamuriel could have been as high as 407 men of all ranks.[130]

As mentioned above, the allies claimed to have captured many more prisoners in their counterattack. In Barnes's Brigade, Douglas stated that very few prisoners were taken, and that most of the French to his front were either killed or wounded.[131] In Pringle's Brigade, the 30th and 44th Foot have been described as taking more than 350 prisoners, although Hopkins of the 4th Foot only mentions the releasing of the allied prisoners taken in the morning.[132] Liñan stated in his report that his brigade had taken 104 prisoners.[133] Hale, attacking with the Spaniards, stated that about 400 French prisoners were taken.[134] This total of more than 850 prisoners is not supported by the regimental or prisoner of war registers referred to above, which suggests that there was some double counting.[135]

As a more detached observer, Bingham from his perspective at Dueñas, perhaps more accurately, put the number of prisoners at 100.[136] Thus it appears that Liñan may have been referring to the prisoners captured by all the brigades in the attack, while the author of Hamilton's obituary and Hale were both perhaps guilty of exaggeration, with Douglas and Hopkins being more reliable.[137]

---

129 If de Tarragon did confuse the killed and wounded of the 15e Ligne, the estimated totals would be 56 killed, 142 wounded and 122 missing.

130 Muir, *Salamanca*, pp.256–7; Muir has the officers underestimated by a third and the other ranks by 20 percent. Both of these figures are only his best estimates and are difficult to substantiate from the sources available to us.

131 Monick (ed.), *Douglas*, p.59.

132 Napier, *History*, 1840, Vol.VI, p.xviii; 'Obituary of Colonel Alexander Hamilton', *United Service Journal* (1838), pt.2, p.431; 'more prisoners than their own force was composed of'.

133 AHNM, *Diversos/Colecciones*/101/n63.

134 Hale, *Journal*, p.95.

135 For example, in the sample of 31 men captured at Villamuriel, in the Portsmouth prisoner of war registers, three of them are recorded as being captured by the Spanish troops.

136 Glover (ed.), *Bingham*, p.162.

137 Hale, *Journal*, p.124; Oman, Vol.VII, p.549; Hale also refers to the 9th Foot taking 400 prisoners during the Battle of the Nive on 10 December 1813, whereas Soult reported 290

Comparing the monthly returns, the net decline in the combat strength of Maucune's 5e Division in the period 15 October to 15 November 1812 amounts to 921 men, however the December return suggests that of these, 409 were in hospital:[138]

	15 October		15 November	15 December	
	Present	Hospital	Present	Present	Hospital
d'Arnauld's Brigade					
15e Ligne					
1er Bataillon	677	414	530	533	474
2e Bataillon	659	352	518	523	422
4e Bataillon	240	60	138	164	98
66e Ligne					
4e Bataillon	515	356	438	433	180
6e Bataillon	467	144	370	377	133
Montfort's Brigade					
82e Ligne					
4e Bataillon	465	117	412	469	199
5e Bataillon	482	129	401	390	231
86e Ligne					
1er Bataillon	641	187	524	538	327
2e Bataillon	604	127	498	481	231
Totals	4,750	1,886	3,829	3,908	2,295

prisoners and 276 missing for 9–13 December.

138 De Tarragon, *Historique*, p.219; Oman, *History*, Vol.VI, p.743; NAFZIGER, *Portugal* 15 October and 15 November; SHD C8 468–9.

13

The End of the Campaign

On 26 October, Wellington directed the retreat to Cabezón de Pisuerga where he crossed the river. Thus, having faced east to confront the French across the Carrión, once the French had crossed the Carrión in pursuit, Wellington now faced west, confronting them across the Pisuerga. This position covered his subsequent retreat south across the Duero.[1] The 6th Division and Reserve Artillery left Cabezón at 4:00 a.m. on 26 October, while the 1st and 5th Divisions left there at 5:00 a.m. on 28 October.[2]

Lieutenant and Captain Henry Packe, of the 1st Foot Guards, who had arrived on the 24th, writing on 31 October, described this second phase of the retreat in a letter home, 'our retreat appears to have been admirably conducted, and great caution, but… little enterprise, has been displayed on the part of the enemy'.[3]

From the environs of Boecillo on the Duero the retreat continued on 30 October towards Tordesillas, the 1st, 6th, 7th and two Spanish divisions leading the way to confront Foy, who had daringly captured the bridge across the Duero at Tordesillas, while the 5th Division, Pack's and Bradford's Portuguese brigades together with two more Spanish divisions formed the rearguard on the river Adaja at Aniago.[4]

Subsequently, Wellington was able to rest his army and the over-all position was somewhat relieved by the 7º Ejército taking Bilbao, in the French rear, causing the contingent from the Armée du Nord to return north to restore order. However, the converging French armies from the east and south soon forced Wellington, after a stand-off on the Tormes at Salamanca, to retire further back into Portugal.[5] The 6º Ejército marched home to Galicia via the road through Bragança.[6]

1 Napier, *History*, Vol.V, plate 5; the river is the Douro in Portugal and the Duero in Spain.
2 Leslie, *Dickson*, Vol.IV, p.779.
3 Glover (ed.), *Packe*, p.53.
4 Leslie, *Dickson*, Vol.IV, p.780; Oman, *History*, Vol.VI, pp.83–5.
5 Esdaile, *Peninsular War*, p.416.
6 A.García Fuertes, F.C.Álvarez, O.G.García, *Más que una Guerra: Astorga y el noroeste de España en el conflicto peninsular (1808–1814)* (Astorga: Centro de Estudios Astorganos Marcelo Macías, 2014), p.220.

As it progressed the conditions of the retreat significantly deteriorated as described by Corporal Samuel Gallagher (5th Dragoon Guards):

> Every day added to our misfortunes. Our route lay over a hilly and mountainous country the greatest part of our retreat, intersected by rapid rivers, woods, morasses, in fact every obstacle we were obliged to encounter. Such roads as we fell in with occasionally were soon cut up and rendered almost impassable by the gun carriages and trampling of the cattle. Numbers of the peasantry which were dispersed by the rapid advance over the face of the country of two contending armies, those poor individuals were flying in all directions exposed to the clemency of a cold winter carrying with them what little property they could get along with them, but when met or overtaken by any of the enemy they were robbed of everything. Our horses and mules worn out and completely exhausted, were no longer able to drag the guns, so that we were compelled to spike them, a great part of our cavalry also were dismounted. In this forlorn condition we could offer but a feeble resistance to the overwhelming forces of the French who never ceased harassing us neither day nor night. Numbers of our infantry were crushed to death by the rapid advance of the enemy's cavalry and artillery and many who were unable to keep up with their columns straggled away and were either cut to pieces or perished with cold and hunger in the woods. The sufferings of our poor women and children were also dreadful in the extreme, but it was out of our power to assist them. Even the very elements seemed to conspire against us, heavy storms of thunder and lightning accompanied by showers of sleet and piercing cold continually bursting over our heads against which we had neither shelter nor cover. Added to this we were emaciated with hunger and worn out with fatigue, many were half naked.[7]

It is unclear which guns Gallagher is referring to here. Neither Dickson, Oman, nor Napier mentions the loss of any field guns during the retreat. Elsewhere Gallagher refers to the rearguard being Ponsonby's Brigade, Anson's Brigade of light dragoons and 'two brigades of artillery' (presumably the troops of Ross and Bull).[8]

Wellington's army had a terrible November with the number of men reported missing rising to nearly 5,000 from an army of 54,000 men, with the Portuguese troops particularly affected. Soult reported capturing 1,700–1,900 men in three days alone.[9]

The experience of an anonymous soldier of the 38th Foot provides a further example of the chaos and brutality of this retreat. This soldier was wounded in the foot at the battle of Salamanca in July and remained there in hospital as the army marched to Burgos via Madrid, before being taken prisoner by the French during the retreat to Portugal:

7 G. Glover (ed.), *The Journal of Trooper Samuel Gallagher 5th Dragoon Guards in Spain, Portugal and France 1810–15* (Godmanchester: Ken Trotman, 2016), pp.51–2; the journal was written in retrospect in the 1840's (G. Glover personal communication).

8 Glover (ed.), *Gallagher*, p.50.

9 Oman, *History*, Vol.VI, p.154.

Our army pursued the French up to Burgos and attempted to besiege the castle, but the French got a strong reinforcement and soon drove them back. As soon as they heard in Salamanca that our army was retreating, they began to send the worst of the cases away to Lisbon and all that they could get conveyances for was sent but my wound had just healed up so I was left until our army came down and then I was ordered to join the regt. I marched, but it was with very great pain, about a mile and a half but when I got to the regt. I was so much spent that I was forced to lie down. I had not lay long before I was seized with a very strong fit of the ague. I was very ill and had to lie on the bald ground all the night. The next morning I was taken and put into one of the sick waggons. I was taken three days in the waggons but when the 4th morning came, the French came upon us so quick that those who were able to get into the waggons did, but I had the ague so bad every day and was so weak that I could not get in of myself, so I was left lying on the ground and was taken prisoner. When I was captured, I felt assured that I must use every exertion in my power to preserve my life for if I had not tried to march I should either been put to death instantly or left to die upon the ground. So I threw all away that I could and went through the French lines about the distance of a mile, then I got into a field where there were many more prisoners that were taken. There they kindled a fire, the night was very wet and cold and I had nothing but the few clothes that I stood in, for while I was going through the French lines one of them stepped out of his rank and came to me and took my big coat and everything I had except some books, which he gave me back again. On account of the wetness of the night, we did not attempt to lay ourselves down until a very late hour so the fire was kept burning until the rain ceased and then they put it out but seeing me so very ill, they laid me on the place where the fire had been that I might get what nourishment I could from the warmth of the ground and the rest of the men lay round me. In the morning the French guard came and collected us together and marched us off, but there were many more among us that was sick and as soon as we began to march the French put many to death that could not keep up. But most of them that were killed were Portuguese and Spaniards and I expected every minute it would be my lot to suffer the same fate. But in that case the Lord was pleased to show mercy unto me in causing one of the sergeants belonging to the French guard to take pity on me, so that when I could not keep up, he would stay for me. We did not go more than one league or three miles that day and that night we were put into a place under cover and had some straw to lie upon. The next morning we marched again but we did not go much more than two miles and there were several put to death that day also. The third day we marched about five mile and I believe that there were 36 put to death that day and one of them was a man belonging to the same regt as myself. But when the fourth morning came we had the longest days march to go to get into Salamanca and I felt so ill that I expected that it would be my lot to suffer the same fate that so many of my fellow prisoners had met with, but when the fourth morning came, we marched and we had a young officer that had the command of the guard and he seemed to be a very feeling man which made the whole of the guard seem to put on a different feeling toward us so that they treated us with more kindness than they did before. So that when any of us got far behind they would halt and let us rest as much as possible they could, so that on that day there was but one put to death and I believe it would not have been only for a circumstance that we saw

> on the road but the Spaniards were cruel people and if they could ever light of any one or two of the French alone they would murder them...[10]

Difficult though the autumn of 1812 had been for Wellington, it could have been much worse. *Général de Division* Foy, writing in Salamanca in November, was disappointed with the outcome:

> We had an army stronger by a third than the enemy's, infinitely superior in cavalry and artillery. Confident expectation of victory was in every man's head. The chance had come of beating the English – perhaps of driving them from the Peninsula. This fine opportunity, so splendid, so decisive, with so few adverse chances has been let slip.[11]

The bloody events at Villamuriel de Cerrato represented just one day in a month-long retreat for Oswald's 5th Division which lost a further 660 men captured by the French.[12] Amongst others Ensign Francis Kelly of the 2/30th Foot died of exhaustion during the retreat, having joined the army only on the day of Villamuriel.[13] The 25 November monthly returns of the division's eight British infantry battalions show that a total of 184 NCOs and other ranks died in the preceding month. By way of comparison the *Gazette* has 33 dying in the period 21 to 29 October, of whom 27 died on 25 October at Villamuriel.

Writing on 27 November 1812 from Gibraltar, where he was serving with the 2/9th Foot, Assistant Surgeon William Dent remarked 'letters from the army received a few days ago mention our first battalion to have lost six or seven officers and upwards of one hundred men, killed and wounded, composing part of the rearguard in the retreat from Burgos.'[14]

Although described in some quarters as disastrous, the retreat had enabled Wellington to escape the stronger and converging French armies with an intact if exhausted army to fight another day.[15] Wellington himself summarised the Burgos campaign in a letter to Edward Cooke, Under-Secretary of State for Foreign Affairs, on 28 November 1812. He was clearly on the defensive, writing more than 800 words to explain not only what happened but how he had anticipated and expected the result. Surprisingly, he says that Souham's more numerous and revitalised army had no part in his decision to retire from Burgos, but then apparently contradicts himself. Wellington goes onto say that Ballasteros was given the role of protecting Hill

10 NAM, Acc. No. 1979-12-21, pp.22–24; for clarity, the original spelling has been corrected and punctuation added. Gareth Glover has recently identified this soldier as Private Joseph Cooley (Waterloo Association, Napoleonic War Archive). The pay-list has him in the first battalion. For context see Oman, *History*, Vol.VI, pp.131–145.

11 Girod, *Foy*, pp.189–190.

12 Oman, *History*, Vol.VI, p.747.

13 Divall, *Redcoats*, p.119.

14 L.W.Woodford, *A Young Surgeon in Wellington's Army* (Old Woking: Unwin, 1976), p.31.

15 Oman, *History*, Vol.VI, p.180; R.D. Henegan, *Seven Years Campaigning in the Peninsula and the Netherlands, 1808–1815* (Stroud: Nonsuch, 2005), Vol.I, pp.146–7.

in Madrid but at the same time had no expectation of Ballasteros fulfilling the role assigned to him:

> You will certainly be disappointed in your expectations of the result of the campaign here; and I am afraid others will be so likewise. Yet I acknowledge that what has at last happened ought to have been expected, and was expected and foretold by me when I thought it probable that Soult would raise the siege of Cadiz, and would evacuate Andalusia.
>
> I entertained hopes that things might have taken a different turn if I could have succeeded at Burgos, and if Ballesteros had come forward as he ought in the end of September. But I believe those hopes are like many others regarding the war in Spain, and ought more properly to be termed wishes. However, this cause bewitches everybody; and nobody that I have seen can form and act upon a cool judgment in almost any case.
>
> I ought to have succeeded at Burgos early in October, and then how should I have stood? I might have driven the Army of Portugal, whose reinforcements were not then organised, beyond the Ebro, and I might have left there or at Burgos an army of 20,000 English and Portuguese (by the by, the worst of that description I have yet had, having nearly all the German troops among them), and from 12,000 to 16,000 Spaniards, against what turned out to be 45,000 French. If I could have stayed with them myself, this might have done; but there is nobody else on whom I could have imposed the charge, or who would have liked to undertake it.
>
> I reckon that the King and Soult brought out of Valencia about 45,000 men, of which from 5,000 to 7,000 cavalry. Hill had on the Tagus about 30,000 of the best we have, and about 10,000 Spaniards of sorts. My plan was to bring Ballesteros upon the left flank and rear of Soult's march out of Valencia, by placing him at Alcaraz, in the Sierra, where he would have been safe, at the same time that nobody could move on the great road from Valencia to attack Hill upon the Tagus.
>
> If this game had been well played, it would have answered my purpose. Soult and the King could not have remained in Valencia, and they must have crossed the Ebro, where I should have assembled all the allies, and should have worked upon their right flank.
>
> Had I any reason to expect that it would be well played? Certainly not. I have never yet known the Spaniards do anything, much less do anything well. Ballesteros has sometimes drawn the attention of a division or two for a moment, but that is all. Everything else you see and read is false and rotten. A few rascals called guerrillas attack one quarter of their numbers, and sometimes succeed, and sometimes not; but as for any regular operation, I have not known of such a thing, and successful, in the whole course of the war.
>
> Under all these circumstances, probably I ought not to have remained so long at Burgos, and ought to have withdrawn Hill at an earlier period from Madrid, and to have taken earlier measures to retire to the Agueda. The way in which matters stood are as follows: I was deceived respecting the numbers in my front in the North. I had no reason to believe that the enemy were so strong till I saw them. Fortunately they did not attack me: if they had, I must have been destroyed.
>
> I raised the siege of Burgos and retired, not because there was any pressure upon me, but because I did not think Hill secure; and I knew that if he was obliged to retire, I should be lost.

> When I saw the enemy in my front, it was clear that I was less able to contend with them than Hill was with those in his front, and that the danger threatened him, the apprehension of which as coming from his quarter had induced me to move from Burgos. I therefore ordered him to move; and I fairly bullied the French into remaining quiet upon the Douro for seven days in order to give him time to make his march. Afterwards our situation on the Tormes depended in some degree on the weather. If the rain which fell on the 15th had fallen on the 13th, the French must have attacked me at St Christoval, or we must have remained in the cantonments on the Tormes; and after all I don't know that we have sustained any great loss or inconvenience by remaining as long as we could in our positions at Madrid and the Tormes.
>
> In short, I played a game which might succeed (the only one which could succeed), and pushed it to the last; and the parts having failed, as I admit was to be expected, I have at last made a handsome retreat to the Agueda, with some labour and inconvenience, but without material loss. I believe I have done right.[16]

'Without material loss' – except of course the thousands of casualties and prisoners of war.

Béchaud received strong praise from the Armée de Portugal's commander-in-chief, Souham, 'this senior officer of rare merit and rock-solid bravery, behaved with the greatest distinction … at the combat of Villamuriel'.[17] Souham recommended Béchaud for promotion to *général de brigade*, based on his performance at Villamuriel.[18] Béchaud was promoted in January 1813 before being killed while leading a charge at the Battle of Orthez on 27 February 1814.[19] Following Béchaud's death *Maréchal* Soult wrote that '*Général de Brigade* Béchaud who was killed leading a charge, was an officer of very distinguished merit and great value: his loss is deeply felt'.[20]

Souham himself however was dismissed from the command of the Armée de Portugal, for 'tardiness and over caution in his manoeuvres since 30th October'.[21]

The significance of Villamuriel to the participants is perhaps shown by the visit of Lieutenant Colonel Craufurd of the 1/9th Foot together with Major General Andrew Hay, his then commander, to the bridge of Villamuriel in June 1813 to see the scene of the action, before moving on to Vitoria and the French border. This visit to the bridge was recorded by Le Mesurier, unfortunately all three men were subsequently killed in action: Craufurd at San Sebastian, Hay at Bayonne and Le Mesurier at the Nive in December 1813.[22]

---

16 Wellington (ed.), *Supplementary Despatches*, Vol.VII, pp.476–8.

17 A. Pigeard, D. Cavalli, A. Chappet, *Les Étoiles de Napoleon – Marechaux, Amiraux et Generaux* (Entremont-le-Vieux: Quatuor, 1996), p.218.

18 Dumay, *Historique*, p.60.

19 Colin, 'Béchaud', p.386.

20 NAM, Acc. No. 1968-07-98; Soult's report of the Battle of Orthez, 6 March 1814, to the Minister of War, included in a volume of papers from the French *Ministère de Guerre* to Napier.

21 Oman, *History*, Vol.VI, p.129.

22 Greenwood (ed.), *Le Mesurier*, pp.170, 213; letter of 7 June 1813 from Palencia.

14

Concluding Remarks

Although the two sides were approximately equal in strength, Maucune's approach of sending only one of his two brigades in strength across the Carrión at Villamuriel enabled Wellington and Oswald to create a superiority of numbers to facilitate their successful counterattack. On the other hand, Maucune's caution needs to be seen in the context of the relative quality and experience of the two sides. Although the two sides had approximately equal numbers of veteran troops, given their respective combat records it is perhaps not surprising that Maucune treated the defenders of Villamuriel with respect. Maucune is almost absent from the accounts we have, with no evidence that he was between the 'skirmishers and the heads of his columns' as he was only a few days before.

In 1836, Weare opined that:

> No guns were brought across, and the enemy seemed satisfied they could not hold their ground, otherwise why not send over more troops. – the French Genl took advantage of the absence of half the division to force the other – and knowing that the French troops had withdrawn and re-crossed the bridges at Palencia he must have anticipated the reunion of our troops and was afraid to run the risk of pushing over any more men.[1]

Alternatively, Maucune may have incorrectly assumed that the allied troops would simply retire once he had forced a crossing. Certainly, Maucune's actions at Villamuriel, where he only fully committed one brigade across the Carrión against the same division that overthrew him at Salamanca, cannot be considered those of the 'very rash leader' described by Oman.

Béchaud, writing in response to Wellington's accounts of the campaign, having compared the Palencia to Dueñas position to that at Buçaco, wrote:

> [O]ur generals only had the intention to explore your [Wellington's] strengths, distinguish your line, see your attitude of defence, in order to manoeuvre

1 TNA, NRA 21704 Oswald, Weare 12 December 1836.

> accordingly if you had not given us the ground; our general in chief did want to leave anything to risk, our *général de division* did not exceed his instructions.[2]

Béchaud also described how Maucune deployed a large proportion of his infantry as skirmishers, at least 33 percent from the beginning of the action, rising to more than 50 percent by the time of the Allied counterattack. These skirmishers were drawn from *voltigeur*, grenadier and fusilier companies. On the left these skirmishers were led by *Chef de Bataillon* Izambard of the 4/66e Ligne and on the right by *Chef de Bataillon* Frémin of the 2/15e Ligne. Both of these men, two of the four battalion commanders in d'Arnauld's brigade, became casualties. By comparison the allied army deployed approximately 15 percent of their men as skirmishers and the provisional light infantry battalions for the 5th Division were led by two majors and a captain.

This study also highlights the difference in the published regulations and instructions for skirmishing between the French and British armies, with the British specifying skirmish screens deployed at significantly smaller intervals (between two and six paces per file) than those of the French (between eight and 20 paces per file).[3] Superficially these differences provide a different lens through which to view the 'denser' British and allied skirmish screens in the Peninsula, which have often been discussed, sometimes unconvincingly, only in terms of the numbers of men deployed to skirmish. In an era when approximately half of all musket shots missed a man-sized target at 100 paces, the trade-off between density of fire and effective use of cover is perhaps represented by these differences in regulations. The greater dispersion of the French tirailleurs enabling better use of available cover, while the closer deployment of the British skirmishers enabling a greater density of fire. The further complication was that the British regulations were written for both the light infantry and the riflemen using the more accurate Baker rifle. The extent to which these publications of regulations and instructions reflect actual practices in combat needs further research.

The success of the allied counterattack was ensured by d'Arnauld's decision to deploy the two battalions of the 15e Ligne entirely as skirmishers, presumably because the ground around and beyond the canal was broken and perhaps based on an assumption that the allies were in the process of a further retirement. The accounts from both sides suggest that the French were somewhat surprised by Wellington's counterattack. The allied assault was received by only a skirmish screen and the French did not attempt to – or could not – establish a close order response until they had retreated across the Carrión. More research is required to establish how typical this tactical style was of Maucune's generalship and whether he tried to fight this way in other actions.

2 Colin, 'Béchaud', p.410.

3 Husson, *Instruction*, pp.13, 23, 47–48; War Office, *Regulations*, p.17; Anon., *Systema de Instrucção e Disciplina para os movimentos e deveres dos Caçadores…* (Lisbon: Regia, 1810), p.47; Neil Campbell, *Instructions for Light Infantry and Riflemen* (London: Egerton, 1813), p.64; Campbell's work was translated to provide the regulations for the Portuguese caçadores, in it he specifies a six pace interval between files or double files.

Another subject for further work relates to the 15e Ligne taking a 'light infantry role' for the division. Five of the eight divisions in the Armée de Portugal had a light regiment in their first brigade. It is commonly stated that the French light infantry regiments had 'levelled down' to the standards of the line regiments by this time with regard to light infantry operations and were used interchangeably, but this is worthy of reconsideration. On first inspection the 5e Division is an example of this interchangeability, but it is interesting that Maucune chose the *voltigeurs* and grenadiers of d'Arnauld's brigade to open the skirmishing at Calabazanos and to lead the assault across the river there in the afternoon rather than those of his left-hand brigade, Montfort's. The subsequent use of the 15e Ligne fully deployed to skirmish may suggest that the interchangeability was more limited than has been suggested and that individual regiments, whether line or light, in the divisions were given this role.

The initial deployment of Pringle's Brigade in columns of attack, ready to advance to the bridge to counterattack the French should the mine fail, and Wellington's choice of an open column formation followed by a wheel into line for Barnes's Brigade in the afternoon counterattack, both within range of the enemy guns, together demonstrate the tactical flexibility of the British infantry.

This study describes how divisional level combat in the Peninsula during the Napoleonic Wars was more complex than simple confrontations between French columns and British lines. The light infantry 'ambitions' of the 1/9th Foot vividly illustrates the continuing development of infantry tactics while the war was progressing. The 1/9th Foot appears to have been used on more than one occasion to reinforce the provisional light infantry battalions of the British brigades, in the skirmish screen, and at Villamuriel appears to have a different role to the other British battalions.

The village of Villamuriel itself did not feature in the fighting on 25 October as did villages in other Peninsular War battles. This was due to a refusal by both sides to garrison it because of the easy availability of wine and the previous drunkenness in both armies. Hence the men of the two much-reduced companies of the Duke of Brunswick Oels Light infantry were able to capture the village during the counterattack. The decision taken to avoid drunkenness seems to have led to several witnesses remarking that the village was not properly defended.

It is a testament to the general confusion that surrounds even a small action like Villamuriel, that, even though Wellington's counterattack was successful in driving the French infantry back across the Carrión, at least two of Oswald's regiments were unable to take all their wounded men with them the next morning.

Although some British observers including Wellington were critical of the order and discipline of the Spanish infantry, their eagerness for action is also remarked on. Moreover, any criticism needs to be viewed in the context that one of the units had only been raised four months before the battle and the other only 12 to 18 months before the battle.

Both sides claimed victory at Villamuriel de Cerrato. Wellington described in his despatch how he had driven the French back across the

Carrión 'with considerable loss' while his own men suffered 'a good deal'. On the other hand, Souham wrote that 'the enemy, seeing that we were masters of the left bank of the Pisuerga, was quick to accelerate his retirement'. Oman concluded 'despite of Maucune's repulse, the result of the day's fighting was much to Wellington's detriment, since… the capture of Palencia ruined his scheme for defending the line of the Carrion. Souham's whole army could follow Foy and turn the left flank of the Allies behind that river'.[4]

In summary, while the French had been forced back across the river at Villamuriel, they had also established that they could cross it at will through the fords and across the bridges at Palencia, Villamuriel, and Tariego. The French also lost considerably fewer men at Villamuriel than claimed by some of the allied sources, and probably fewer than the allied army. Wellington therefore determined to continue his retreat steadily through Dueñas to a stronger position beyond the Duero.

4 Oman, *History*, Vol.VI, p.81.

15

Wargaming the Action

'... it all stands on the hazard of a die'
– Ensign John Mills, Coldstream Guards, 28 October 1812[1]

This chapter provides the key information for recreating the action of Villamuriel with miniatures on the tabletop.

Scenarios

The combat for Villamuriel can be divided into three main scenarios for gaming the action:

1. Morning, Initial French Attack.
2. Afternoon, Main French Attack.
3. Afternoon, Allied Counterattack.

The generals can be represented using the following ratings which have been chosen to best represent their performance on the day. Wellington is not represented as he left Oswald to fight his division, while he was equally concerned about the action at Palencia and Tariego:

General	Black Powder™	General de Brigade®	Comment
Maucune	Staff Rating=7; +1 to break test within 12"	Average	Inspirational but unusually remained aloof
D'Arnauld	SR 8; 1 bonus attack	Average	
Montfort	SR 7	Average	Passive and defensive
Blanzat	SR 7	Average	Static during the action
Desfossés	SR 8; 1 bonus attack	Average	
Oswald	SR 8; 1 bonus attack	Average	
Barnes	SR 8; +1 to charge; 1 bonus attack	Average	Aggressive
Pringle	SR 8; 1 bonus attack	Average	
Spry	SR 6	Poor	Did not get involved
Liñan	SR 7	Average	

1 Divall, *Scrape*, p.119.

The following tables detail which units are included in each scenario, their quality and strengths, expressed in the figure scales of 33 and 20 men represented per figure:

French	Quality	Strength	Figures		Scenario		
Général de Division A.L. Maucune			1:33	1:20	1	2	3
Brigade d'Arnauld							
15e Ligne							
1er Bataillon	Veteran	677	21	34	Y	Y	Y
2e Bataillon	Veteran	659	20	33	Y	Y	Y
4e Bataillon	Veteran	240	7	12	Y	Y	Y
66e Ligne							
4e Bataillon	Veteran	515	16	26	Y	Y	Y
6e Bataillon	Veteran	467	14	23	Y	Y	Y
Brigade Montfort							
82e Ligne							
4e Bataillon	Veteran	455	14	23	Y	Y	Y
5e Bataillon	Veteran	471	14	24	Y	Y	Y
86e Ligne							
1er Bataillon	Veteran	563	17	28	Y	Y	Y
2e Bataillon	Veteran	526	16	26	Y	Y	Y
Light Cavalry Brigade Desfossés							
3e Hussards	Veteran	249	8	12	N	Y	Y
22e Chasseurs à Cheval	Veteran	330	10	17	N	Y	Y
26e Chasseurs à Cheval	Veteran	356	11	18	N	Y	Y
28e Chasseurs à Cheval	Veteran	21	1	1	N	Y	Y
Artillery							
11/8e Artillerie à Pied (2x 8pdrs, 2x 4pdrs, 2x 6-inch how.)	Veteran	77	2	4	Y	Y	Y
6/2e Artillerie à Cheval (4x 8pdrs, 1x 6-inch how.)	Veteran	88	3	4	Y	Y	Y
Totals		5,694	173	285			

Allied	Quality	Strength	Figures		Scenario		
			1:33	1:20	1	2	3
5th Division, Maj. Gen. J. Oswald							
1st Brigade, Brig. Gen. E. Barnes							
3/1st Foot	Veteran	376	11	19	N	N	Y
1/9th Foot	Veteran	304	9	15	Y	Y	Y
1/38th Foot	Veteran	284	9	14	Y	N	Y
2/38th Foot	Veteran	158	5	8	Y	N	Y
Brigade light companies	Veteran	172	5	9	Y	Y	N
2nd Brigade, Maj. Gen. W. Pringle							
1/4th Foot	Veteran	356	11	18	Y	Y	Y
2/4th Foot	Inexp'd	302	9	15	Y	N	Y
2/30th Foot	Veteran	206	6	10	Y	Y	Y
2/44th Foot	Veteran	149	5	7	Y	Y	Y
Brigade light companies	Veteran	151	5	8	Y	Y	N
Brunswick Oels Light Infantry*	Veteran	86	3	4	N	N	Y

Brigada N.3, *Brigadeiro* W.F. Spry							
1/RI N.3	Veteran	410	12	21	Y	Y	Y
2/RI N.3	Veteran	296	9	15	Y	Y	Y
1/RI N.15	Veteran	434	13	22	Y	Y	Y
2/RI N.15	Veteran	307	9	15	Y	Y	Y
Caçadores N.8	Veteran	426	13	21	Y	Y	N
Royal Artillery, Major R. Lawson (4x 9pdrs, 1x 24pdr how.)	Veteran	127	4	6	Y	Y	Y
1ª Sección, 1ª Division, 6º Ejército *Brigadier* Don P. Liñan							
Regimiento 1º Asturias	Inexp'd	534	16	27	Y	Y	Y
2º Voluntarios de Corona	Inexp'd	534	16	27	Y	Y	Y
Totals		5,142	156	257			

Note:

*the Duke of Brunswick Oels Light Infantry companies are subsumed into the Brigade light infantry battalions in the first two scenarios. For Scenario 3, this table follows Kortzfleisch, Liñan, Burgoyne and Le Mesurier, alternatively the brigade light infantry battalions could be used instead.

Using the definitions in the Black Powder™ rules (BP), all the French troops should be given the special rules 'reliable' and 'elite 5+'. The French cavalry should also be given the special rule 'marauders'. The British and Portuguese troops should all be given the special rules 'first fire', 'reliable' and 'elite 4+', except for the 2/4th which should instead have the special rule 'unreliable'. To represent their performance on the day, the Caçadores N.8 should also be given the special rule 'valiant'. The Spanish infantry should be given the 'wavering' and 'unreliable' special rules.

Using the definitions in the General de Brigade® rules (GdB), none of the units meet the criterion for 'Veteran' status. The French units would all be classified as 'Line', with the 6/66e Ligne possibly being considered '2nd Line'. Given their history the battalions of the 66e and 82e Ligne cannot be considered '2nd Line' based simply on their battalion number. On the allied side the Spanish units would be considered 'Conscript'. The 2/4th Foot could be '2nd Line' but all other units would be 'Line'. Alternatively, in both armies, promote the 'Line' units to 'Veteran' and the '2nd Line' units to 'Line'.

Scenario One: Morning – Initial French attack

This scenario covers the initial probing attacks by the French towards and across the river. The starting positions for this scenario are as per Map 10:

The scenario maps have been designed for a table of 6 x 4 feet using a ground scale of 1mm to 2 paces for 15- or 18-mm figures. For 25- or 28-mm figures the table would be approximately 10 x 6½ feet at a ground scale of 1 inch represents 30 paces or 24 yards.

Game Duration: The scenario lasts 3 hours or 12 game turns, from 9:00 a.m. The French move first.

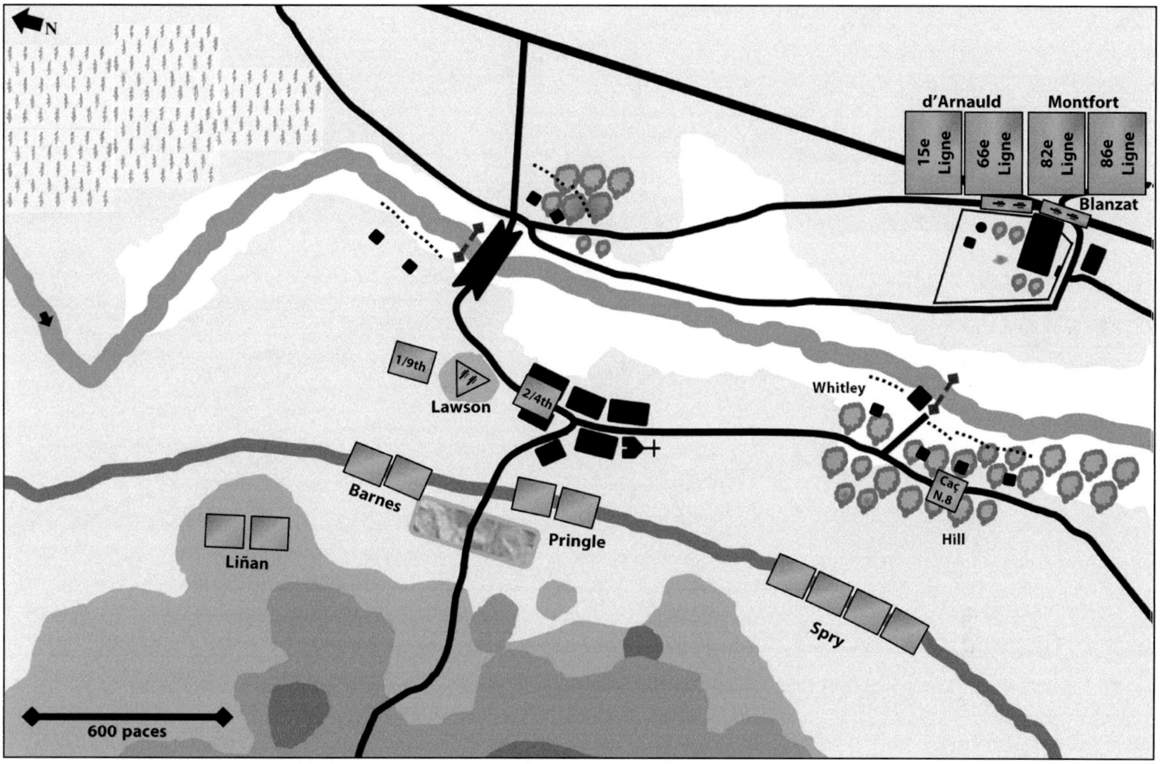

Map 10 Scenario One.

Special Feature: Wellington was clearly nervous about the effectiveness of the mine at the bridge and this should be represented in the game by a die roll. To initiate the detonation of the mine the British and Allied player rolls a D6:

Score	Effect
4+	Detonation initiated immediately.
2–3	Detonation initiated at the start of next move.
1	Detonation initiated at the start of the move after next.

Once the demolition is initiated, the British and allied player should roll another D6. On a score of one, the mine is deemed to have failed, and the bridge remains intact. Only one attempt is allowed. If the attempt is successful, the bridge is destroyed and any unit on the bridge at the time of the explosion is broken (BP) or dispersed (GdB) and removed from play.

Victory Conditions: Souham in his report, described Maucune as 'vigorously attacking' ('*attaquer vivement*') at Villamuriel, while only sending a reconnaissance to Dueñas. Thus, it is reasonable to assume that Maucune was ordered to force the crossing, establishing his division on the right bank. On the other hand, Béchaud, later stated that the objective was only to probe the British and Allied positions, establishing their strength and line, a view supported by Girard, who described Souham as ordering a 'false

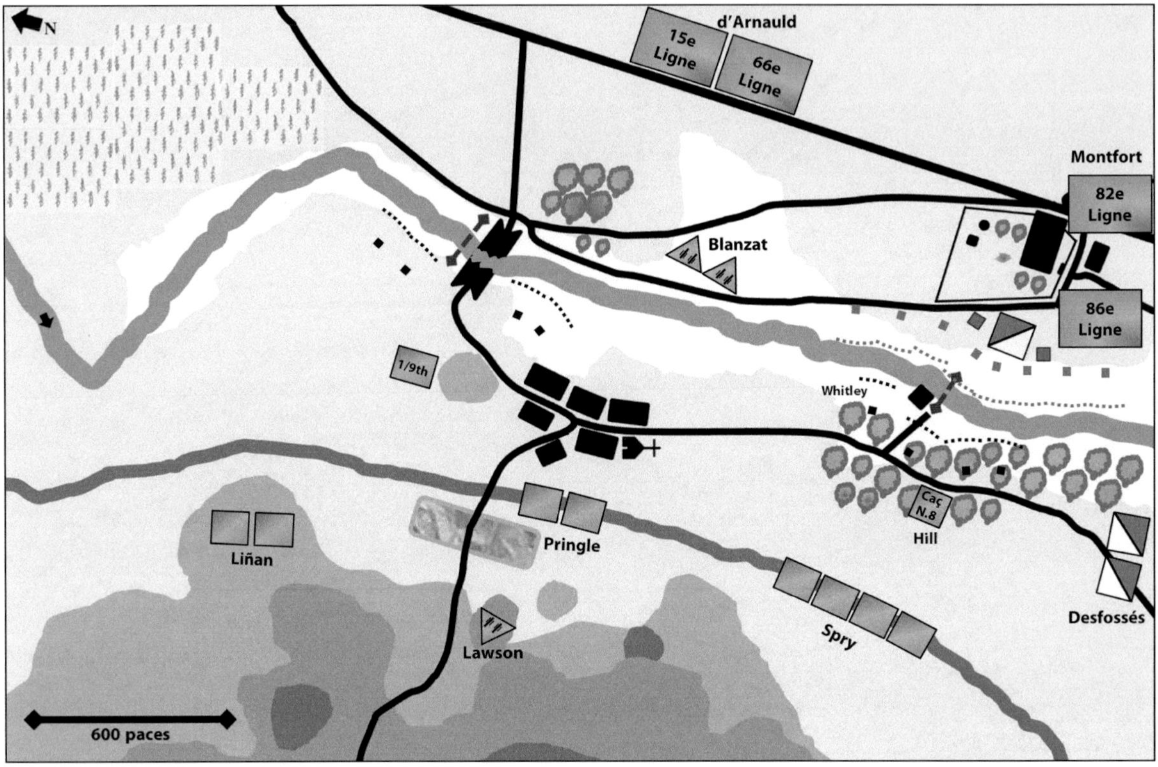

Map 11 Scenario Two.

attack'.[2] From the allied perspective, Wellington hoped and expected that the successful detonation of the mine and destruction of the bridge would prevent the French from crossing the river at all. In this context the French can claim victory if, at the end of the game, one or more of their brigades has successfully crossed the river with more than half of its units. The allies can claim victory if they can prevent the French from fulfilling their victory conditions.

Scenario Two; Afternoon – Main French Attack

This scenario covers the main French attacks across the river. For this scenario a large part of Barnes's Brigade has been detached and is on its way towards Palencia. The French player has been reinforced by the light cavalry brigade and has a free choice of how to divide them between Calabazanos or off the table ready for the flank attack.

The starting positions for this scenario are as per Map 11:

Game Duration: The scenario lasts 2 hours or 8 game turns, from 1:00 p.m. The French move first.

2 Desachy, *Girard*, p.206; Colin, 'Béchaud', p.410.

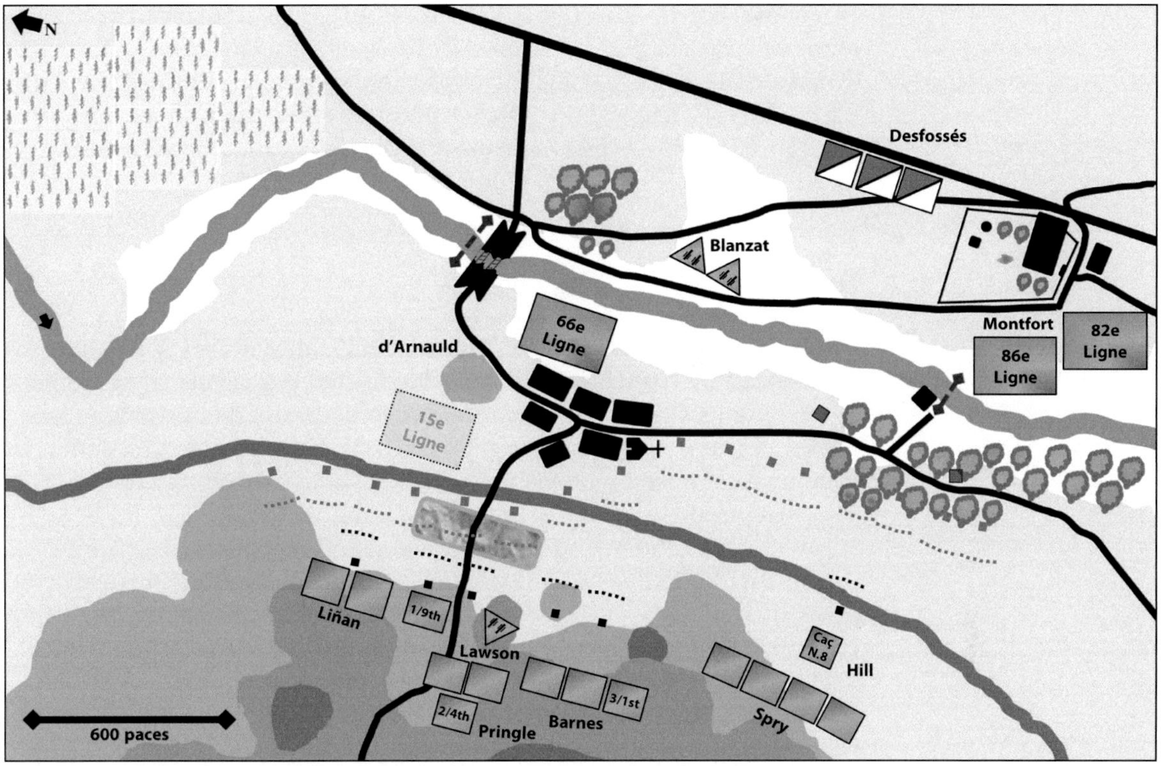

Map 12 Scenario Three.

Victory Conditions: The French can claim victory if at the end of the game, one or more of their infantry brigades has successfully crossed the river with more than half of its units. The allies can claim victory if they can prevent the French from fulfilling their victory conditions.

Scenario Three; British and Allied Counterattack

This scenario covers Wellington's counterattack designed to drive the French back across the river. Barnes's Brigade re-joined the 5th Division at approximately 3:00 p.m.

The starting positions for this scenario are as per Map 12:

Game Duration: The scenario lasts 2 hours or 8 game turns, from 4:00 p.m. The allied army moves first.

Victory Conditions: For the allies, Oswald described his orders as 'to drive the enemy from the right bank of the river'.[3] Oswald can therefore claim victory if he can advance to the banks of the Carrión without his division being broken. The fate of Liñan's brigade does not count towards the army morale of the allies.

3 Oswald, 'Affair at Villa Muriele', p.267.

For the French, once Foy had got across the Carrión at Palencia the urgency of the other probes receded, however Béchaud's account clearly shows that d'Arnauld attempted to hold the crossing and bridge at Villamuriel. Therefore, the French can claim victory if they repulse the allied attack, breaking both of the British brigades, while remaining on the right bank of the Carrión.

All other results should be considered a draw.

Terrain

Fords: the fords were both reported to be 'difficult' and that at Calabazanos was apparently particularly difficult due to the level of the river. In Black Powder™ units attempting to cross either ford, cannot do so using initiative moves. Those units attempting to cross at Calabazanos also suffer an additional command modifier of -1. The crossings themselves both count as a normal linear obstacle (BP) or as difficult terrain (GdB).

Canal: should be treated as two parallel linear obstacles approximately 30 paces apart, the bed of the canal is approximately 20 paces wide. The depth (2–3 m) is such that units in the canal bed cannot see or fire out of the canal.[4]

Village Buildings: the village was well stocked with wine and, given the widespread drunkenness that had occurred at Torquemada, both sides were prevented from garrisoning the village.[5] Only skirmish order units or units in march column may move through the village, treating it as rough ground.[6]

Bodegas or Wine Vaults: should be treated as rough ground, and like the village buildings, the vaults themselves cannot be occupied.

Watermill: in our game, the mill is too small to be considered a built-up area and therefore cannot be occupied.

Hillside: Douglas describes the hillside as being very steep and broken. Furthermore, Oswald describes the Caçadores N.8 being pushed back to 'broken ground'.[7] Therefore the ground above the 750m contour should be considered as rough ground (BP) and difficult terrain (GdB).

Wood: the woods should be considered as open, or as rough ground which blocks line of sight (BP) and as difficult terrain (GdB).

4 Napier, *History*, 1993, Vol.V, p.300; Guía Canal de Castilla 2018, available at <http://www.canaldecastilla.org/Docs/guia/CdC_Introduccion.pdf>, accessed 12/09/2013.

5 Colin, 'Béchaud', p.408; Leslie, *Dickson*, Vol.IV, p.712.

6 Colin, 'Béchaud', p.409.

7 Monick (ed.), *Douglas*, p.59; Oswald, 'Affair at Villa Muriele', p.267.

Uniform Notes

There are plenty of readily available resources describing the uniforms likely to have been worn by the participants at Villamuriel, consequently this section includes notes on specific points of interest.

French Infantry

The 15e Ligne regiment was one of the regiments given the 1806 white uniforms and initially went to Spain wearing them.[8] However given that the regulation life of the long tailed coat or *habit-longe* was three years, they would have been expected to change to the pre-Bardin blue *habit-longe* during 1809.[9] The 1812 Bardin uniforms based on the short tailed *habit-veste* were unlikely to have been worn in the Peninsula in 1812.

French Eagles, Flags and Fanions

From 1808, it was expected that each regiment would carry only one eagle into the field. Béchaud mentions that the 66e Ligne carried one eagle into battle at Villamuriel.[10] Letrun states that the fourth battalion of the 66e Ligne was given an eagle in Bordeaux in 1808, although Charrié records that this happened in 1810 and that the eagle in service with the regiment in 1812 was that of the 'old' third battalion.[11] Eagles were also carried by the 1/15e Ligne, the 4/82e Ligne and the 1/86e Ligne.[12] Muzás has the 86e Ligne losing its eagle in a shipwreck on the voyage from Portugal to France following the Convention of Cintra in 1808. However, this is not supported by either Charrié or the regimental history.[13] Although the regimental headquarters was involved in the sinking of their transport, the schooner the *Three Brothers*, the *colonel* and other officers escaped and returned to France, presumably taking the precious eagle with them.[14]

In December 1811, the new tricolour-based flags to be used with the eagles were decreed, however it is unlikely that any flags of the new design were sent to units in the Peninsula in 1812.[15]

The battalions that did not carry eagles, were intended to have carried simple plain unmarked ensigns or *fanions* on a staff with a simple spearhead. According to the 1811 decree and the February 1812 order of the day, they would have carried; 2/15e Ligne – a white *fanion*; 6/66e Ligne – a yellow

8 M. Windrow, G. Embleton, *Military Dress of the Peninsular War* (London: Ian Allen, 1974), Plate 1, figure 1, p.22; G. Dempsey, *Napoleon's Army 1807–1814* (London: Arms and Armour, 1997), plates 107/34, 109/36.

9 Crowdy, *Handbook*, p.58; P. Haythornthwaite, *Napoleon's Line Infantry* (London: Osprey, 1983), pp.9, 20.

10 Colin, 'Béchaud', p.408.

11 L.Letrun, *French Infantry Flags* (Paris: Histoire et Collections, 2009), pp.18, 170, 172; P. Charrié, *Drapeaux et étendards de la Révolution et de l'Empire* (Paris: Copernic, 1982), p.210.

12 Charrié, *Drapeaux*, pp.205, 211; Arvers, Brecht, *Historique*, p.127.

13 L.S. Muzás, *Trophies Taken by the British from the Napoleonic Army during the War of Spanish Independence (Peninsular War) 1808–1814*, at <https://www.napoleon-series.org/military-info/battles/c_capturedflags.html>, accessed 21 June 2017.

14 Anon., *Historique du 86e*, p.21.

15 Charrié, *Drapeaux*, p.140.

fanion; 5/82e Ligne – a green *fanion*; 2/86e Ligne – a white *fanion*. However, Charrié states that it is unlikely that any of the official *fanions* were sent to the regiments in Spain in 1812, thus leaving the regimental colonels to make their own if they so desired. The known unofficial *fanions* were of various combinations of blue and red and various tricolour designs. However, it is likely that the plain green flag taken by the 11th Foot at Salamanca, was such a *fanion*. A drawing of this captured flag, by William Thomas Fitzgerald, that was published by Edward Orme in August 1812, is consistent with the 1811 decree.[16] The only fifth battalions present with the French Army were the 5/26e Ligne from Ferrey's division and the 5/66e Ligne and 5/82e Ligne from Maucune's division.[17] Orme's illustration also shows a similar white ensign that would have belonged to a second battalion. Regardless of which battalion was involved, the capture of these flags is evidence that the new pattern *fanions* were available in Spain in 1812, locally produced or otherwise. Robinson suggested that the green flag belonged to a foreign unit in the French army, however the order of battle contains only a small detachment of the *Régiment de Prusse* or *4e Régiment d'Étranger*, which, if it had a flag, would have been one of the standard French pattern.[18]

French 3e Hussards

The uniform of the 3e Hussards is the subject of significant discussion regarding the colour of the cloth used, which is described as *gris argentin* or silver grey.[19] The main issue regards how blue the silver grey cloth was, with some sources opting for more blue than grey.[20] Three illustrations demonstrate the variety; Vernet's and Martinet's contemporary representations along with Knötel's more recent one.[21]

Brigadier General Edward Barnes

It was common, given the temporary nature of their appointments, for British brigadier generals to wear their regimental uniforms as colonel or lieutenant colonel, while serving as brigadier generals. Barnes, however, was sent to the Peninsula without his regiment, the 46th Foot, which went to Jersey on its return from the West Indies. Consequently, Barnes served on Wellington's

16 The Royal Collection Trust, RCIN 750679, *Battle of Salamanca: trophies taken from French, 22 July 1812*.

17 Crowdy, *Handbook*, p.107; Charrié, *Drapeaux*, pp.90–91, plate facing p.224; P. Haythornthwaite, *Uniforms of the Retreat from Moscow 1812* (Poole: Blandford, 1976), plate 13, p.114; Letrun, *Flags*, p.169.

18 R.E.R. Robinson, *The Bloody Eleventh, History of the Devonshire Regiment, Volume 1, 1685–1815* (Exeter: Devon and Dorset Regiment, 1988), p.430; Cannon, *Historical Record of the Eleventh Foot*, pp.65, 68.

19 *Gris argentin* is sometimes translated as Argentine Grey, but the *Larousse English-French Dictionary* suggests that Argentine Grey would be *gris d'Argentine*.

20 A. Jouineau, *Officers and Soldiers of the French Hussars, 2: 1st to 8th Regiments, 1804–1812* (Paris: Histoire et Collections, 2006), pp.38–43.

21 Musée de l'Armée, Paris, C. Vernet, Planche 180 du volume IV du projet de règlement sur l'habillement du Major Bardin; Dempsey, *Army*, print 89; R. Knötel, *Uniformenkunde*, Vol.13, plate 8; at <https://commons.wikimedia.org/wiki/File:3e_r%C3%A9giment_de_hussards,_1806-1814.jpg>.

staff and could have worn the uniform of a brigadier general on the staff as described by Haythornthwaite:

> Uniform distinctions for … brigadier general were first published in 1804, when it was specified that their coats should resemble those of major generals, but for the loops on the sleeve and skirt, where instead of two pairs there should be three set two over one, with the lowest sleeve loop on the cuff. … [T]he regulation button bore a crossed sword and baton surrounded by a laurel wreath in gilt. The order of 1811 which replaced epaulettes with the single aiguillette [on the right shoulder] must have applied to brigadiers.[22]

Portuguese Infantry

The Caçadores N.8 were created on 4 May 1811 from the 2/Leal Legião Lusitana. In July 1811 new uniforms were introduced for the *caçadores*. A veteran of the Leal Legião Lusitana confirmed that the new uniforms had replaced the green of the Legião by the beginning of 1812.[23] At the same time, a new British style stovepipe shako was being introduced to replace the 1806 Barrentina, consequently these would have been worn by the Caçadores N.8.

The line infantry also adopted the British style stovepipe shako as the war progressed.[24] Spry's Brigade were reported by Le Mesurier to have gone to get new clothing in May 1812, therefore they were most likely wearing the new shako at Villamuriel.[25]

Spanish Infantry

Given that both the Spanish battalions were relatively recently raised, it is likely that the uniforms worn by these men were from the shipments provided by the British government during 1811 and 1812. These were of blue jackets and blue or blue-grey trousers with sky blue (1° Asturias) or red facings. The units would also have worn stovepipe shakos.[26]

If they had flags, the two battalions would have carried the 1762 model *coronela* design, a white flag bearing the royal arms in the centre, or the newer non-regulation designs based on the *coronela* but including the red cross of burgundy in the background. Alternatively, they could have carried a *sencilla* design, a white flag with just the red cross of burgundy, as carried by the 2° Asturias.[27]

---

22 P. Haythornthwaite, *Wellington's Army, the uniforms of the British soldier, 1812–15* (London: Greenhill, 2002), Plate 3 commentary.

23 Santos, *Ordens*, 1811, pp.72, 139–140; W. Mayne, J.S. Lillie, *Loyal Lusitanian Legion during the years 1809, 1810 and 1811* (London: T. Egerton, 1812), pp.116–7.

24 Windrow, *Military Dress*, plate 6, figures 44, 42, pp.74–5; Portuguese Line and Caçadores.

25 Greenwood, *Le Mesurier*, p.108.

26 R. Chartrand, B. Younghusband, *Spanish Army*, pp.12–13, 16; citing TNA, WO1/270; *Estado*, 1815, p.54; Conde de Clonard, *História*, Vol.VIII, p.13.

27 L.S. Muzás, *Banderas, estandartes y trofeos del Museo del Ejército 1700–1843, Catálogo razonado* (Madrid: Ministerio de Defensa, 2000), pp.57, 196 and p.540 on accompanying CD, Inventory no. 40748.

Appendix I

French Staff, Regimental and Battalion Commanders

Staff

Chief of Staff

***Chef de Bataillon* Étienne-François Girard** born 7 November 1766 in Châteaudun, he volunteered as a *soldat* in the de Neustrie (later the 10e) régiment d'infanterie on 27 July 1785 having been rejected as too small the year before. He was promoted to *sergent* 4 June 1792 and was wounded while serving with the Armée du Midi. Promoted to *sergent major* on 7 March 1793, he was wounded again in the assault on Fort Mulgrave at Toulon 16–17 December 1793. He was promoted to *sous-lieutenant* 20 December 1793 and joined Dugommier's staff. Distinguished at the Combat of Boulou against the Spanish on 1 May 1794, he was promoted to *lieutenant aide de camp* to *Général de Brigade* François Guillot on 2 December 1794. He was promoted to *capitaine* on 5 May 1796 while serving in the Armée d'Italie. He then joined the Armée d'Angleterre/Armée de l'Ouest and then the Grande Armée for the campaigns of 1805, 1806 and 1807, on the staff of VI Corps. He was then promoted to *chef de bataillon* on 22 March 1807. He then joined the staff of VI Corps, Armée d'Espagne in November 1808 and then the 5e Division, Armée de Portugal on 13 March 1812 as chief of staff.[1] Desachy provides the following description of Girard; 'his size is small: five feet, one inch… round, full, colourful face, marked by smallpox and by a scar above the right eyebrow. Mouth wide, raised nose, small forehead. Hair and eyebrows black. Eyes blue'.[2]

Girard was supported in his role as chief of staff by *Lieutenant Adjoint* Vincent Python who was born in Lisbon in 1772.[3]

1 Quintin, *Colonels*, pp.378–9.
2 Desachy, *Girard*, Preface p.iii.
3 SHD C8 468; LEONORE LH/2242/97.

Divisional Artillery Commander

***Chef de Bataillon* Charles Ursin Blanzat**: 2e Régiment d'Artillerie à Cheval, born 9 November 1779, entered service 6 August 1792, seniority 29 January 1812.[4]

Divisional Engineer

***Capitaine* Benoît Placide Génot**: born in Dijon 27 June 1782, *sous lieutenant* 22 November 1801, *lieutenant d'état major* 23 October 1802, *capitaine en second* 1 January 1807, *capitaine de première classe* 1 January 1812. He served in the Grande Armée 1805–8, the Armée d'Allemagne 1809, and then the Armée de Portugal, 1810–12. He was awarded the *Legion d'Honneur* in 1810.[5]

Maucune's Aides de Camp

***Capitaine* Pierre Abraham Lafont**: born on 2 August 1777, joined the army as a *soldat* in 1793; he served in the Pyrenees and Italy before joining the Grande Armée for the campaigns of 1806 and 1807. He then went to Spain and Portugal for all the campaigns from 1808 until 1813, before following Maucune to Italy in 1814 as *chef de bataillon*. In all he was wounded six times. He was awarded the *Legion d'Honneur* in 1807.[6]

***Capitaine* Alexandre Jean François Lesueur LaChapelle**: born 27 November 1779, volunteered as *soldat* 25 June 1804. In 1805–7, he served with the Grande Armée and he then served in Spain and Portugal from 1808 to 1813, before re-joining the Grande Armée in 1814. He was appointed lieutenant *aide de camp* to Maucune in November 1808 and was then promoted to *capitaine aide de camp* in June 1811. Having been appointed a *Legionnaire* in 1807, he became an *Officier de la Legion d'Honneur* in 1815.[7]

15e Ligne

***Major* Jacques-Louis Dornier**: born 13 February 1774, son of a Swiss soldier, *caporal* 3e Bataillon de la Republique 17 October 1792; seniority as *major* 21 June 1811, killed in action at Troyes in March 1814 as *général de brigade*.[8] In his biography, Six does not include Dornier's service with the 15e Ligne, however, he does mention the incident at Arroyo del Puerco, 28 August 1811, when Dornier distinguished himself while serving with the 69e Ligne, before he joined the 15e Ligne in November 1811. Dornier served in several infantry regiments, 2e Grenadiers de la Garde Consulaire, 43e Ligne, 15e Légère, 69e Ligne and 15e Ligne before becoming *colonel* of the 26e Légère.[9]

---

4 LEONORE LH/255/44.

5 LEONORE LH/1111/28.

6 LEONORE LH/1436/67.

7 LEONORE LH/1618/55.

8 G. Six, *Dictionnaire Biographique* des *Généraux et Amiraux Français de la Révolution et de l'Empire, 1792–1814* (Paris: Historique et Nobiliaire, 1934), Vol.I, pp.368–9.

9 De Tarragon, *Historique*, p.216; *Historique du 69e Régiment d'infanterie* (Paris: Charles-Lavauzelle, 1890), p.54.

***Capitaine* Jean Lafitte**: born 27 March 1773, *sergent major* 21 September 1793, seniority as *capitaine* 20 December 1805.[10]

***Chef de Bataillon* Alexandre François Frémin**: born 31 December 1782, joined as *soldat* 20 December 1803, seniority as *chef de bataillon* 4 December 1809. He 'disappeared' after the Battle of Leipzig when *colonel* of the 153e Ligne, while serving in Maison's 16e Division, Lauriston's V Corps.[11]

66e Ligne

***Colonel* Jean Pierre Béchaud**: born 17 February 1770, joined as a *soldat* 7 June 1787, seniority as *colonel* 8 December 1808. He fought with the Armée du Rhin in 1792–6, the Armée d'Angleterre in 1797, the Armée d'Italie in 1798–1801, before serving in the West Indies in 1802–3. He was seriously wounded on the bridge over the Cõa in July 1810 and wounded again at Buçaco in September. In 1804 he was appointed *Legionnaire de la Legion d'Honneur* and an *Officier* in 1810.[12]

***Chef de Bataillon* Michel Izambard**: born 27 May 1773, joined as a *soldat* 27 September 1792, seniority as *chef de bataillon* 2 March 1811.[13]

***Capitaine* Leopold Daniel Charlemont**: born 21 October 1773 in Nancy, appointed *lieutenant* by the King in 1792, seniority as *capitaine* 19 June 1794.[14]

82e Ligne

***Colonel* Joseph Jacob van Geen**: born 1 September 1775, enlisted as a *soldat* 15 July 1791. He fought in Flanders and Holland in 1792–5, in Germany in 1796, from 1797–9 in North Holland. He then served in Germany in 1805–9 and in Zeeland in 1811. Seniority as *colonel* 29 August 1809. He first served in Spain in 1812. He was wounded five times.[15]

***Chef de Bataillon* Michel Lefizelier**: born 12 April 1768, enlisted as *soldat* 14 September 1792, seniority as *chef de bataillon* 23 August 1809.[16]

***Chef de Bataillon* Jean Baptiste Dupré**: born 14 October 1767, enlisted as *soldat* 3 January 1793, seniority as *chef de bataillon* 19 April 1812.[17]

---

10 SHD 2Yb 157, p.63, *contrôle des officiers* 15e Ligne.

11 Quintin, *Colonels*, p.345–6; a third of his officers were casualties at Leipzig.

12 A. Liévyns, J.-M. Verdot, P. Bégat, *Fastes de la légion-d'honneur: biographie de tous les décorés accompagnée de l'histoire législative et réglementaire de l'ordre* (Paris: Bureau d'Administration, 1844), Vol.IV, p.458; SHD 2Yb 349, p.3, *CdO* 66e Ligne.

13 SHD 2Yb 349, p.21.

14 SHD 2Yb 349, p.139.

15 Quintin, *Colonels*, p.367; SHD 2Yb 397, p.155, *CdO 82e Ligne*; the *CdO* gives only four wounds.

16 SHD 2Yb 397, p.162.

17 SHD 2Yb 397, p.152.

86e Ligne

***Colonel* Claude Joseph Pélecier**: born 3 October 1774, enlisted as *soldat* 6 June 1792. He served with the Armées du Rhin (1792–3), du Rhin-et-Moselle (1794–7, 208e Demi-brigade de bataille and 56e Ligne), d'Italie (1797–9), de l'Oeust (1800–3, 56e Ligne) and d'Italie (1805, 3e Légère). He then served in the Grande Armée from 1806–7. He went to Spain in 1808 where he served in both the 113e Ligne and 103e Ligne, before his promotion to *colonel* in the 86e Ligne 15 April 1811.[18]

***Chef de Bataillon* Jean Luzinier**: born 17 August 1769, enlisted as *soldat* 8 October 1793, seniority as *chef de bataillon* 20 September 1809.[19]

***Chef de Bataillon* François Adam Eys**: born 6 November 1771, enlisted as *sous lieutenant* 26 September 1788, seniority as *chef de bataillon* 2 March 1811.[20]

3e Hussards

***Major* Amedée Marie Joseph Heina**: born 29 September 1769, enlisted as *cavalier* in the Division de la Cavalerie de Paris 18 October 1789, *sous lieutenant* 1 May 1793, seniority as *major* 7 April 1809.[21]

22e Chasseurs à Cheval

***Colonel* François Michel Desfossés**: see Chapter 3.

26e Chasseurs à Cheval

***Capitaine* Jacques Felix Franquin Govon**: born 25 July 1779, joined as *soldat* in Régiment de la Reine Infanterie 8 March 1795, seniority as *capitaine* 17 November 1808.[22]

28e Chasseurs à Cheval

***Sous Lieutenant* Joseph Pinelli**: born 16 March 1777 in Tuscany.[23]

11/8e Artillerie à Pied

***Capitaine* Joseph Marie Alexis Vincent Genta**: born 19 February 1787 on Sardinia, enlisted 12 August 1800, wounded 15 January 1814, Isle of Wilhelmsburg, Hamburg.[24]

6/2e Artillerie à Cheval

***Capitaine* Joseph Viard**: served in the Garde Impériale from April 1813 and was killed in action at Dresden in August 1813.[25]

---

18 SHD Yb21 411, p.16, *CdO 86e Ligne*; Quintin, *Colonels*, p.672; LEONORE LH/2082/21.
19 SHD Yb21 411, p.50.
20 SHD Yb21 411, p.48.
21 SHD 2Yb 953, p.52; LEONORE LH/1277/82.
22 LEONORE LH/1183/32.
23 LEONORE LH/2166/5.
24 LEONORE LH/1112/20; Martinien, *Tableaux*, p.646.
25 SHD 2Yb 1015; Martinien, *Tableaux*, p.107.

Appendix II

Allied Staff, Regimental Commanders and Officers

Staff

The staff of the Anglo-Portuguese 5th Division comprised the following officers;

Assistant Adjutant General	Lieutenant Colonel George Henry Frederick Berkeley	35th Foot
Deputy Assistant Adjutant General	Captain Henry Craig	30th Foot
Assistant Quartermaster General	Lieutenant Colonel William Maynard Gomm	9th Foot
Deputy Assistant Quartermaster General	Captain Nathaniel Gledstanes	68th Foot
Aide de Camp to Oswald	Captain Thomas Weare	35th Foot
Aide de Camp to Pringle	Captain George Davis Wilson	4th Foot
Aide de Camp to Barnes	Captain Andrew Hamilton	4th West India Regiment
Aide de Camp to Spry	*Capitão* Thomé de Avelar da Silva Capèto	RI N.3
Brigade Major to Pringle	Captain Robert Anwyll	4th Foot
Brigade Major to Barnes	Brevet Major James Taylor	48th Foot
Brigade Major to Spry	*Capitão* Charles John Fitzgerald	82nd Foot/RI N.15

Sources

Berkeley: Wellington Papers, Lawson's report to Oswald; CHALLIS.
Craig: TNA, WO17/138, October monthly return, 2/30th Foot (this record does not specify his assignment as the 5th Division, but this is confirmed by CHALLIS).
Gomm: Carr-Gomm, *Gomm*, pp.242, 288.
Gledstanes: Carr-Gomm, *Gomm*, p.293; TNA, WO25/798, p.153, Statement of service.
Weare: CHALLIS.

Wilson: TNA, WO17/101, October monthly return, 1/4th Foot.

Hamilton: Philippart, *Calendar*, 1820, Vol.V, p.102. This Andrew Hamilton (as opposed to Andrew Hamilton of the 3/1st Foot) is omitted from CHALLIS. He served with Barnes in the 46th Foot in the West Indies.[1]

Thomé de Avelar da Silva Capèto: Santos, *Ordens*, 1810, p.78, 1812, p.147; PT/AHM/G/LM/B/03/07/0134, *Projecto Germil (Livros Mestros)*; AHM PT/AHM/DIV/3/12/07/17, *List of Officers under the command of Brigadier Sprye*; appointed *Ajudante de Ordens*, 25 August 1812. *Capitão* Capèto was born in 1776 and joined the army as a cadet in 1793 then became an *alferes* in 1797, before joining the new *caçadores* in Alorna's Legião de Tropas Ligeiras in 1801. Subsequently, he was appointed *capitão* of the second company of RI N.3 in April 1810, following service as *ajudante* in the first battalion of that regiment. *Capitão* Capèto became *a.d.c.* to Spry in November 1810.

Anwyll: TNA, WO17/101, monthly return, 1/4th Foot; Anwyll replaced Richard Machell (2/30th Foot) whom Challis has still in his staff role in October, however the October monthly return of the 2/30th (WO17/138) describes how Machell had resigned his role on the staff and was 'absent without lea*ve*' before returning in November.

Taylor: Philippart, *Calendar*, 1820, Vol.V, pp.234–5.

Fitzgerald: CHALLIS; Centeno, *Exército*, 2011, p.113.

Regimental Officers

3/1st Foot (Royal Scots)[2]

Brevet Lieutenant Colonel Colin Campbell commanded the battalion until Waterloo, the officers present (including those in the light company) were:

> Captains; Andrew Hamilton, Lawrence Arguimbeau, Abraham Logan, John Cameron, John O. Glover, James Stewart.
> Lieutenants; George Glover, John Armstrong, William Rea, John N. Ingram, Richard Vallancey, John Anderson, John M. Balfour, John McKilligan, John Holebroke, Thomas B. Wall, Samuel Clarke, James Cluffe (Adjutant).
> Ensigns; Joseph Jeffries, J.H. Thompson, Thomas Weir.
> Staff; Surgeon Thomas Forster.
> (23 officers in all).

1/9th Foot (East Norfolk)[3]

Commanded by Brevet Lieutenant Colonel Henry Craufurd, the officers present, including those in the light company, were:

1 Cannon, *Forty Sixth*, p.45.
2 TNA, WO17/96, October monthly return.
3 TNA, WO17/110, October monthly return.

Captains; Thomas Ferrars, William Percival.[4]

Lieutenants; James Whitley, John Shelton, John Ackland, John Reed, Richard Dale, Jeremiah Taylor, John Ogle, Thomas Sheppard, Hon. William Curzon, John B. Ford, Peter Le Mesurier, Alexander Fraser, Edward Ross Lewin.[5]

Ensigns; William Brookes, William Telford.

Staff; Assistant Surgeon James Bulkeley.

(19 officers in all).

1/38th Foot (1st Staffordshire)[6]

Commanded by Lieutenant Colonel Charles Greville, the officers present, including those in the light company, were:

Brevet Lieutenant Colonel Edward Miles.[7]

Captains; Thomas Willshire, James Annesley, Andrew Todd, James Baillie, George Hussey.

Lieutenants; William Ince, Rodrick Macleod, Frederick B. Sandwith, Samuel Green, William Hopper (Adjutant).

Ensigns; James F. Magee, William D. Lawrence, Robert Willcocks, Edward Byam, George Freer.

Staff; Paymaster Valerius Skipton, Quartermaster Thomas Southall, Surgeon Donald Macleod, Assistant Surgeon Robert Todd.

(21 officers in total)

2/38th (1st Staffordshire) Foot[8]

Commanded by Lieutenant Colonel John Nugent, the officers present, including those in the light company, were:

Major William F.B. Loftus.

Captains; Charles L. Barnard,[9] William Nihill, John B. Perry, Matthew Forster.

Lieutenants; John Magill, John Miller, John M. Tittle, William Harrison, Edward Hopper, Worsopp D. Lawrence, Thomas G. Twigg, Thomas M. Oliver, James Matthews (Adjutant).

Ensign George Young.

Staff; Surgeon Dillon Jones.

(17 officers in total).

4 Greenwood, *Le Mesurier*, p.153; however, Le Mesurier places him with the baggage guard.

5 Greenwood, *Le Mesurier*, p.153; Robert Dallas is also given as present in the monthly return, but Le Mesurier has him absent sick.

6 TNA, WO17/148, October monthly return.

7 *Hart's New Army List*, 1840, pp.34, 46, note 21.

8 TNA, WO17/148, October monthly return

9 G. Glover, *The Waterloo Archive, Volume 1 British Sources* (Barnsley: Frontline, 2010), p.57; Barnard was killed in action at Waterloo while serving with the Scots Greys.

1/4th Foot (King's Own)[10]

Commanded by Lieutenant Colonel Francis Brooke, the officers present, including those in the light company, were:

Brevet Lieutenant Colonel John Piper.
Major George O'Halloran.
Captains; John Williamson, James Ward, James C. Edgell, William L. Wood, John W. Fletcher.
Lieutenants; George Thorne, Elers P. Hopkins, Jeffrey Salvin, Patrick Conroy, Francis Maguire, John Read Vincent, Benjamin Martin, W.B.C. Edgell, Jonas Fawson, Edward Guichard, John K. Mackenzie, John Stavely, Francis Le Blanc, John P. Jameson, George Haywood, William Ramsden,[11] Thomas Barker (Adjutant).
Ensigns; Henry C. McVaugh, James White, Edward Bowlby, William H. Clarke.
Staff; Paymaster James Lonsdale, Surgeon Theodore Gordon, Quartermaster John Jenkins.
(32 officers in total).

James Ward's seniority as captain dated from November 1804. Challis shows that he was wounded at Vitoria, however Hall excludes him, assigning his wound to Lieutenant John Warde, whom Challis has at Belem throughout 1810-1814. Ward was promoted to brevet major in June 1814 and served with the regiment in North America until 26 November 1814, but in January and February 1815, he was serving as the Adjutant of the Camp d'Orique depot in Lisbon, Portugal and therefore missed New Orleans. The Army List 1816 records James Ward's death, which, as the London Gazette reported, was before 5 May 1815.[12]

Edward Bowlby's name is spelt 'Boulby' in the *Army List* (e.g. 1815, p.167) but it is spelt correctly in the monthly return of the first battalion. Peter Bowlby refers to Edward as his brother in his account of the Waterloo Campaign; he also describes how Edward, having been placed on half pay, studied Theology at Cambridge University.[13]

2/4th Foot (King's Own)[14]

Commanded by Brevet Lieutenant Colonel David Williamson,[15] the other officers present, including those in the light company, were:

---

10 TNA, WO17/101, October monthly return.

11 Ramsden was promoted to lieutenant on 8 October, but this was not reflected in the monthly returns until November.

12 *Army List*, 1816, casualties' section; TNA, WO17/1218, monthly returns to the Adjutant General, America North; Hall, *History*, p.584; *London Gazette*, 17,011, 13 May 1815, p.891.

13 G. Glover (ed.), *Walcheren, Spain, America and Waterloo, The Memoir of Captain Peter Bowlby, 4th Foot (1791–1877)* (Godmanchester: Ken Trotman, 2016), p.61; between 1838 and 1860, Edward Bowlby was the rector at St. Mary the Virgin church, Little Thurrock where he is now buried (see website at <http://www.essex100.com/rector.html>, accessed 7 May 2016, which cites the *Southend Telegraph*, 10 July 1915).

14 TNA, WO17/101, October monthly return.

15 See first battalion returns, 'occasional remarks'.

Major Alured D. Faunce.

Captains; David S. Craig, Eusby S. Kirwan, Richard Moore, James Jameson, Henry Brereton.

Lieutenants; Lewis M. Bennet, Peter Bowlby, John Renny, John Caulfield, John Clarke, John R. Marsden, Benjamin M. Collins, William Squire, John Bushell, Richard Mulholland, William Lonsdale.

Ensigns; Thomas Woodward, Edward Rawling (Rawlings in CHALLIS), Henry Andrews, Denis E. McCrohan, William Richardson (Adjutant).

Staff; Paymaster Christopher Hancorne.

(24 officers in total)

2/30th Foot (Cambridgeshire)[16]

Commanded by Lieutenant Colonel Alexander Hamilton, the other officers present, including those in the light company, were:

Captains; Thomas B. Bamford, John Hitchen, Thomas W. Chambers (light company).[17]

Lieutenants; J. Loraine White, Richard Mayne, Matthias Andrews, Richard Heaviside, John F. Garvey, James Eager, Arthur W. Freear, John Rumley, George W.A. Brisac, Andrew Baillie, William Campbell, John Garland (Adjutant).[18]

Ensigns; Henry Beere, Francis Tincombe.

Staff; Paymaster Hugh B. Wray, Surgeon Dennis Hughes.

(20 officers in total, plus the five joining on the 25th; Captain Thomas G. Richardson, Lieutenant Theophilus O'Halloran, Ensigns Samuel R. Poyntz, George Madden and Francis Kelly).

Although Challis and his own obituary record Adjutant John Garland as present, the monthly return records him as 'sick absent', with Bannatyne describing him as 'down country sick'.[19]

2/44th Foot (East Essex)[20]

Commanded by Brevet Lieutenant Colonel George Harding, the other officers present, including those in the light company, were:

Captains; John C. Guthrie, Thomas A. Ballard (commanded light company at Salamanca), Thomas A. Dudie.

Lieutenants; Robert Russell, Frederick Hemming, William F. Lennon, John Connor, William Pearce, Henry Elwin, Robert Grier, Dering Carey, William H. Meade (Adjutant).

Ensigns; John O'Reilly, William Tomkins, James Smith.

Staff; Surgeon Henry Jobb, Assistant Surgeon John Collins.

(18 officers in total).

16 TNA, WO17/138, October monthly return; Bannatyne, *Thirtieth*, pp.285–289.

17 C. Divall, *Napoleonic Lives* (Barnsley: Pen and Sword, 2012), pp.136–9.

18 *Hart's New Army List*, 1840, pp.318, 339, note 30.

19 'Obituary', *The Gentleman's Magazine*, May 1851, Vol.CLXXXIX, p.554.

20 TNA, WO17/156, October monthly return.

The Duke of Brunswick Oels Light Infantry[21]

2nd Company (Barnes's Brigade); Captain Georg David von Sternfeld, Lieutenant Friedrich S. Häusler (recorded in the Adjutant's Roll as Lewis Häusler).

10th Company (Pringle's Brigade); Captain Ludwig von Nassau, Lieutenant Carl Hartwig.

Mackenzie described Lieutenant Hartwig as 'a fine young man… who behaved most gallantly, and was killed in the village, to the great regret of the brigade, by whom he was called John Bull owing to his fat, plump and sturdy appearance.'[22]

Lawson's Company, 8th Battalion Royal Artillery

Lawson's other officers in 1812 were:[23]

> 2nd Captain Alfred Thompson (1,141).[24]
> Lieutenants; James William Johnston (1,193), Basil Robinson Heron (1,285).
> 2nd Lieutenant Archibald MacBean (1,529 later lieutenant general).

However, Challis specifically only records Lawson, Johnston and Sinclair as present at Villamuriel and this is supported by the Lawson's report to Oswald.[25]

Lieutenant James Sinclair (1,207) was assigned from Ilbert's Company, Fifth Battalion, pending their arrival in the Peninsula and he was present in June 1812. Although he does not feature in Lawson's muster roll for October 1812, Sinclair's presence is confirmed by his obituary.[26]

Johnston joined the brigade on 7 September. Thompson left the brigade on sick leave in July. Lieutenant William B. Ingilby (1,464 later general) had been in Lawson's Brigade until May 1812 when he transferred to Gardiner's Brigade in the 1st Division.[27] Ingilby was replaced in Lawson's Brigade by MacBean, who was absent 'on command' in October 1812.

According to Lawson's muster roll, Heron had replaced Lieutenant Henry Festing (1,192). The muster roll records Heron's presence in October 1812, but Lawson's own report states he was absent on the 25th for some undeclared reason. Lawson's diary records Heron's pending arrival with remounts on 5 September 1812 and his delayed return with the 'store carriage' on 20 November 1812, which may give us an indication of Heron's role in the brigade.[28]

---

21 TNA, WO12/11654.
22 TNA, WO12/11654; 'McK', 'The Affair of Villa Muriel', p.543.
23 Leslie, *Dickson*, Vol.IV, pp.696, 699, 704, 709.
24 Askwith, *List*; the numbers in parentheses refer to the officer's number in this edition. Lawson is number 943.
25 Wellington Papers, Lawson to Oswald, 27 October 1812.
26 'Obituary', *The Gentleman's Magazine*, August 1851, p.218.
27 Glover (ed.), *Ingilby*, 2014, p.40.
28 TNA, WO10/916, muster roll for October 1812; Leslie, *Dickson*, Vol.IV, pp.709, 714, 730.

Spanish

Coronel Pedro Dejoui, 1° Asturias. Born in France, 18 August 1762, in March 1783 he was named a *soldado distinguido* in the Regimiento de Infanteria de Flandes and between then and 1792 he rose to *sargento 1°* in the Regimiento de Infanteria de Hibernia. Promoted to *2° subteniente* in 1793, *1° subteniente* in 1798, *teniente* in 1800, he became *teniente coronel* in 1808 and *coronel* in 1809. He fought in the wars against France in 1792–4, and in the battles of Cabezón de la Sal, Medina del Campo, Alba de Tormes, Ronquillo, Aracena, Pajares and the siege of Astorga during the Peninsular War before Villamuriel. He became a *brigadier* in 1816.[29]

29 Martinez, *Diccionario*, p.256–7.

Appendix III

Ensign George Young, 2/38th Foot

In her article 'Some Peninsular Letters', K.E. Younge does not specifically name the officer who wrote the letters,[1] but in her notes describes him as being the 'senior major' in the 38th Foot in 1839. Younge also refers to an article in the *Freeman's Journal* regarding the presentation of new colours to the regiment, at which the senior major played a central role.[2] This directly identifies the officer as George Young, who was an ensign in 1812.[3] However, this attribution is not without its apparent difficulties.

Challis dates Young's arrival in the Peninsula to April 1811 and Young received a clasp to his Military General Service Medal for the Battle of Fuentes de Oñoro, which was fought on the 3–5 May 1811. However in Young's first letter he stated 'I arrived at the army on the 19th May after a very long and fatiguing march and joined my Regt. at Nava d'Aver, near Almeida on the frontiers of Spain…' The monthly returns for the battalion do not resolve this apparent contradiction, since the return for 25 April 1811 states that George Young was 'absent with leave; not joined since appointed – supposed to be in England', while that for 25 May confirms his presence with the regiment.[4] So all we can say is that it is unlikely that Young had written May when he meant April in his letter. A further source gives Young's departure for the Peninsula as January 1811.[5]

In a letter written in Lamego, 10 December 1811, the writer of the 'Peninsular letters' describes how he had been in Lamego 'some time' since leaving the regiment when wounded and that the regiment would not reach Lamego until 11 December.[6] However the monthly return for 25 November 1811 has Ensign George Young as present for duty with the regiment at Ituero

1 Younge, 'Some Peninsular Letters', pp.508–517; assuming that Younge was Miss K.E. Younge of the Irish Antiquarian Society.

2 *Freeman's Journal*,16 February 1839, p.4.

3 *Hart's New Annual Army List*, 1840, p.189.

4 TNA, WO17/148, monthly returns 38th Foot, 1762–1812.

5 Dix Noonan Webb, Lot 2, 28 March 2002, at <https://www.dnw.co.uk/auction-archiv/lot-archiv/lot.php?department=Medals&lot_id=73330>, accessed 7 March 2017.

6 Younge, *'Some Peninsular Letters'*, p.512.

(60 miles south east from Lamego) while Lieutenant Thomas Milward Oliver (also wounded) is recorded as absent with leave at Coimbra (100 miles from Ituero and 60 miles southwest from Lamego).

Thomas Milward Oliver, who was a newly promoted lieutenant at Villamuriel, is the most obvious alternative candidate, within the 38th Foot, as the author of Younge's 'Peninsular Letters'. However, Oliver's own letters home were privately published by his family in 1930.

Younge clearly knew who the writer of the letters was having seen both the letters and the addresses on the covers, as well as a miniature painting of the officer. As she stated in her notes, the letters she published were not a complete set and we must assume that, if Ensign George Young arrived in time for the battle, a letter immediately following Fuentes de Oñoro is among the missing ones. Despite the above discrepancies, the author of Younge's 'Peninsular Letters' is most likely to have been Ensign George Young, as she implied.

Appendix IV

The identity of 'McK'

'McK' are the initials at the end of a key source, 'The Affair of Villa Muriel', which was published in the *United Service Magazine* in 1850.[1] The identity of 'McK' is not immediately apparent but the evidence suggests that he was Lieutenant (later Lieutenant Colonel) John Kenneth Mackenzie of the 1/4th Foot. An analysis of the 1812 and 1813 Army Lists for the regiments present, cross referencing them with the muster rolls for October 1812, looking for surnames which might reasonably have been shortened to McK, identified only two candidates who were present at Villamuriel; Lieutenant John McKilligan (3/1st Foot) and Lieutenant John Kenneth Mackenzie (1/4th Foot).

Of these gentlemen, Mackenzie appears on the medal roll of the recipients of the Military General Service Medal 1793-1814, in 1847, while McKilligan does not.[2] Mackenzie's name on his medal is spelt McKenzie. The *United Service Magazine* account refers to the 4th Foot six times while all other regiments – including the Royal Scots, the 3/1st Foot – are mentioned only once.

Mackenzie joined the 4th Foot as an ensign at 16 years old in 1807. He served in the Peninsula from August 1808 until January 1809 and from June 1812 until April 1814.[3] He was wounded at Bladensberg in August 1814. After the war he went with the 4th Foot to Australia in 1831 and remained there on leaving the army in 1834. He was promoted to lieutenant colonel in 1832.[4]

Mackenzie was born in 1791 and would therefore have been 58 or 59 when he wrote his account of Villamuriel.[5]

John McKilligan does not appear in the Army List after 1817, and the National Archives' copy of that list includes an additional handwritten note that McKilligan unfortunately died on 3 April 1817.

---

1 McK, 'The Affair of Villa Muriel', *United Service Magazine* (1850), pt.1, p.542.

2 MGSMR; available online, at <http://www.dnw.co.uk/resources/medal-rolls/entry.php?medalroll_id=1&entry_id=15867> accessed 6th January 2015; Photographs of the medal from Jager Medals and Militaria.

3 CHALLIS.

4 'Promotions and Appointments', *United Service Magazine* (1832), pt.1, p.429.

5 *Sydney Morning Herald*, 20 August 1857, p.1, 29 August 1857, p.5.

Appendix V

Killed on a forgotten field in Spain…

During the research for this book the names of those killed at the Battle of Villamuriel have been identified and they are reproduced here together as a roll of honour. Unfortunately, the sources consulted were not so forthcoming with respect to 46, so far un-named, Portuguese and Spanish soldiers killed in action that day.

<table>
<tr><td>3/1st Foot
Sergeant William Le George
Corporal John Johnston
Private John Caine
Private Thomas Jones
Private Mark Kealing
Private William Kirk
Private William Rogers</td><td>1/38th Foot
Captain Andrew Todd
Private Joseph Barlow
Private James Murdock
Private Robert Norbury
Private William Rowley
Private John Spencer
Private Thomas Woodhouse</td></tr>
<tr><td>1/4th Foot
Sergeant George Rea
Corporal Robert Archer
Corporal David Hopkins
Private Michael Donahoe
Private James Ellingham
Private Patrick McLoughlin</td><td>2/38th Foot
Major Edward Ovens (RI N.3)
Private James Moore</td></tr>
<tr><td>2/4th Foot
Private John Crany</td><td>2/44th Foot
Lieutenant William Lennon
Lieutenant Henry Elwin
Ensign James Smith
Sergeant Thomas Brooks
Corporal Patt Martin
Private William Murray</td></tr>
<tr><td>1/9th Foot
Sergeant Thomas Barefot
Corporal Richard Willcox
Private James Buy
Private James Clarke
Private Edward Davis
Private John Kennedy
Private William Smith</td><td>8/Royal Artillery
Gunner John Davidson
Gunner John Hardy
Gunner Edward Rogers</td></tr>
</table>

2/30th Foot Sergeant James Keith Sergeant John Nightingale Private Patrick Shearin Private Rodney Tansey	The Duke of Brunswick Oels Light Infantry Captain Georg David von Sternfeld Lieutenant Carl Hartwig Corporal Karl Lindner
Caçadores N.8 *Tenente* João Baptista Ferreira	

15e Régiment d'Infanterie de Ligne *Capitaine* Jean Lafitte *Grenadier* Jacques Bourget *Grenadier* Jean Eustache Delafoy *Grenadier* Jean Baptiste Dubois *Voltigeur* Guillaume Arodeaux *Voltigeur* Claude Étienne Durand *Soldat* Pierre François Caillaud *Soldat* Joseph Crecy *Soldat* Jacques Marie Delaporte *Soldat* Joseph Escoland *Soldat* François Petit *Soldat* Jacques Ré	66e Régiment d'Infanterie de Ligne *Sous Lieutenant* Georges Portenseigne *Sergent Major* Jacques M. Bosco *Sergent Major* Auguste Mathieu *Sergent* Jean Pierre Bousquet *Caporal* François Jean Hubis *Tambour* Jacques Carbone *Tambour* Jean J. Valery *Soldat* Jean Bobineau *Soldat* Pierre M. Gratarollo *Soldat* Joseph Moun *Soldat* Georges Mosteau *Soldat* Jean Marot *Soldat* Guillaume Richard *Soldat* Jean Rivel *Soldat* Jean François Roussel *Soldat* Thermidor H. Simonet
82e Régiment d'Infanterie de Ligne *Sergent* Pierre Dupuy *Soldat* Louis Cynard *Soldat* Victor Piger *Soldat* Jean Pierre Sudre	86e Régiment d'Infanterie de Ligne *Soldat* Louis Daveau *Soldat* Dominique-C. Lebbe
Staff *Capitaine* François Basile Burgevin de Lesme	

Bibliography

Archives

Archivo Histórico Militar, Lisbon (AHM)

PT/AHM/G/LM/B/03/07/0134: Projecto Germil (Livros Mestros).

PT/AHM/DIV/3/12/07/17: List of Officers under the command of Brigadier Sprye.

PT/AHM/DIV/3/12/09/7: Combate de Carrion– 25 de Outubro de 1812, Minuta de oficiais mortos ou feridos.

PT/AHM/G/LM/B-03/09: Livro nº 9 – Livro de Registo do Regimento de Infantaria, de 1812 a 1814.

Archivo Histórico Nacional de Madrid (AHNM)

Diversos/Colecciones/144/n32: October Monthly State.

Diversos/Colecciones/101/n63: Liñan's report.

Archives of the Museum of the Staffordshire Regiment, Lichfield (AMSR)

Acc. No. 13: Digest of the 38th Regiment, 1804–1885.

Hartley Library, University of Southampton

MS 61 Wellington Papers WP1/353 (Wellington Papers).

National Archives, Kew (TNA)

ADM 103/8, 86, 165, 216, 264–7, 337–8, 364–8, 391, 408, 443, 448, 454: Registers of Prisoners of War.

PROB 11/2111/265: Will Alured Dodsworth Faunce.

NRA 21704 Oswald; Oswald Correspondence.

WO1/256, p.103: War department in-letters and papers, Morning state 23 October 1812.

WO1/256, pp.117–119: War department in letters and papers.

WO10/916: Lawson's muster roll for October 1812.

WO12/2012: Pay-list 24 December 1812, 3/1st Foot.

WO12/2206: Pay-list 24 December 1812, 1/4th Foot.

WO12/2265: Pay-list 24 December 1812, 2/4th Foot.

WO12/2665: Pay-list 24 December 1812, 1/9th Foot.

WO12/4646: Pay-list 24 December 1812, 2/30th Foot.

WO12/5184: Pay-list 24 December 1812, 1/38th Foot.

WO12/5245: Pay-list 24 December 1812, 2/38th Foot.

WO12/5715: Pay-list 24 December 1810, 2/44th Foot.

WO12/5716: Pay-list 24 December 1812, 2/44th Foot.

WO12/5713–6: Pay-lists 44th Foot.

WO12/10053: Muster Rolls, 1794–5, 110th – 135th Foot.

WO12/11654: October 1812 Adjutant's Roll, Brunswick Light Infantry.

WO17/96: October 1812 Monthly Return, 3/1st Foot.

WO17/101: October 1812 Monthly Return, 4th Foot.

WO17/110: October and November 1812 Monthly Return, 1/9th Foot.

WO17/138: October 1812 Monthly Return, 2/30th Foot.

WO17/148: October and November 1812 Monthly Return, 38th Foot.
WO17/156: October and November 1812 Monthly Return, 2/44th Foot.
WO17/200: August 1800 Monthly Return, 79th Foot.
WO17/221: August 1794 Monthly Return, 99th Foot.
WO17/1218: Monthly Returns to the Adjutant General, America North.
WO22/180, p.118: Morgan Blakeney Pension records.
WO25/770/57: Oliver's 1828 service return.
WO25/771: Pickering's Statement of service 1828.
WO25/798, p.153: Gledstanes Statement of service.
WO25/915: Pickering's Statement of service 1806.
WO25/982: 1806 statement of service.
WO25/1506: Casualty return, 3/1st Foot.
WO25/1522: Casualty return, 1/4th Foot.
WO25/1527: Casualty return, 2/4th Foot.
WO25/1556: Casualty return, 1/9th Foot.
WO25/1695: Casualty return, 2/30th Foot.
WO25/1742: Casualty return, 1/38th Foot.
WO25/1750: Casualty return, 2/38th Foot.
WO25/1795: Casualty return, 2/44th Foot.
WO97: Royal Hospital Chelsea Soldiers Service Statements.
WO97/484/77: Morgan Blakeney Discharge papers.
WO97/1219/061: Chapman's discharge papers.
WO164/108: Prize records Demerara.

National Army Museum, London (NAM)
Acc. No. 1968–07–362–1: Whitley's parole pass at Verdun.
Acc. No. 1979-12-21: Memoir of unidentified soldier of 38th Foot.
Acc. No. 2002-02-729: Memoir of Captain Peter Bowlby.

Service Historique de la Défense, Paris (SHD)
2Yb 157: *Contrôle des Officiers*, 15e Ligne.
2Yb 349: *Contrôle des Officiers*, 66e. Ligne.
2Yb 397: *Contrôle des Officiers*, 82e Ligne.
2Yb 411: *Contrôle des Officiers*, 86e Ligne.
2Yb 928: *22e Chasseurs à Cheval; Registre des Services des Officiers*
2Yb 953: *Contrôle des Officiers, 3e Hussards.*
2Yb 1015: *Contrôle des Officiers*, Artillery.
2Yb 1050 *Contrôle des Officiers*, Train battalions
C8 462: *Situation Armées en Espagne,* 15 January 1812.
C8 466: *Situation Armées en Espagne,* 15 August 1812
C8 467: *Situation Armées en Espagne*, 1 November 1812
C8 468: *Situation Armées en Espagne*, 1 January 1813.
C8 469 *Situation Armées en Espagne*, 15 February 1813

University of Manchester Library (UML).
GB 133 Eng MSS 1273: Correspondence of Sir William Henry Pringle.

Books and Articles

Anon., *Army List* (London: War Office, 1784–87, 1792–96, 1798, 1800–03, 1808–17, 1822).
Anon., *Biographie universelle et portative des contemporains, ou Dictionnaire historique des hommes vivants et des hommes morts depuis 1788 jusqu'à nos jours* (Paris: Levrault, 1834).
Anon., *Estado militar de España* (Madrid: Imprenta Real, 1811, 1812, 1815, 1816, 1833).
Anon., *Estados de la Organizacion y Fuerza de los Ejercitos Espanoles Beligerantes en la Peninsula, Durante la Guerra de Espana contra Bonaparte* (Barcelona: Viuda e hijos de Antonio Brusi, 1822).
Anon., *État des donataires totalement dépossédés: qui en droit á l'indemnité fixée par la loi proposée aux Chambres en 1821* (Paris: Imprimerie Royale, 1821).

Anon.,'Fourth (or the Kings Own) Regiment of Foot', *United Service Magazine* (1830), pt.2, pp.558–67.

Anon., *Historique du 118e régiment d'infanterie* (Paris: Charles-Lavauzelle, 1893).

Anon., *Historique du 86e régiment d'infanterie* (Paris: Charles-Lavauzelle, 1886).

Anon., *Historique du 69e régiment d'infanterie* (Paris: Charles-Lavauzelle, 1890).

Anon., *Journals of the House of Commons* (London: House of Commons, 1813, 1814).

Anon., 'Notes on the History and Services of the Fifty-Eighth Regiment of Foot', *United Service Magazine*, 1878, Vol.CXLVII, pt.2, pp.84–9.

Anon., 'Obituary of Colonel Alexander Hamilton', *United Service Journal*, July 1838, pt.2, pp.430–1.

Anon., *Parliamentary Papers 1780–1849, Estimates of Army Services for the year 1816* (London: House of Commons, 1816).

Anon., *Parliamentary Papers, House of Commons, Finance accounts of Great Britain and Ireland, Session 8th November 1814 to 12th July 1815* (London: House of Commons, 1815).

Anon., 'Record of the Services of the 51st (Second West York) or King's Own Light Infantry Regiment', *United Service Magazine* (1869), pt.1, pp.223–235.

Anon., *Revue Savoisienne: Journal publié par l'Association Florimontane d'Annecy: histoire, sciences, arts, industrie, littérature* (Annecy: Perrissin, 1876).

Anon., *Systema de Instrucção e Disciplina para os movimentos e deveres dos Caçadores…* (Lisbon: Regia, 1810).

Anon., *The confidential correspondence of Napoleon Bonaparte with his brother Joseph, sometime King of Spain* (New York: Appleton, 1856)

Ardenne, Armand Léon Baron von, *Bergische Lanziers, Westfälische Husaren nr.11* (Berlin: Mittler, 1877).

Arvers, Paul and Brecht, Charles Frédéric, *Historique du 82e Régiment d'Infanterie* (Paris: Lahure, 1876).

Askwith, W.H. and Kane, John, *List of Officers of the Royal Regiment of Artillery from the Year 1716 to the Year 1899* (London and Beccles, William Clowes, 1900).

Bannatyne, Neil, *History of the Thirtieth Regiment now the First Battalion East Lancashire Regiment, 1689–1881* (Liverpool: Littlebury, 1923).

Bardin, Étienne-Alexandre, *Manuel de l'Infanterie* (Paris: Magimel, 1813).

Bardy, Henri, *La dernière campagne du général Lecourbe: Belfort en 1815* (Saint-Dié: Humbert, 1889).

Beauvais de Préau, Charles-Théodore (ed.), *Victoires, conquêtes, désastres, revers et guerres civiles des …* (Paris: C.L.F. Panckoucke, 1820).

Belmas, Jacques-Vital, *Journaux des sièges faits ou soutenus par les Français dans la Péninsule* (Paris: Firmin Didot, 1836).

Bromley, Janet and David, *Wellington's Men Remembered* (Barnsley: Pen and Sword, 2015).

Brown, Steve, *By Fire and Bayonet, Grey's West Indies Campaign of 1794* (Solihull: Helion and Company, 2018).

Buckley, Roger Norman (ed.), *The Napoleonic War Journal of Captain Thomas Henry Browne 1807-1816* (London: Bodley Head, 1987).

Burke, Edmund, *The Annual Register* (London: Rivington, 1842).

Burnham, Robert, *Charging against Wellington* (Barnsley: Frontline, 2011).

Burnham, Robert and McGuigan, Ron, *The British Army Against Napoleon: Facts, Lists and Trivia, 1805–1815* (Barnsley: Frontline, 2010).

Burnham, Robert and McGuigan, Ron, *Wellington's Brigade Commanders: Peninsular and Waterloo* (Barnsley: Pen and Sword, 2017).

Burroughs, George Frederick, *A Narrative of the retreat of the British army from Burgos: in a series of letters: an introductory sketch of the campaign of 1812 and military character of the Duke of Wellington* (Bristol: Joseph Routh, 1814).

Cadell, Charles, *Narrative of the Campaigns of the 28th Regiment… from 1802 to 1832* (London: Whittaker, 1835).

Caldwell, George and Cooper, Robert, *Rifle Green in the Peninsula* (Leicester: Bugle Horn, 2006).

Campbell, Neil, *Instructions for Light Infantry and Riflemen* (London: Egerton, 1813).

Cannon, Richard, *Historical Record of the Eighty-Eighth Regiment of Foot, or Connaught Rangers* (London: William Clowes, 1838).

Cannon, Richard, *Historical Record of the Eighty-Sixth or the Royal County Down Regiment of Foot* (London: John W.Parker, 1842).

Cannon, Richard, *Historical Record of the Eleventh or North Devon Regiment of Foot* (London: Parker, Furnivall and Parker, 1845).

Cannon, Richard, *Historical Record of the Fifth or Princess Charlotte of Wales Dragoon Guards* (London: William Clowes, 1839).

Cannon, Richard, *Historical Record of the Forty Sixth or South Devonshire Regiment of Foot* (London: Parker, Furnivall and Parker, 1851).

Cannon, Richard, *Historical Record of the Fourth Regiment of Foot* (London: William Clowes, 1839).

Cannon, Richard, *Historical Record of the Ninth or East Norfolk Regiment of Foot 1685–1847* (London: William Clowes, 1848).

Cannon, Richard, *Historical Record of the Seventy First Regiment, the Highland Light Infantry* (London: Parker, Furnivall and Parker, 1852).

Cannon, Richard, *Historical Record of the Seventy Third Regiment* (London: Parker, Furnivall and Parker, 1851).

Cannon, Richard, *Historical record of the Sixteenth, or Queen's Light Dragoons, Lancers; containing an account of their formation in 1759 and their subsequent services to 1841* (London: J.W.Parker, 1842).

Cannon, Richard, *Historical Record of the Twenty First Regiment or Royal North British Fusiliers* (London: Parker, Furnivall and Parker, 1849).

Carr-Gomm, Francis C. (ed.), *The Earlier Letters and Journals of Sir William Maynard Gomm* (London: John Murray, 1881).

Carter, Thomas, *Record Forty-Fourth or East Essex Regiment of Foot* (Chatham: Gale and Folden, 1887).

Casse, Albert du (ed.), *Mémoires et correspondance politique et militaire du roi Joseph* (Paris: Perrotin, 1854).

Castel, Pierre, *Relation de la bataille et retraite des Arapiles...* (Toulouse: Caseaux, 1854).

Centeno, João T., *O Exército Aliado Anglo-Português 1808–1814* (Parede: Tribuna da Historia, 2011).

Charrié, Pierre, *Drapeaux et étendards de la Révolution et de l'Empire* (Paris: Copernic, 1982).

Chartrand, René and Younghusband, Bill, *The Spanish Army of the Napoleonic Wars (3) 1812–15* (Oxford: Osprey Military, 1999).

Chuquet, Arthur, *Dugommier* (Paris: A. Fontemoing, 1904).

Colin, Lieutenant Colonel Jean (ed.) 'Journal du Colonel Béchaud de l'Armée de Portugal Octobre 1812', *Revue des études napoléoniennes*, 1912, vol.II, pp.385–411; 1913, vol.I, pp.89–114.

Clonard, Serafín María de Sotto y Abbach, Conde de, *História orgánica de las armas de infantería y caballería españolas desde la creación del Ejercito permanente hasta el día* (Madrid: Castilla, 1855, 1858).

Cooper, Thomas Henry, *A Practical Guide for the Light Infantry Officer* (London: T.Egerton, 1806).

Courcelles, Jean Baptiste Pierre Jullien de, *Dictionnaire historique et biographique des generaux Francais: depuis le onzième siècle jusqu'en 1820* (Paris: Author, Arthus Bertrand and Treuttel and Wurtz, 1822).

Cowper, L.I., *The King's Own the Story of a Royal Regiment* (Oxford: University Press, 1939).

Crowdy, Terry, *Napoleon's Infantry Handbook* (Barnsley: Pen and Sword Military, 2015).

D'Alton, John, *History of Drogheda with its Environs...* (Dublin: Author, 1844).

Dalton, Charles, *The Waterloo Roll Call* (London: Eyre and Spottiswoode, 1904).

Daney de Marcillac, Sidney, *Histoire de la Martinique: depuis la colonisation jusqu'en 1815* (Fort Royal: E.Ruelle, 1846).

Daniel, John Edgecombe, *Journal of an Officer in the Commissariat Department of the Army: Comprising a Narrative of the Campaigns Under His Grace the Duke of Wellington, in Portugal, Spain, France, and the Netherlands, in the Years 1811, 1812, 1813, 1814, and 1815; and a Short Account of the Army of Occupation in France, During the Years 1816, 1817, and 1818* (London: Author, 1820).

Dempsey, Guy, *Napoleon's Mercenaries: Foreign Units in the French Army under the Consulate and Empire* (London: Greenhlll, 2002).

Dempsey, Guy, *Napoleon's Army 1807–1814* (London: Arms and Armour, 1997).

Depping, Georges-Bernard, *Dictionnaire géographique de l'Espagne et du Portugal* (Paris: Masson et Yonet, 1829).

Desachy, Paul, *Les Cahiers du Colonel Girard, 1766–1846* (Paris: Plon, 1951).

Divall, Carole, *Napoleonic Lives* (Barnsley: Pen and Sword, 2012).

Divall, Carole, *Redcoats against Napoleon* (Barnsley: Pen and Sword, 2009).

Divall, Carole, *Wellington's Worst Scrape–The Burgos Campaign 1812* (Barnsley: Pen and Sword, 2012).

Dumay, Alfred-Hippolyte, *Historique du 66e régiment d'infanterie, 1672–1900* (Tours: E.Arnault, 1900).

Dupuy, Raoul, *Historique du 3e Régiment du Hussards de 1664 à 1887* (Paris: Piaget, 1887).

Elting, John R., *Swords around the Throne* (London: Weidenfeld and Nicolson, 1989).

Esdaile, Charles Joseph and Freeman, P., *Burgos in the Peninsular War, 1808–1814; Occupation, Siege, Aftermath* (Basingstoke: Palgrave Macmillan, 2015).

Esdaile, Charles Joseph, *The Peninsular War* (London: Allen Lane Penguin, 2002).

Esdaile, Charles Joseph, *The Spanish Army in the Peninsular War* (Nottingham: Partizan Press, 2012).

Fabry, Gabriel Joseph, *Rapports historiques des régiments de l'armée d'Italie pendant la campagne de 1796–1797* (Paris: R.Chapelot, 1905).

Fletcher, Ian (ed.), *The Peninsular War–Aspects of the Struggle for the Iberian Peninsula* (Staplehurst: Spellmount, 1998).

Fletcher, Ian, *Wellington's Regiments–The Men and Their Battles from Roliça to Waterloo, 1808–1815* (Staplehurst: Spellmount, 1994).

Folliet, André, *Révolution française: les volontaires de la Savoie, 1792–1799* (Paris: L.Baudoin, 1887).

Fortescue, John William, *A History of the British Army* (Uckfield: Naval & Military, 2004).

Franklin, Carl, *British Napoleonic Field Artillery* (Staplehurst: Spellmount, 2007).

Freer, William J., 'The Thirty-Eighth Regiment of Foot, now the First Battalion of the South Staffordshire Regiment', *British Numismatic Journal* (1915), vol.XI, pp.298–303.

Fuller, John Frederick Charles, *Sir John Moore's System of Training* (London: Hutchinson, 1924).

García Fuertes, Arsenio and Álvarez, F.C. and García, O.G., *Más que una Guerra: Astorga y el noroeste de España en el conflicto peninsular (1808–1814)* (Astorga: Centro de Estudios Astorganos Marcelo Macías, 2014).

García Fuertes, Arsenio, *Nos Sin Nosotros: La aportación militar española a la victoria aliada en las campañas de 1811 y 1812 de la guerra peninsular*, volumen 1 (Astorga: CSED Historia, 2018).

Gates, David, *The British Light Infantry Arm* (London: Batsford, 1987).

Gates, David, *The Spanish Ulcer, A History of the Peninsular War* (London: Allen and Unwin, 1986).

Girod de l'Ain, Maurice, *La Vie Militaire du Général Foy* (Paris: Plon Nourrit, 1900).

Glover, Gareth (ed.), *Eyewitness to the Peninsular War and the Battle of Waterloo, the Letters and Journals of Lt. Colonel the Honourable James Stanhope, 1803–1825* (Barnsley: Pen and Sword, 2010).

Glover, Gareth (ed.), *Personal Adventures of a Young Officer during Walcheren and the Peninsular War* (Godmanchester: Ken Trotman, 2017).

Glover, Gareth, *The Forgotten War against Napoleon, Conflict in the Mediterranean 1793–1815* (Barnsley: Pen and Sword, 2017).

Glover, Gareth (ed.), *The Journal of Trooper Samuel Gallagher 5th Dragoon Guards in Spain, Portugal and France 1810–15* (Godmanchester: Ken Trotman, 2016).

Glover, Gareth (ed.), *The Letters of Lt. Colonel Sir John Cameron, 1st Battalion, 9th Regiment of Foot, 1808–14* (Godmanchester: Ken Trotman, 2013).

Glover, Gareth (ed.), *The Peninsular War and Waterloo Journals of Lieutenant William Ingilby, Royal Horse Artillery, 1810–15* (Godmanchester: Ken Trotman, 2014).

Glover, Gareth (ed.), *The Waterloo Archive, Volume 1 British Sources* (Barnsley: Frontline, 2010).

Glover, Gareth (ed.), *Walcheren, Spain, America and Waterloo, The Memoir of Captain Peter Bowlby, 4th Foot (1791–1877)* (Godmanchester: Ken Trotman, 2016).

Glover, Gareth (ed.), *Wellington's Lieutenant, Napoleon's Gaoler–The Peninsular War Letters and St. Helena Diaries of Sir George Ridout Bingham* (Barnsley: Pen and Sword, 2004).

Glover, Gareth (ed.), *Wellington's Voice, The Candid Letters of Lieutenant Colonel John Freemantle, Coldstream Guards 1808–1837* (Barnsley: Frontline, 2006).

Glover, Gareth (ed.), *With the 1st Foot Guards in the Peninsular and at Waterloo, The Letters of Lieutenant Colonel Henry Packe, 1806–16* (Godmanchester: Ken Trotman, 2016).

Glover, Michael (ed.), *A Gentleman Volunteer, The Letters of George Hennell from the Peninsular War 1812–1813* (London: Heinemann, 1979).

Gómez de Arteche y Moro de Elexabeitia, José, *Guerra de la independencia, historia militar de España de 1808 á 1814* (Madrid: Credito de Comercial, 1875).

Grattan, William, *Adventures with the Connaught Rangers, 1809–14* (London: Edward Arnold, 1902).

Green, John, *The vicissitudes of a soldier's life; or, A series of occurrences from 1806 to 1815* (Louth: Author, 1827).

Greenwood, Adrian (ed.), *Through Spain with Wellington, the letters of Lieutenant Peter Le Mesurier of the fighting Ninth* (Stroud: Amberley, 2016).
Grehan, John and Mace, Martin, *British Battles of the Napoleonic Wars, 1793–1806* (Barnsley: Pen and Sword, 2013).
Günther, Reinhold, *Der Feldzug der Division Lecourbe im Schweizerischen Hochgebirge 1799* (Frauenfeld: J.Huber, 1896).
Gurwood, John (ed.), *Dispatches of Field Marshal the Duke of Wellington…* (London: Parker, Furnivall and Parker, 1845).
Gurwood, John (ed.), *Selections from the Dispatches and General Orders of Field Marshall the Duke of Wellington* (London: John Murray, 1851).
Gurwood, John (ed.), *The General Orders of Field Marshal the Duke of Wellington* (London: W. Clowes, 1832).
Hale, James, *Journal of James Hale, late Sergeant in the Ninth Regiment of Foot* (Cirencester: Philip Watkins, 1826).
Hall, John Alexander, *A History of the Peninsular War, vol.VIII; the Biographical Dictionary of British Officers Killed and Wounded, 1808–1814* (London: Greenhill, 1998).
Halliday, Andrew, *The present state of Portugal, and of the Portuguese Army* (Edinburgh: G.R.Clarke, 1812).
Hamilton, Frederick William, *The Origin and History of the First or Grenadier Guards* (London: John Murray, 1874).
Hart, Henry George, *New Army List* (London: John Murray, 1840, 1845, 1850).
Haslewood, Francis, *The Genealogy of the family of Haslewood, Staffordshire and Warwickshire branches* (London: Author, 1881).
Haverfield, Captain John and Hofmann, Lieutenant Henry, *Scharnhorst's Military Field Pocket Book* (London: Vogel and Schulze, 1811).
Hay, William (ed. Andrew Bamford), *Reminiscences 1808–1815 under Wellington* (Solihull: Helion and Company, 2017).
Haythornthwaite, Philip, *Napoleon's Line Infantry* (London: Osprey, 1983).
Haythornthwaite, Philip, *Uniforms of the Retreat from Moscow, 1812* (Poole: Blandford, 1976).
Haythornthwaite, Philip, *Wellington's Army, the uniforms of the British soldier, 1812–15* (London: Greenhill, 2002).
Henegan, Richard D., *Seven Years Campaigning in the Peninsula and the Netherlands, 1808–1815* (Stroud: Nonsuch, 2005).
Hodge, William Barwick, 'On the Mortality Arising from Military Operations', *Journal of the Royal Statistical Society* (1856), Vol.XIX, p.219–71.
Hopton, Richard, *The Battle of Maida 1806 – Fifteen Minutes of Glory* (Barnsley: Pen and Sword, 2002).
Hourtoulle, François-Guy, *1814, The Campaign for France* (Paris: Histoire et Collections, 2005).
Hugo, Abel, *France militaire: histoire des armées françaises de terre et de mer, de 1792 à 1833* (Paris: Delloye, 1837).
Hunter, Archie, *Wellington's Scapegoat, the tragedy of Lieutenant Colonel Charles Bevan* (Barnsley: Pen and Sword, 2003).
Husson, Eugène Alexandre, *Instruction pour les Voltigeurs de l'infanterie légère et de ligne* (Paris: Cordier, 1822).
Jomini, Antoine Henri, *Critique et Militaire des Guerres de la Revolution* (Brussels: Petit, 1840).
Jones, Colin, *The Longman Companion to the French Revolution* (Harlow: Addison Wesley Longman, 1988).
Jones, John T., *Journals of the Sieges Undertaken by the Allies in Spain: In the Years 1811 and 1812, with Notes* (London: T. Egerton, 1814).
Jouineau, André, *Officers and Soldiers of the French Hussars, 2: 1st to 8th Regiments,1804–1812* (Paris: Histoire et Collections, 2006).
'T.E.K.', 'Sketch of the Formation and Services of the various regiments of the line raised and disbanded since the commencement of the Seven Years War', *USM*, 1851, pt.1, pp.554–9.
Keltie, John, *A History of the Scottish Highlands, Highland Clans and Highland Regiments* (Edinburgh: A.Fullerton, 1875).
Kortzfleisch, Gustav von, *Geschichte des Herzoglich Braunschweigischen Infanterie-Regiments und seiner Stammtruppen 1809–1867* (Braunschweig: Limbach, 1896).
Lachouque, Henri and Brown, Anne S.K., *The Anatomy of Glory* (London: Arms and Armour, 1978).
Lacour, Auguste, *Histoire de la Guadeloupe* (Basse Terre: Gouvernement, 1858).

Lemonnier-Delafosse, Jean-Baptiste, *Campagnes de 1810, 11, 12, 13, 14 1815 en Portugal, Espagne, France, Belgique ou Souvenirs Militaires* (Havre: Lemale, 1850).

Le Noble, Pierre-Madeleine, *Mémoires sur les opérations militaires des Français: en Galice, en Portugal, et dans la Vallee du Tage, en 1809, sous le commandement du maréchal Soult, duc de Dalmatie, avec un atlas militaire* (Paris: Barrois, 1821).

Leslie, John H., *The Dickson Manuscripts* (Cambridge: Ken Trotman, 1988 and 1990).

Leslie, John H., *The Services of the Royal Regiment of Artillery in the Peninsular War, 1808–1814* (London: H.Rees, 1908).

Letrun, Ludovic, *French Infantry Flags* (Paris: Histoire et Collections, 2009).

Levinge, Richard George Augustus, *Historical records of the Forty Third Monmouthshire Light Infantry* (London: W. Clowes, 1868).

Liddell Hart, Basil Henry (ed.), *The Letters of Private Wheeler, 1808–1828* (Adlestrop: Windrush, 1993).

Liévyns, A. and Verdot, Jean Maurice and Bégat, Pierre, *Fastes de la légion-d'honneur: biographie de tous les décorés accompagnée de l'histoire législative et réglementaire de l'ordre* (Paris: Bureau d'Administration, 1844).

Lindau, Friedrich, *A Waterloo Hero – The reminiscences of Friedrich Lindau* (Havertown: Frontline Books, 2009).

Lipscombe, Nick, *Wellington's Guns–The Untold Story of Wellington and his Artillery in the Peninsula and at Waterloo* (Oxford: Osprey, 2013).

Longford, Elizabeth, *Wellington–Years of the Sword* (Frogmore: Panther, 1971).

Low, Charles Rathbone, 'Memoir of General Sir Thomas Willshire', *United Service Magazine*, 1879, pt.2, pp.59–80.

Low, Charles Rathbone, *Soldiers of the Victorian Age* (London: Chapman and Hall, 1880).

Luz Soriano, Simão José da, *Historia da guerra civil e do estabelecimento do governo parlamentar em Portugal, comprehedendo a historia diplomatica, militar e politica d'este reino desde 1777 até 1834, Guerra da Peninsula* (Lisbon: Imprensa Nacional, 1876).

Lynn, John, *Bayonets of the Republic* (Urbana: University of Illinois, 1984).

Mackenzie, Thomas Arthur and Ewart, John Spencer and Findlay, C., *Historical Records of the Seventy-Ninth Queens Own Cameron Highlanders* (London: Hamilton, Adams, 1887).

MacKinnon, Daniel, *Origins and Services of the Coldstream Guards* (London : Richard Bentley, 1883).

Maclean, Loraine, *Indomitable Colonel* (London: Shepheard-Walwyn, 1986).

Madoz, Pascual, *Diccionario geografico estadistico-historico de Espana y sus posesiones de ultramar* (Madrid: Author, 1849).

Magon de la Giclais, Henri, *Historique du 15e Régiment de Chasseurs à Cheval* (Paris: Berger-Levrault, 1895).

Maldonado, José Muñoz, Conde de Fabraquer, *Historia política y militar de la guerra de la independencia de España contra Napoleon Bonaparte desde 1808 á 1814* (Madrid: José Palacios, 1833).

Marcel, Nicolas, *Campagnes du Capitaine Marcel, du 69e de ligne, en Espagne et en Portugal (1808–1814)* (Paris: Plon-Nourrit, 1913).

Marmont, Auguste Frederic Louis Viesse de, *Memoires du Maréchal Marmont, Duc De Ragusa* (Paris: Perrotin, 1857).

Martin, Emmanuel, *La Gendarmerie Française en Espagne et en Portugal (Campagnes de 1807 à 1814)* (Paris: Léautey, 1898).

Martinez, Alberto Martín-Lanuza, *Diccionario Biografico del Generalato Español: Reinados De Carlos IV Y Fernando VII (1788–1833)* (Villatuerta: Foro para el Estudio de la Historia Militar en España, 2012).

Martinien, Aristide, *Tableaux, par corps et par batailles, des officiers tués et blessés pendant les guerres de l'Empire (1805–1815)* (Paris: Charles-Lavauzelle, 1899).

Martinien, Aristide, *Tableaux, par corps et par batailles, des officiers tués et blessés pendant les guerres de l'Empire (1805–1815): Supplément* (Paris: L.Fournier, 1909).

Mayne, William and Lillie, John Scott, *Loyal Lusitanian Legion during the years 1809, 1810 and 1811* (London: T. Egerton, 1812).

'McK', 'The Affair of Villa Muriel', *United Service Magazine* (1850), pt.1, pp.542–4.

Mericourt, André Baron de, *Mémoires du Général Noguès, 1777–1853: sur les guerres de l'empire* (Paris: Lemerre, 1922).

Miñano y Bedoya, Sebastián de, *Diccionario geografico-estadistico de España y Portugal* (Madrid: Pierart-Peralta, 1828).

Mockler-Ferryman, Augustus Ferryman (ed.), *The life of a regimental officer during the great war, 1793–1815 comp. from the correspondence of Colonel Samuel Rice, C.B., K.H. 51st Light Infantry, and from other sources* (Edinburgh: W. Blackwood and Sons, 1913).
Monick, Stanley (ed.), *Douglas's Tale of the Peninsular War and Waterloo, 1808–1815* (London: Leo Cooper, 1997).
Muir, Rory (ed.), *At Wellington's Right Hand – The Letters of Lieutenant Colonel Alexander Gordon* (Stroud: Sutton, 2003).
Muir, Rory, *Salamanca 1812* (New Haven: Yale University, 2001).
Muir, Rory and Burnham, Robert and Muir, Howie and McGuigan, Ron, *Inside Wellington's Peninsular Army, 1808–1814* (Barnsley: Pen and Sword, 2006).
Muir, Rory and Reiter, Jacqueline, 'A New Letter on the Battle of Salamanca 22 July 1812', *Journal of the Society for Army Historical Research* (2018), vol.XCVI, no.385, pp.21–32.
Mullié, C., *Biographie des célébrités militaires des armées de terre et de mer…* (Paris: Poignavant, 1851).
Muzás, Luis Sorando, *Banderas, estandartes y trofeos del Museo del Ejército 1700–1843, Catálogo razonado* (Madrid: Ministerio de Defensa, 2000).
Nafziger, George, *The Armies of Spain and Portugal 1808–1814* (West Chester: Author, 1993).
Nafziger, George and Gioannini, M., *The Defense of the Napoleonic Kingdom of Northern Italy, 1813–14* (Westport: Praeger, 2002).
Napier, William Francis Patrick, *History of the War in the Peninsula and in the South of France from the year 1807 to 1814* (London: Constable, 1993).
Nicols, Alistair, *Wellington's Mongrel Regiment* (Staplehurst: Spellmount, 2005).
O'Keefe, Eamonn, 'The Old Halberdier: From the Pyrenees to Plattsburgh with a Welshman of the 39th', *Journal of the Society for Army Historical Research* (2017), Vol.XCV, no.381, pp.17–33, no.382, pp.141–160.
Oman, Charles, *History of the Peninsular War* (London: Greenhill, 1995–7).
Oman, Charles, *Wellington's Army 1809–1814* (London: Edward Arnold, 1913).
Oswald, John, 'Affair at Villa Muriele', *United Service Journal* (1837), p.266–7.
Partridge, Richard and Oliver, Michael, *Napoleonic Army Handbook – British Army and her Allies* (London: Constable, 1999).
Pérez, Bernardo Blanco, *Pascual Sebastian de Liñan* (Madrid: Lit. de J. Donon, 1856).
Petre, Francis Loraine, *The History of the Norfolk Regiment, 1685–1918* (Norwich: Jarrold, 1924).
Philippart, John, *The Royal Military Calendar* (London: Valpy, 1815, 1820, 1821).
Phipps, Ramsay Weston, *The Armies of the First French Republic and the Rise of the Marshals of Napoleon 1* (London: Oxford University, 1931).
Pigeard, Alain and Cavalli, Daniel and Chappet, Alain, *Les Étoiles de Napoleon – Marechaux, Amiraux et Généraux* (Entremont-le-Vieux: Quatuor, 1996).
Poyen-Bellisle, Henry de, *Les Guerres des Antilles, 1793–1815* (Paris: Berger-Levrault, 1896).
Queypo de Llano y Ruiz de Saravia, José María, Conde de Toreno, *Historia del Levantamiento, Guerra y Revolucion de Espana* (Paris: Europea de Baudry, 1838).
Quintin, Danielle and Bernard, *Dictionnaire des Colonels de Napoléon* (Paris: S.P.M., 2013).
Reid, Stuart, *British Redcoat (2) 1793–1815* (London: Osprey, 1997).
Robinson, Roger E.R., *The Bloody Eleventh, History of the Devonshire Regiment* (Exeter: Devon and Dorset Regiment, 1988).
Ross-Lewin, Harry, *With the 32nd in the Peninsular and other Campaigns* (Dublin: Hodges, Figgis and Company, 1904).
Sañudo, Juan José, *Base de datos sobre las unidades militares en la guerra de la independcia española* (Madrid: Ministerio de Defensa, 2012).
Santos, António Nunes dos, *Collecçao das Ordens do Dia do… Guilherme Carr Beresford…* (Lisbon: Quartel General, 1810, 1811, 1812, 1813).
Schaumann, August Ludolf Friedrich, *On the Road with Wellington, the diary of a war commissary* (London: Greenhill, 1999).
Simón y Nieto, D. Francisco, *Estudio Médico-Topográfico de Villamuriel de Cerrato* (Palencia: Alonso y Z. Menéndez, 1886).
Six, Georges, *Dictionnaire Biographique* des *Généraux et Amiraux Français de la Révolution et de l'Empire, 1792–1814* (Paris: Historique et Nobiliaire, 1934).
Smith, Digby, *Napoleon's Regiments* (London: Greenhill, 2000).
Smith, Digby, *The Greenhill Napoleonic Wars Data Book* (London: Greenhill, 1998).
Susane, Louis, *Histoire de l'artillerie française* (Paris: J. Hetzel, 1874).

Ch. Talandier, *Mémoires relatifs aux opérations du deuxième corps d'armée en Espagne et en Portugal, sous les ordres du Maréchal Soult dans les années 1808, 1809, 1810, et 1811* (Verdun: Lippmann, 1835)

De Tarragon, Marie Louis Adrien, *Historique du 15e Régiment d'Infanterie* (Paris: Charles-Lavauzelle, 1895).

Thompson, Mark S., *Wellington's Engineers, Military Engineering in the Peninsular War, 1808–1814* (Barnsley: Pen and Sword, 2015).

Thompson, W.F.K., *An Ensign in the Peninsular War* (London: Michael Joseph, 1981).

Trimen, Richard, *An Historical Memoir of the 35th (or Royal Sussex) Regiment of Foot* (Southampton: Southampton Times Newspaper, 1873).

Urrecha, Gonzalo Serrats, *El general Álava y Wellington: de Trafalgar a Waterloo* (Legardeta: Foro para el Estudio de la Historia Militar de España, 2015).

Vane, Charles William (Marquess of Londonderry), *Story of the Peninsular War* (London: Henry Colburn, 1848).

Vaudoncourt, Frédéric François Guillaume, Baron de, *Histoire des campagnes de 1814 et 1815, en France* (Paris: De Gastel, 1826).

Vidal de la Blache, Joseph, *L'évacuation de l'Espagne et l'invasion dans le Midi, juin 1813–avril 1814* (Paris: Berger-Levrault, 1914).

Vivien, Jean Stanislas, *Souvenirs de ma Vie Militaire, 1792–1822* (Paris: Hachette, 1907).

War Office, *Regulations for the exercise of riflemen and light infantry* (London: T. Egerton, 1803, 1814).

War Office, *Return of the Names of the Officers in the Army* (London: House of Commons, 1818).

Wellington, 2nd Duke of (ed.), *Supplementary Despatches, Correspondence and Memoranda of Field Marshal Arthur, Duke of Wellington, K. G.* (London: John Murray, 1860).

Wheater, William, *A Record of the Services of the Fifty-first (Second West York), the King's Own Light Infantry Regiment* (London: Longman, 1870).

Windrow, Martin and Embleton, Gerry, *Military Dress of the Peninsular War* (London: Ian Allen, 1974).

Woodford, Leonard W., *A Young Surgeon in Wellington's Army* (Old Woking: Unwin, 1976).

Woollright, Henry Herriott, *Records of the Seventy-seventh (East Middlesex): The Duke of Cambridge's Own Regiment of Foot* (London: Gale and Polden, 1907).

Wrede, Alphons Freiherr von, *Geschichte der K. und K. Wehrmacht* (Vienna: Seidel 1898).

Wrottesley, George, *Life and Correspondence of Field Marshal Sir John Burgoyne, Bart* (London: Richard Bentley, 1873).

Younge, K.E., 'Some Peninsular Letters', *United Service Magazine*, Vol.LII (New Series), October 1915–March 1916, p.508–17.

Periodicals

The Gentleman's Magazine Or, Monthly Intelligencer for the Year

The Royal Military Chronicle; or, British Officers Monthly Register and Mentor

The Scots Magazine

Online Resources

A História do Regimento de Infantaria N°15, at <http://ri15.paraquedistas.com.pt/publicacoes/livro200anos/200anos.html>

Archives Nationale, Paris, *Base de Données Léonore* (LEONORE) at<http://www2.culture.gouv.fr/documentation/leonore/recherche.htm>

Gill, John H., 'Fuentes de Oñoro, 1811: The French Order of Battle', at <http://www.sammustafa.com/honour/wp-content/uploads/downloads/2010/08/Fuentes-Gill.pdf>

Lagos Militar, at <http://lagosmilitar.blogspot.co.uk/>

Guía Canal de Castilla 2018, at <http://www.canaldecastilla.org/Docs/guia/CdC_Introduccion.pdf>

Mapa Topográfico Nacional, Primeras Ediciones (MTN), available via SIGNA at <http://signa.ign.es/signa/>

Military General Service Medal Roll (MGSMR), *Dix Noonan Webb*, at <http://www.dnw.co.uk/resources/medal-rolls/medal-roll.php?medalroll_id=1>

Morand's instructions for skirmishers, 1811, at <http://www.demi-brigade.org/tirdaven.htm>

Service Historique de la Défense, Registres Matricules at <http://www.memoiredeshommes.sga.defense.gouv.fr/fr/arkotheque/inventaires/ead_ir_consult.php?fam=10&ref=23>

SHD GR21YC 133–137 (15e Ligne); SHD GR21YC 551–556 (66e Ligne)

SHD GR21YC 632–636 (82e Ligne); SHD GR21YC 666–669 (86e Ligne)

Nafziger Orders of Battle (NAFZIGER)

French Army of Italy, 21 March 1797 at <http://usacac.army.mil/sites/default/files/documents/carl/nafziger/797CAD.pdf>

Distribution of Spanish Forces, Zaragosa, Valencia and Murcia, June 1808 at <http://usacac.army.mil/sites/default/files/documents/carl/nafziger/808FSBK.pdf>

Battle of Medina del Rio Seco, 14 July 1808 at <http://usacac.army.mil/sites/default/files/documents/carl/nafziger/808GSAT.pdf>

French II Corps, 15 January 1809 at <http://usacac.army.mil/sites/default/files/documents/carl/nafziger/809ASBN.pdf>

Order of Battle for the Spanish Army of the Centre for December 1809 at <http://usacac.army.mil/sites/default/files/documents/carl/nafziger/809LSAA.pdf>

Artillery of the French Army in Spain, 1 March 1810 at <http://usacac.army.mil/sites/default/files/documents/carl/nafziger/810CSXA.pdf>

The Spanish Army of the Centre for September 1810 at <http://usacac.army.mil/sites/default/files/documents/carl/nafziger/810ISAS.pdf>

French Army in Spain, 15 July 1811 at <http://usacac.army.mil/sites/default/files/documents/carl/nafziger/811GSAK.pdf>

French Army of Portugal, 1 March 1812 at <http://usacac.army.mil/sites/default/files/documents/carl/nafziger/812CSAC.pdf>

French Army of Portugal, 15 July 1812 at <https://usacac.army.mil/sites/default/files/documents/carl/nafziger/812GSAQ.pdf>

French Army of Portugal after Salamanca, 1 August 1812 at <https://usacac.army.mil/sites/default/files/documents/carl/nafziger/812HSAR.pdf>

The Grande Armée, 1 August 1812 at <http://usacac.army.mil/sites/default/files/documents/carl/nafziger/812HAB.pdf>

French Army of Portugal after Salamanca, 1 August 1812 at <https://usacac.army.mil/sites/default/files/documents/carl/nafziger/812HSAR.pdf>

Army of Portugal, 15 October 1812 at <http://usacac.army.mil/sites/default/files/documents/carl/nafziger/812JSXI.pdf>

Army of the North, 15 October 1812 at <http://usacac.army.mil/sites/default/files/documents/carl/nafziger/812JSXJ.pdf>

French Army of Portugal, New Organisation, 1 January 1813 at <http://usacac.army.mil/sites/default/files/documents/carl/nafziger/812ASXH.pdf>

French Corps d'Observation de Italie, 15 June 1813 at <http://usacac.army.mil/sites/default/files/documents/carl/nafziger/813FDI.pdf>

French Army of Italy, 11 February 1814 at <http://usacac.army.mil/sites/default/files/documents/carl/nafziger/814BDF.pdf>

The French Army of Italy, 1 April 1814 at <http://usacac.army.mil/sites/default/files/documents/carl/nafziger/814DFC.pdf>

The Army of Italy, 1 April 1814 at <http://usacac.army.mil/sites/default/files/documents/carl/nafziger/814DFD.pdf>

Napoleon Series Online Articles

Bamford, Andrew, 'British Army Unit Strengths: 1808–1815, The Peninsular War', at <http://www.napoleon-series.org/military/organization/Britain/Strength/Bamford/c_BritishArmyStrengthStudyPeninsular.html>

Brown, Steve, 'British Regiments and the Men Who Led Them 1793–1815: the "Ephemeral Corps"1793-1796', at <http://www.napoleon-series.org/military/organization/Britain/Infantry/Regiments/c_ephemeral.html>
Challis, L.S., 'Peninsula Roll Call' (CHALLIS) at <https://www.napoleon-series.org/research/biographies/GreatBritain/Challis/c_ChallisIntro.html>
Foster, Ray, 'Duke of Brunswick Oels (Jäegers)', at <http://www.napoleon-series.org/military/organization/Britain/Infantry/WellingtonsRegiments/c_BrunswickOels.html>
Foster, Ray, 'Notes on the Portuguese Infantry of the Peninsular War 1807-1814: 3rd Regiment of Olivenza (Beira) and 15th Regiment of Olivenza (Beira), and 8th Caçadores', at <http://www.napoleon-series.org/military/organization/portugal/Infantry/Notes/c_NotesonPortugueseInfantry3.html>
Muzás, L.S., 'Trophies Taken by the British from the Napoleonic Army during the War of Spanish Independence (Peninsular War) 1808–1814', at <http://www.napoleon-series.org/military/battles/c_capturedflags.html>
McGuigan, Ron, 'British Regiments in the Peninsular War 1808-1814', at <http://www.napoleon-series.org/military/organization/Britain/Strength/c_RegimentsinPeninsula.html>